FROM HELL TO REDEMPTION

FROM HELL TO REDEMPTION

A Memoir of the Holocaust

by BORIS KACEL

University Press of Colorado

Published by the University Press of Colorado
P.O. Box 849
Niwot, Colorado 80544

The University Press of Colorado is a cooperative publishing enterprise supported, in part, by Adams State College, Colorado State University, Fort Lewis College, Mesa State College, Metropolitan State College of Denver, University of Colorado, University of Northern Colorado, University of Southern Colorado, and Western State College of Colorado.

The paper used in this publication meets the minimum requirements of the American National Standard for Information Services—Permanence of Paper for Printed Library Materials. ANSI Z39.48-1984

Library of Congress Cataloging-in-Publication Data

Kacel, Boris, 1921–
        From hell to redemption : a memoir of the Holocaust / Boris Kacel.
            p. cm.
        Includes index.
        ISBN 0-87081-460-5 (cb)
        1. Kacel, Boris, 1921– . 2. Jews—Latvia—Riga—Biography.
        3. Holocaust, Jewish (1939–1945)—Latvia—Riga—Personal narratives.
        4. Riga (Latvia)—Biography. I. Title.
        DS135.L33K33   1988
        940.53'18'092—dc21   97-35507
                                                                                CIP

10 9 8 7 6 5 4 3 2 1

Dedication

❧

I dedicate this book in everlasting memory of my mother, Fanja, my sisters, Dora and Ljuba, and my brother, Leiba, all of whom perished in the Riga massacre of November 30, 1941. I also dedicate this book to my father, Abram, with whom I spent my entire incarceration period and who passed away on April 19, 1990, in the United States.

I also dedicate this book to all my relatives and friends who perished during the Holocaust.

I sincerely hope my children, Sharon and Steven, and my son-in-law and daughter-in-law, Robert and Robin, will fully understand and respect the cruel exploitation their father had to endure during the Nazi era and that, despite this hardship, he ultimately found the strength to build a new life.

It is my heartfelt wish that my grandchildren, Benjamin, Elizabeth, and Aaron, will understand the evil power of man's inhumanity to man, which haunted their innocent grandfather as a youth. I also want them to be aware that such crimes should never again be committed, against the Jews or any other group of people.

I want especially to express profound appreciation to my wife, Tamara, also a Holocaust survivor, for her extensive cooperation and for accepting my absence for innumerable hours while I was occupied with writing my memoirs.

Contents

Preface

As incredible as it may seem, many people deny that the awesome event known as the Holocaust ever happened, despite the existing proof. It is, therefore, incumbent upon every survivor to tell his or her story for the sake of posterity; as an eyewitness, I want to share my experiences. Since the human memory is relatively short, I consider a written history to be the best way to preserve the past for the enlightenment of the future.

I wrote this book in my senior years, not because I wanted to but because I felt obligated to speak for the now-muted voices of my family and friends lost in the war. I am one of the few to be able to tell what happened to me and to thousands of other Jews under Nazi occupation in Riga, Latvia, and in other countries. My own suffering began soon after high school, when I was caught between two powerful forces—Stalin's communism and Hitler's Nazism. Ruthlessness and repression were characteristic of both of these ideologies, and the stories told here represent many years of battling to overcome these evils.

Creating this book was a monumental undertaking, as these unpleasant experiences of the past had faded away. I had to face the pain associated with them and relive the darkest days of my life. The process was torturously long, as the details had to be retrieved and sorted out, one episode at a time. I wrote these memoirs not in the comfort of my living room, in full view of the beauty of my backyard, but in the sub-basement, where natural light does not penetrate. Only this subdued atmosphere, so similar to my former surroundings, allowed my thoughts to flow freely. Sitting alone in the dimly lit basement, I thought about my family and friends who had perished. I considered my happy and carefree life as a youngster, playing lovingly with my younger brother and sisters. My caring family did not expose me to the negative forces I would soon have to face.

My mother was the guiding force of my youth. When she and my siblings were taken away from me, my father took her place, helping me in any way he could. He often thought more about my comfort than about his own. I would never have survived such a loss without his complete devotion to me. Also aiding my survival was my firm belief in Darwin's theory of the survival of the fittest. In these pages, I have tried to describe some of the means I used to adapt to the mistreatments and hunger I had to endure. I am grateful that a lesson learned in high school helped me to accept my difficult circumstances with dignity while resisting the kind of life my enemies tried to force upon me.

Perhaps the most trying time I experienced was triggered by the separation from my father shortly before our liberation. Until that point, we had managed to remain together and to survive our inhuman ordeal, buoyed only by mutual caring and the hope that we might soon be released. When I thought I had lost this great man, I began an intensive search, even jeopardizing my own life by working for our second-worst enemies, the Soviets. When I finally found him, I attempted to resume my life as normally as possible.

My traumatic experiences under Nazi slavery destroyed my belief in a compassionate God. Nature has a way of healing old wounds, however, and after I became a free man again, I returned to the traditions and customs of Judaism so deeply ingrained in me. I not only regained my faith but became aware of a greater force that I believe guided me through my trials.

In my newly adopted homeland, the United States of America, I have often thought of my friends and acquaintances from Riga, none of whom survived the Holocaust. I was the sole heir to their legacies and felt I was responsible for honoring their memories. Some of them died before the German SS Einsatzkommando or the gestapo could kill them; it is not widely known that Riga was terrorized by local mobile killing squads before the Germans arrived. To this day, the Latvians do not admit their culpability and instead blame others for the crimes committed against the Jews.

I hope this book will not only serve as a memorial to those who perished but will also shed light on the dark, forgotten corners of history. In the small Baltic country of Latvia, the Jewish community was nearly annihilated. Only by learning from mistakes of the past can we prevent another mass genocide such as the Holocaust. The Germans killed twenty million people, six million of whom were Jews. I hope the time will come when the disease we know as anti-Semitism will be eradicated and tolerance will reign with peace in every part of the world. It is my fervent desire that sharing my experiences and thoughts will help in some small way and that it will be unnecessary for books such as this one to ever again have to be written in a civilized society.

> *In Germany they came*
> *first for the Communists,*
> *and I didn't speak up*
> *because I wasn't a*
> *Communist. Then they*
> *came for the Jews, and I*
> *didn't speak up because*
> *I wasn't a Jew. Then they*
> *came for the trade*
> *unionists, and I didn't*
> *speak up because I wasn't*
> *a trade unionist. Then they*
> *came for the Catholics, and*
> *I didn't speak up because*
> *I was a Protestant. Then*
> *they came for me, and by*
> *that time, nobody was left*
> *to speak up.*

This statement was made by Pastor Martin Niemoeller, a German theologian who was president of the World Conference of Churches from 1961 to 1968. He was incarcerated in Sachsenhausen and Dachau, German concentration camps, from 1937 to 1945.

CONCENTRATION CAMPS
IN OCCUPIED EUROPE
1939-1945

Sonda
Leningrad
Nerete
Klooga Vaivare
ESTONIAN
S.S.R.

------ Borders in 1933
✳ Extermination Camp
★ Concentration Camp
◩ Ghetto
▼ Transit Camp
○ Labor Camp

Riga Kaiserwald
LATVIAN S.S.R.

LITHUANIAN S.S.R.
★ Pravjeniskis
Kaunas Vilna
Stutthof

BELORUSSIAN
S.S.R.

ka ✳ Bialostok
rsaw ◩ POLAND
Trawniki ◩
z • Poniatova
Plaszow ✳★ Lublin-Majdanek
Cracow ✳ Belzec
Janovska
Lvov ◩

✳ Sobibor

SOVIET UNION

UKRAINIAN S.S.R.

○ Vrhne

Budapest

MOLDAVIAN S.S.R.

RY

RUMANIA

Bucharest •

BLACK SEA

AVIA

BULGARIA
• Sofia

Istanbul TURKEY

Salonika

GREECE

0   350
Scale of miles

FROM HELL TO REDEMPTION

1

German Troops March Into Riga

My life story begins in apartment 30 on Aizsargu Street 20 in Riga, Latvia, where my family had lived for as long as I could remember. Aizsargu was a peaceful residential street, and the various ethnic groups in this middle-class neighborhood were friendly to each other. Within days of German occupation, however, the friendships that had existed for decades were destroyed. On Sunday, June 22, 1941, under the code name "Operation Barbarossa," German troops attacked the Soviet Union, crossing the border from the Baltic to the Ukraine. Taken completely by surprise by the blitzkrieg, the slow, ill-prepared Red Army surrendered en masse. Within a week, war activity could frequently be heard and felt in the surrounding area. Heavy artillery bombardment began in the old part of Riga, and the bombs were soon falling all over the city. My family and I could hardly sleep at night, often going to the window to see whether any shells had landed in the courtyard below or if any damage had been done to the front of the building.

My mother protected my younger brother, Leiba, and my sister Ljuba by drawing them close to her; she also made sure they were fully clothed at all times in case we had to evacuate our apartment. I was already on my own, as was my sister Dora, the elder of the two girls, and we could take care of ourselves. It was very frightening when the whole building started to shake. My father was very calm, since he had experienced fighting during World War I; his only concern was his family's safety. To ease his nervousness, which he tried to hide, he constantly checked our food supplies and the two baskets of clothes we kept on hand for an emergency. At sunrise, Mother prepared a hearty breakfast to make sure we were fed in case of any unexpected disturbances.

Early each morning, I was filled with suspense and curiosity about what was going on in the streets. I wanted to see the results of the previous night's heavy bombardment and wondered what a German soldier looked like or whether the army was in Riga yet. Before I ventured outdoors, my mother advised me not to go far. When I came downstairs, several young people were already on the street with the same intention—to see what was going on. Everything was calm outside. I walked over to the bulletin poster on the corner, on which several mobilization orders had been posted by the Soviet authorities. My age group was included in one order, but I had no intention of registering for this mandatory army draft. Despite all of the threats mentioned on the poster, I did not take the order to mobilize seriously. That corner soon became the observation point for the disarrayed Soviet Army, whose soldiers retreated on foot and by truck. Large artillery was pulled slowly by small, dehydrated horses; a foamy saliva dripped from their mouths, and their bodies were steaming from heavy perspiration and exhaustion. At times, I would see the same units over and over, as though they were lost. It seemed that they were going in circles to find a way out of their entrapment.

Communist Party members and their sympathizers were looking for a way to escape to the Soviet Union, not knowing the once glorious Red Army was speedily retreating, leaving everything behind. The easiest escape route would have been by rail, had the rail system been well organized, but word had spread that the railroad station was overcrowded with people trying to leave, and very few trains were expected to depart from the Riga station. In desperation, some people decided to flee on foot or by bicycle, and a large majority of the population left from their workplaces in trucks.

People gathered in small groups to discuss the situation. I lived in a neighborhood heavily populated by Jews, who were frightened by Nazi Germany, which they knew was their enemy. They wanted to escape German occupation, which would be difficult since nobody had the necessary means of transportation or a truly safe place to go. Unfortunately, the existing Soviet political system in Latvia was not ideal either, as the government was unconcerned about the fate of its citizens. Within a matter of hours, the Jews had to decide whether to run to Stalin's Russia or stay in Hitler's Germany and hope for the best. In the midst of this crisis, my father maintained his composure and weighed the options for our well-being. My mother, whom we considered an angel, gathered her children around her. She praised us for our brave behavior and in a soft, convincing voice tried to assure us that everything would work out.

I was nineteen years old, the oldest child. In this time of distress, I found I was an innocent, frightened young man with no practical life experience. My parents had given me the opportunity to attend private schools, where I could obtain the best education available; in 1940, I had graduated from one of the most prominent private high schools in Riga. This was during the time the Soviet Union occupied Latvia, which had formerly been independent. After graduation, I was not permitted to enroll in the university because I was the son of a businessman, which, to the Soviets, meant I was the son of a capitalist.

I was also prevented from getting a job to try to earn a living. On the recommendation of a good friend of my father's, however, I was hired as a draftsman right before the war broke out. To begin work, I had to submit to an interrogation by the Narodniy Komissariat Vnutrenich Del (People's Commissariat on Interior Matters [NKVD]), the predecessor to the well-known Komissariat Gosudarstvenoj Bezopasnosti (Commissariat of Government Securities [KGB]), to determine the depth of my loyalty to the Soviet Union. I anticipated that my interrogation would be lengthy and thorough, but it lasted only fifteen minutes. I regretted that I had gone there, for I received a lecture that contained threatening words I remember to this day. The hostilities on the fighting front advanced so quickly that I was never able to start work. When the war broke out and the Nazis' military operations were successful, I hoped their hatred of Jews would subside. I thought they would no longer need a scapegoat for the problems in their country and that I would be able to lead a normal life.

With the rapid advancement of the German armed forces, the tension in our house rose steadily. My father did not know what to undertake first, so he decided to seek advice from my oldest uncle, Wulf, a successful jewelry businessman, who was considered the wisest man in the family and was always the main speaker at family gatherings. My father asked, "Wulf, what did you decide to do? Are you staying in Riga?

What would you advise me to do with the family?" After a lengthy discussion, Uncle Wulf said, "Living under the Germans will not be rosy, but it will certainly not be as bad as living in Stalin's Siberia. Under the Germans, our way of life will be extremely restricted, but we will still have our freedom and the means for survival." I soon learned how little my "wise" Uncle Wulf knew of what Adolf Hitler had in store for us and the dreadful consequences we would have to face. My father took my uncle's advice and abandoned the idea of running to Russia. He again checked our plentiful food supplies and the essential clothing that had been packed in boxes and baskets. Only two weeks earlier—on June 14, 1941—the Soviet authorities had forcibly removed "enemies of the Soviet society," sending them to Siberia in boxcars. Among them were prominent businessmen, rabbis, industrialists, and Zionist leaders. My father made sure everything was in order in case he was ever included in this mass evacuation.

On July 1, 1941, after the heavy shelling had subsided, the Germans entered Riga. I could not suppress my desire to see the victorious German Army. I was rather naive to venture outside in such a tense and unpredictable atmosphere, but I walked less than a hundred feet to the main street called Terbatas. I thought I would be the only one there, but a few other people seemed as curious as I was about what was happening. Unexpectedly, around the corner the first German soldiers appeared in battle gear in a column of motorcycles, which had buggies attached to them. I rushed to the curb to get a closer look. In addition to the driver, every motorcycle had two soldiers seated in its buggy; all of the men were fully armed. The passengers and vehicles were covered with a heavy layer of dust. They had likely been on the road all night, for they looked tired. I initially thought they would greet the civilian bystanders with a smile or a wave, but their intentions were now clear to me. These men were in pursuit of the enemy, and there was no time to be lost; in a blitzkrieg, time was essential to a victory. It shocked me to see the stern-looking soldiers, ready for their next assault. Assault on whom, on the fleeing Red Army or on the Jews? I was afraid because I did not know what to expect from the occupying forces, but one thing was clear—whatever they did would not be good.

After the motorized column had passed, I ran home to tell my family what was going on, shouting, "The Germans are here—the Germans are in Riga!" Mother and the children wanted to know what was going on outside, so I told them everything I had seen. Not realizing the seriousness of the situation, my brother and sisters wanted to go outside to see a foreign army, which was a unique sight, but my mother did not allow them to do so. I had seen very little, but it was enough to make me realize how impossible it was going to be to defeat this enemy. I soon went back out to see if there were any more German soldiers; everything on the street seemed calm, and very few people were visible. With such a strange calmness, I felt very uncomfortable being outdoors; it seemed as though I was experiencing the calm before the storm. Since no military units were on the street, I returned home.

In a way, I was happy to see our country be rid of the Communist regime, although I could not guess how the Germans would treat the Jewish population. I was left trembling by the rough physical appearance of the German soldiers I had seen for the first time that morning and by not knowing what their future actions might be. Their faces stuck in my young mind. I remembered the stories my father used to tell about World War I—how it had started so innocently and had ended with tragedy in every household, including his own. I thought about everything we had heard on the German program on the radio. In his loud, vulgar voice, Hitler had given nationalistic speeches about the glorious "Deutsches Reich"; he said the Germans were the pure Aryan people of the world and that the Jews were a plague on Germany. Father once told me that after the armistice agreement that ended World War I, everyone had assumed all nations would live in peace and harmony. I could see, however, that this was clearly not the case; this world war would be a continuation of the unfinished business from the first one.

By that afternoon, the calm and peaceful streets of Riga had become crowded and filled with violence. The Latvians were celebrating independence from Communist repression, flying their large national red, white, and red flags over buildings and waving smaller ones by hand. I saw happy faces everywhere, which I understood, since I, too, was glad to see the fall of the Soviet system. To my surprise, though, I also saw anger and irrational behavior on the streets. The Latvians expressed their hatred of the Jews through physical acts and angry words. They accused the Jews of being Communists and blamed them for all the ills to which they had been subjected during Soviet rule. In my wildest dreams, I could never have imagined the hidden animosity the Latvians had for their Jewish neighbors. I had hoped the liberation celebration would have passionate meaning for the Jews. Instead, the Latvians saw themselves as the messengers of Nazi evil and began to govern the city as if they had received consent from Berlin to do so. They eventually learned this was not the case; their country became no more than one of Germany's pawns. Nonetheless, members of the Jewish community were in deep distress, as their lives, security, and freedom were at stake. At the time, I could not imagine what would happen to the Jews of Riga when the Germans had the ruling hand.

Trucks appeared carrying small vigilante groups of ten to fifteen armed Latvians, who wore armbands in their national colors of red, white, and red. These men intended to kidnap Jews off the street and take away their personal belongings. The prisoners were then forcibly loaded onto the trucks, taken to the woods, and killed. It was terrifying to go outside, as one had to be aware of the vigilante groups that drove around the streets. The mobile killing squads, as I called them, were in full command of the city, and nobody challenged their presence or their unconscionable killings. I did not expect such a severe assault; after all, the Jews had lived among the Latvians for many years. The two groups had always tolerated each other and had lived together in a friendly, harmonious atmosphere. My maternal grandparents had settled in Riga at the turn of the century, and I had lived my entire life there among Latvians, who now considered me their mortal enemy and were prepared to kill me. No one was willing to protect my life.

After a few days, our household began to run out of fresh produce. Although every Jew in town was aware of the mobile killing squads, my father decided to go to the Widzemes produce market two blocks from our house. I went with him to help carry the groceries home. For many years, Father had often gone to the market before going to work at the shoe store he owned, so he knew the contents of every stall, as well as each proprietor. He was, therefore, not afraid—he expected to see the friendly faces of people with whom he had dealt for a long time. When we approached the main entrance of the market, we noticed that the large iron gate was closed; only the small pedestrian door was open. A large sign stated that "Jews and dogs are not allowed in the market." We could not believe what we saw. Dogs had never been allowed inside, but

I was shocked that the word "Jews" had been added. I thought, our friendly Latvian neighbors, whose goods we have bought all these years, are now ready to stick a knife in our backs. These stallkeepers want to deprive us of fresh food and even starve us to death. With sad faces and empty hands, Father and I returned home. My mother was very disappointed to hear about the sign. She, too, was upset that she had supported the stallkeepers all these years and that in this time of distress they did not want to help us in return.

Later that day, I went across the street to purchase milk from a small grocery store where we shopped regularly. The owner was a Latvian, well liked and well-known throughout the neighborhood. He was as polite as always and sold me everything I requested. After I had paid him, he remarked, "Next time you come to the store, please use the rear door so nobody will see you coming here." For the next few days I did as he asked, for I was glad I could get the groceries my mother needed; at least I had found one Latvian in the neighborhood who was less hostile to us than the others. Unfortunately, his friendliness did not last long; eventually, the grocer told me I could no longer come to his store and that he would be unable to sell me any groceries. Disappointed, I asked him, "You are the only grocery store in the neighborhood—where shall I go now? My mother has been shopping here for many years, and you know me, my sisters, and my little brother—I have been coming to your store since I was a little boy." "Sorry," he replied. "I do not want you in my store anymore." I left with tears in my eyes, for I knew there would be no more fresh bread, milk, or other dairy products for me and my family.

As the days passed, the Latvian vigilante groups did not stop their despicable murders but merely improved their tactics. They became better organized and more sophisticated. A truckload of men would pull up to an apartment building, and one man would call on the janitor to find out which apartments were occupied by Jews. The janitor would reveal where the Jews lived, and the vigilante groups would split up; a few men would enter each apartment, which was searched and stripped of any valuable items. All men and teenage boys were ordered to follow the men to the truck. These murderers went systematically from one building to another until the truck was full. The innocent Jews were then delivered to the closest police station the vigilantes controlled.

At night, some were sent to police headquarters, called the Prefecture; others were brought to the nearby forest, called Meza Park, and shot. The Prefecture was a nightmare for the Jews; some were lucky enough to be sent to work, but the majority wound up murdered in Meza Park. It was estimated that approximately ten thousand Jews were killed by the volunteer Latvian squads in Riga within a few weeks. The insanity did not stop with robbing and killing Jews. Houses of worship, such as the beautiful Gogol and Zeilen synagogues, were burned with people in them. Latvians scorched their own soil with the blood of the Jewish people, and nobody said a word. The Latvians proved to the world and to future generations that they were unable to govern themselves but needed a guiding hand and an education in human relations.

My parents were constantly in touch by telephone with our large family in different neighborhoods all over the city. We found out that five of our relatives had been kidnapped. They were never heard from again. The madness and evil did not stop in the capital city of Riga but spread to smaller towns throughout Latvia. The news came from small Jewish communities that citizens were being brutally harassed by self-styled vigilante groups who called themselves Latvian partisans and went so far as to arrest and kill entire Jewish communities. The greatest tragedy was that these crimes were committed not by strange, invading forces but by the local Latvians, who knew their victims by their first names. This was the case with my relatives in the town of Rezekne, where my family roots could be traced back a few hundred years. Golanske was a household name in the small town.

As the authorities of the German occupation were setting up their offices, the Latvian assaults on Jews became unbearable. The mobile killing squads were still in control of the streets of Riga, walking and driving around the city with smoking guns. The Jews soon had to seek German protection from the vicious Latvian hordes. The Germans were well informed about the crimes against the Jews in the city but chose not to stop them until the Jews went to work for them and sought their help. I went to work for a military unit whose duty was to furnish living quarters and offices for the new administration. I received a written order stating that I should not be apprehended, as my employment with this army unit was crucial. This document was stamped and signed by my German commanding officers and served as my new passport for protection. The Latvian forces honored the order, and I could freely walk the streets without being harassed by anyone.

My father was not as lucky. While I was at work one morning, a vigilante group, with the help of our janitor, invaded our apartment and those of other Jewish tenants in the building. My family was not ready to receive these uninvited "guests" at such an early hour, and Father was unwilling to let them in, but since the janitor was with them he reluctantly opened the door. Several Latvian men walked in and began to ransack the apartment. They found hidden Soviet money, various textile pieces for suits and dresses, and a large variety of groceries packed in boxes. They accused my father of being a Soviet collaborator and arrested him, putting everything they had found into their truck. After the search-and-arrest operation had ended, all of the Jewish men had to congregate on the street and were led under heavy guard to the local police station a few blocks away. They forced my father to walk at the head of the group, holding a ten-ruble bill in his mouth so Lenin's picture could be seen.

When they arrived at the station, all of the rooms were occupied by previously arrested Jews. Our confiscated items were brought into the station, and the police chief was pleased to have so many valuables. My father knew he was in trouble; to escape from this place alive would be possible only if he could make a deal with the chief. At an appropriate time, he quietly approached the office and made a proposal: The chief could keep all of the money and goods—no questions asked—if he would release my father. Furthermore, if he did so immediately, he would receive an additional gift. The police chief was pleased with my father's offer but refused it. A short while later, however, he called my father aside and informed him that he was to be transferred to the Prefecture, where he would be much safer. Before Father boarded the police van, the chief gave him a loaf of bread. The rest of the men who remained at the police station were never seen again; my father saved his own life with quick thinking and a passionate plea.

When my father arrived at the Prefecture, he found a building filled with arrested Jews whose fates were in the hands of unreasonable men. He spent the night locked up in a large room. The following morning, a Latvian baker came to request the help of the police. He needed someone to repair his bread oven, which had broken down, so the guard in charge asked if anyone knew anything about masonry. My father immediately jumped up and answered, "I am an experienced bricklayer."

Before Father was released, he requested two helpers for the job. With the guard's consent, he picked two men with whom he had become acquainted during the night. He had saved his life again, as well as two others, by being in the right place at the right time.

He went straight to work, although he knew nothing about laying bricks or mixing cement. When he came home that evening, we were all delighted, since we had not been sure we would ever see him again. I exclaimed happily, "Oh, Papa, I love you—you were lucky to get out of the devil's hands!" Father was glad to be back home and to see that we were unharmed. He calmly told us the whole story of how he had spent the last day and night among the most vicious men he had ever met. The account of his ordeal in the Prefecture was chilling; he said the building was like a huge torture chamber. He felt very sorry for the captive Jews, for the Latvian guards took advantage of their inability to defend themselves. The prisoners were constantly interrogated and beaten for no reason except that they were Jews. Food was denied them, so he had shared his loaf of bread with the other inmates.

Very few people got out of the Prefecture alive; most were taken to the woods to be shot. I was glad to hear that my father had not been harmed. "Maybe the police chief at the local station put in a good word for me, for I was certainly not in charge of my own destiny," said my father. "I was very lucky. I suppose God was with me—He was the one who decided not to deliver me to the devil. Not only did I save my life but also those of two other Jewish souls." Father's clothes and face were dirty because when he was at work, he told us, he had to crawl into a wood-burning baking oven and scrape off all of the soot on the surface so the damaged bricks could be replaced. Mother helped him wash up and change his clothes, unable to express her happiness; our family was reunited and ready to challenge the unknown future. Another miracle had taken place: I had a father again, and as head of the household, he had a job. Every morning the Latvian baker came to pick him up and brought him back in the evening. Father did not get paid for his work but as compensation received one or two loaves of bread a day, more than enough for our family. The most important thing was that he was safe from being kidnapped by the mobile killing squads.

By the end of July 1941, a German civilian administration had taken over Riga; the Schutzstaffel, or SS, an elite Nazi guard unit, had set the gestapo (an organization of secret police) and the Einsatzkommandos (special command units) in place to govern the Jews. Germans who had left Latvia for Germany in the late 1930s were called back to serve in their native country. The top positions of many administration agencies were occupied by newly arrived Baltic Germans: the Reichskommisar of Ostland was Heinrich Lohse, and the new head of police was SS General Friedrich Jackeln. They established law and order in the country. No more Latvian vigilantes and murder squads were seen on the streets of Riga, no more robbing and kidnapping of Jews occurred, and Latvians could no longer abuse or assault the Jewish population. The inhuman treatment of recent weeks had already set an unfortunate precedent, however.

The Latvians received the Nazis willingly and tried to follow in their footsteps, especially in their handling of the Jews. Their primary goal was to reestablish an independent Latvian state and government, but after the German occupying forces had begun their work, disappointment was soon evident. Latvian flags disappeared from Riga's skyline, the national anthem was no longer sung on the radio, and Latvian was recognized only as a second language. The unrestricted police power was ended, the nationalistic armbands were changed to plain green, and the customary army uniform was no longer worn. Latvian youths were now part of the German Army and dressed in German uniforms; the new recruits were part of the German armed forces serving the Third Reich. The first administrative orders were handed down to the Jewish population: Jews could no longer use public places and parks, and they would have to wear a ten-centimeter yellow Star of David on their left breasts. To determine how many Jews still lived in Riga, we all had to register; another order then followed that Jews would only get 50 percent of the food ration the rest of the population was to receive. The drastic decrees continued: Jews had to wear a second yellow star on their backs, and they were forbidden to use the sidewalks. We became the "gutter Jews," for we could only walk on the cobblestone pavement in the streets. At first, it was very difficult to accept the fact that I was no longer as free as the rest of the people in town, but I had no options.

The gestapo was in charge of all police activities and of the implementation of the Nuremberg racial laws. A small-scale Latvian government was created in appreciation of faithful Latvian cooperation with the Hitler regime. In command was a Latvian general named Dankers, who was half German and sympathized more with the Germans than with the Latvians. Included in his administration were the past president of Latvia, Kvesis, and the state's attorney, Valdmanis. These and other prominent Latvians were considered good men and were members of the intelligentsia, but in the end they proved to be as cruel as the Nazis.

Even with all of the restrictive orders, our lives had to go on. We could sometimes forget about the tension for a day or two, and we slowly got used to the unpleasant routines. My father worked for the bakery as a bricklayer and cleaning man. Mother took care of my brother, Leiba, and my sisters, Dora and Ljuba. I was working for a Wehrmacht (army) unit that provided furnishings for the apartments and offices of newly arrived administration officials. One day, something very significant happened that changed my future and became a dominant factor in my surviving the Holocaust. My work crew had just finished work on the living quarters of a high-ranking officer. Before we left, the German lieutenant in charge of our crew checked to see if everything was in its proper place. At the end of his inspection, he turned on the lights and noticed that two wall sconces over the grand piano did not light up. He became very upset about this problem and asked if anyone could fix the sconces.

I volunteered although I knew nothing about electrical repairs, and the lieutenant gave me some tools, which I took as if I were a knowledgeable electrician. I removed both sconces and checked them thoroughly, then took the wires apart and wiggled the sockets. I could not see anything wrong and decided to hang the sconces back on the wall the way I had found them. I did not know what the problem could be and became very nervous, for the lieutenant was depending on me. When the sconces were hung on the wall, I turned on the switch and was amazed to see that both of them lit up. I was very relieved and happy that the beautiful, black grand piano would be illuminated by the fixtures I had repaired. Another miracle had happened, since I did not know what I had done to solve this problem. The lieutenant was even happier than I; he could now report that the apartment was ready for occupancy. He praised me in front of my co-workers for a job well done and said, "From now on, you will be my personal electrician."

It was a few more weeks until all outstanding orders were finished and the crew ran out of work. The lieutenant was forced to let go of all of the other men; then he assigned me to a new position: washing cars for high-ranking officers in his unit. I spoke perfect German and could easily converse with the other soldiers who were doing repair work. Some of them were very nice. They felt sorry for me because they knew I was not being paid, and they often gave me cigarettes and bread to take home. Several asked about my family, and others spoke about theirs, but our conversations were always short because the soldiers were afraid to talk long to a Jew who was marked with a yellow star. One day my friendly lieutenant asked me if I knew how to repair bicycles. "Jawohl, lieutenant!" I replied with a stern voice. "I sure can repair bicycles!" He drove me to the old Latvian Fifth Army base, on the outskirts of Riga, where a small German Wehrmacht unit was stationed. He showed me two huge piles of broken bicycles left by the Soviet Army; I was to repair or reassemble them so they were usable. I liked this assignment because it would last for a long time and I was my own boss. It was also less strenuous; I did not have to carry heavy pieces of furniture up and down stairs or wash cars under constant supervision.

The only thing I did not like about this new job was that it was very far from my house, and on my long walk to and from work I had to pass Riga's city jail, known among Jewish people as Centralke. I soon developed a daily route. After leaving the army base gate, I crossed a long field dotted with small private vegetable gardens. The only building I faced was Centralke, which was a large, three-story, red brick building surrounded by a high fence. It was difficult to look at the observation tower, bar-covered windows, and tall, iron entrance gate. I always tried to pass by quickly. The most unpleasant aspect was the sad, crying faces of the people at the gate; I could see some Jewish faces, but most were gentile. Whenever I went by, a large crowd of people was always congregated outside. Some had come to visit loved ones, and others to find out if their missing relatives were here, for the jail held the political prisoners arrested by the Germans. The only joy I found was in walking freely with everyone else on the natural walkways, for there were no sidewalks around the jail. After I had passed Centralke, I was on the main street, Matisa, which eventually brought me within a block of my house. The difficult journey took over an hour each way.

As I was walking home on Matisa Street one day, I had an unusual confrontation. I noticed that a tall, middle-aged German officer from the air force was following me, occasionally glancing my way. He walked on the sidewalk and I on the pavement; when I sped up, he did likewise. I suspected that he was up to something—why would a German officer follow me for so long? I had to get rid of him. As I neared my house, I started to run and ducked into the building next to ours to confuse him. From here I knew a route to our courtyard, from which I could enter our building and climb to our third-floor apartment. When I got home, I told my mother what had happened. After supper, there was a knock at our door; my mother opened it, as I looked to see who was there. I could see the German officer who had followed me, and he saw me. He told my mother he had a job for me and that I should come with him right away. Mother started to cry and begged him not to take me away. When I did not move, he flipped open his leather revolver case and pointed to his gun. He was clearly prepared to use his loaded weapon on me or my mother if we did not cooperate; I had no choice but to follow him outside. He gave me strict orders to behave and warned me not to get any ideas about running away.

We walked a long way until we reached a slum neighborhood, an area with which I was familiar because my grandfather had once lived nearby. When we reached one building, he stopped and told me to follow him; we walked up to the second floor and entered an apartment that was empty except for a wooden cane and an old chair. The officer ordered me to take off my pants and lean over the chair; when I did, he began to swat me on my seat with his cane. It was very painful, and I started to cry and yell; the louder I cried, the harder he hit me. At times, he would examine the condition of my seat, say that it did not look sore enough, and resume the punishment. After a long time, he was finally satisfied with the damage he had done and released me. As I slowly staggered home, I realized that this German officer was a true psychopath, for he had enjoyed inflicting pain. My mother and siblings were very happy to see me return in one piece; they thought something terrible would happen to me when I left. As I told them what had happened, Mother tried to smother the pain by treating me with medication and compresses. I suggested that the officer might come after me again, so after a lengthy discussion it was decided that I should leave our apartment for a while.

Mother made arrangements for me to stay with the new tenants on the floor above ours for the next few days. The Kussmans were a young

Jewish couple with a beautiful three-year-old daughter. For the next two weeks, I had to sit on down pillows, since even a padded chair was too painful. As I had suspected, the officer soon knocked on our apartment door and asked for me. My mother started to cry, asking what he had done to her son, who had never come home the day he was taken away. The officer did not respond to Mother's story but simply left. For the next several days, he snooped around the neighborhood, hoping to catch me and prove that my mother had been lying. I did not dare to go out on the street, and all of our neighbors kept a close watch on him. He eventually left for good, and the embarrassing and painful experience was finally behind me.

I went back to assembling bicycles at the army base. I had initially been able to put together three or four bicycles a day; when I had used up all of the good parts, though, my production dropped to one a day. Soon only broken, unusable parts were left, so I had to be released from my job. I was eager to find new work, but I was unable to find a job with a German employer on my own. A Jewish Community Committee was being established to serve the needs of the people and to act as a legal representative to the German authorities. The committee provided us with food ration cards and an employment service; I registered and had to appear daily until noon, at which time I was free to leave. All of the men seeking work congregated in the large yard in front of the office building. German representatives would come in and request a certain number of laborers; the chosen workers would then be called inside to meet their employers. A representative from the employment office was always present during this process, which resembled a slave market to me, for it was actually forced labor without pay.

On my second day at the employment office, a group of Germans requested fifty men to dig up and dry peat moss. The finished product—turf—was rolled into logs and used to replace wood as heating fuel. The men were needed to replace an existing work crew in a small town called Sloka. The Germans claimed the site would have good working conditions and that the men would receive very good food, but their promise was not honest. Every Jew in town knew it was a terrible place to work; the job was exhausting and strenuous, with very little food and poor accommodations. Under no circumstances would I have considered working out of town, no matter how good the conditions or the food. The rest of the men felt the same way, and nobody volunteered for this work. The Germans waited, then became angry and very disappointed.

This negative response by the unemployed men made the employees of the Community Committee very uncomfortable; they were obliged to furnish fifty workers at any cost. The employment officials closed the entrance gate and surrounded the people congregated in the yard. As they started to pick out men who seemed capable of handling such a difficult assignment, I jumped over the high iron fence that surrounded the yard and ran away. I went home, hoping they would be able to find fifty strong men and would then take my name off the unemployment registration list. Before long, a messenger was at my house looking for me, but luck was with me again. When he came for me I was not home, but I was now forced into hiding again. The Kussmans agreed to keep me once again until the search was over, which meant I had to wait until the employment office could find the fifty men it needed. After a few days, the Sloka work crew was organized, and I could return to my job search.

I was very anxious to find work, so I did not miss a day in the employment office. One day, a large truck pulled up to the gate. Out stepped two SS storm troopers in green uniforms with skull insignia on their jackets and caps. They walked up to the Jews congregated in the yard, and one said, "I need ten musicians." I immediately volunteered, although I did not play any instrument. I was convinced that they did not need any performing musicians; if they had, they would have asked each of us what we played. This led me to believe they were up to something, but I volunteered because the situation would protect me from the vicious environment that surrounded me. Nobody would dare to harass or hurt a worker in a storm trooper unit. Ten men from the yard quickly climbed into the troopers' truck and were on their way. I soon realized I had made the right decision; they did not need musicians, just workers to transport pianos.

Our job consisted of delivering the pianos confiscated from Jewish homes to various German military establishments. The list of addresses was prepared in advance—how the SS men knew which homes had pianos was a puzzle—and we merely had to go into an apartment and remove the piano. A few fine musicians were among our group, and they had a difficult time with the physical labor. The lifting and carrying were done manually—we had no equipment designed for this type of work. I thought this job would last for a while, but after a few days I was on the street again. Father lost his job as well, because the bakery damaged during the war had been cleaned and restored. It was ready for business, so the Latvian baker had no need of my father's help.

The traffic on the streets of Riga had become very heavy, with German military trucks coming and going everywhere. Many carried furniture taken from Jewish homes. We almost lost a piece, but my father outwitted the Germans. One afternoon we heard knocking at the door; when my father opened it, he was confronted by a German officer, who said politely that he would like to check the bedroom. My father knew the officer was going to confiscate some furniture, but he let him in. The officer announced that he would have to take my parents' bed for a short time. My father complained, but the officer paid no attention; he went downstairs and told the soldiers waiting in the courtyard to come and remove the bed. Father pulled my mother aside and said in a subdued voice, "Fanja, he is taking our bed away. Now we will have to sleep on the floor."

A sudden grief-stricken look and glassy eyes changed Father's facial expression. He started to rub his forehead, as if he were desperately searching for a solution to his problem. He rushed into the kitchen, opened the pantry door, and saw a large clay jug filled with Mother's homemade preserves. He took out a few of the little cranberries that were mixed with other fruits. He ran back to the bedroom and smeared them on the wooden headboard. When the officer returned with his soldiers, Father approached him. "You do not want a bed that has wanzen [bedbugs]," he said. "Does this bed have wanzen?" asked the German officer. "Take a look for yourselves," said my father, pointing to the marks the red berries had made. "No, I cannot use a bed with wanzen," replied the officer, and he ordered his soldiers to leave. We were all very proud of my father and his quick, innovative idea. He later told us he would have been unable to bear seeing Mother sleep on the floor. His love for his family had avoided another tragedy. We were lucky again, but other Jewish families in the building were less fortunate.

2

My Move to the Ghetto

The summer of 1941 was almost over, and the cool fall weather was upon us. The poor living conditions for the Jews in Riga had gone from bad to worse. The Community Committee received notification from the gestapo High Command that a ghetto was to be established by October 25 in which the entire Jewish population would have to live. The news swept through our community like a devastating hurricane, and it brought our household to a complete standstill. We were unfamiliar with the exact location of the ghetto but knew the general area in which it would be established. In Yiddish it was called the Mascower Forstadt (Moscow suburb); it was not actually a suburb but was a part of Riga. The area was considered a slum in which mostly poor Russians and Jews lived.

In addition to being in a state of shock, my family had a dilemma: What were we to do with our substantial household belongings and the furniture we had accumulated during the many years of living in the apartment? I had lived my whole life there, and the other children had been born there; we knew no other home. The idea of moving was very scary. Since we had a deadline by which we had to move, it was decided that I would go with Father to the newly designated ghetto to find a place to live. Early the following morning we undertook the long, difficult walk on the streets of Riga; Father knew some shortcuts, but it still took us two hours to get there. Father remembered that some shoemakers who worked for him lived in that area. As we got closer to the ghetto, we saw long streams of people coming from the surrounding side streets.

They were Jews, coming to see their future "neighborhood" and the barbed-wire fence that was being erected.

Our first stop was to visit a female shoemaker who had made baby shoes for us. Her house was on the edge of the ghetto but was not included in it. She received us very cordially and expressed sympathy for the way the Jews were being treated by the Germans, as well as a desire to help us in any way she could. My father asked if she would store some of our belongings in her house, since we would have very limited space in the ghetto; if anything happened to us, she could keep them. She agreed to do so and promised that if there were a shortage of food in the ghetto, she would get some food to us through the barbed-wire fence that stretched almost through her backyard. Father was very happy that she showed such friendship and willingness to help us in our time of need. We left to see another shoemaker who had made water-resistant boots for us in the past. He and his family lived inside the ghetto boundaries in a small frame bungalow with an adjacent yard, which was used as a vegetable garden in the summer. He was happy to see Father, although he and his family were greatly disturbed by the threatening situation we faced, and he expressed sorrow over the way we were being treated.

He and his wife told us tearfully that they had to leave their house and beautiful garden. They described how much work they had put into the little bungalow; they were constantly repairing and remodeling something to keep it in good shape. For many years, this had been their dream house, and they now had to give it up with no compensation to make space for the ghetto.

This would be the ideal home for our family if Father could make some kind of deal with the shoemaker, I thought. Apparently, Father had the same idea; he asked me, "Bora, would you like to live here?" I replied, "This would be just perfect, and the children could play in the beautiful yard." Father immediately proposed a trade: our apartment, fully furnished, in exchange for renting the shoemaker's house. He promised that he would take care of the house, their pride and joy, as if it were his own. "It would be in very good hands," Father assured them. The shoemaker was happy with the proposition and agreed to let us have the house, but he did not want to take our apartment. His family was planning to leave the city and move to a relative's farm, which would be much safer for them. The deal was struck—all that was left was to find out when the

Russian family would vacate their house. The shoemaker agreed to let us know within a few days. We left with hearty embraces, handshakes, and smiles on everybody's faces.

Father and I walked home, proud that we had found living quarters for our family. Mother and the children were waiting and were delighted to hear that we had successfully secured a house in the ghetto. Mother was very pleased that our former workers were willing to help our family. She proudly said to Father, "You see, Abrasha, it always pays to be nice to your workers. You treated them with dignity and respect, and you were helpful to them when they were in need. Now they are returning the favor when you need them." Mother was so happy that she got on the telephone immediately to tell her brothers and sisters the good news. She learned that some of them were not as fortunate; they had either found only very small apartments or were going to be sharing an apartment with another family.

My parents were faced with the task of a lifetime: where to put all of the furniture and other household goods. There was no time to sell them, so we were forced to give them away with the agreement that if we survived the war we would get them back. People consented to that arrangement and seemed glad to help us, but I would not have been surprised if some who received Father's hard-earned belongings had no intention of returning them. Why should they not take them for free with worthless promises and meaningless smiles, I thought to myself. My parents set aside the furniture and other goods they would take to the ghetto; then came all of the people who were taking our belongings. First came a lady shoemaker with a large two-wheeled buggy, which she filled to capacity with the sewing machine and other valuable appliances, as well as some furniture. The piano was given to our next-door neighbor, the dining room furniture to the neighbor upstairs, and the pieces from the living room to some other people in the building. Within a few days, all of the excess items had been given away in good faith to our gentile friends. We were left with very little furniture and the stored food, which consisted of flour, beans, toasted bread, and other preserved food.

I decided to give away my bicycle and my sister Dora's. I was very fond of my new bike, which my parents had given to me when I graduated from high school. I went down to the main floor where our bicycles were kept in a small private storage room. I had to get the door key from the janitor, who informed me that the bicycles were gone. I became very angry and said, "You are the only one who has the keys to this room. How could the bicycles disappear without your knowing about it?" The janitor, who had known me from infancy, innocently replied, "I do not know." I said, "You took our bicycles. All these years I thought you were our friend, but now I know better." I left him standing at his apartment door; he had nothing to say for himself, so that was the way I said good-bye to the "friendly" Latvian janitor in our building.

The ghetto would be closed in two days. Everything in our house was packed and ready to go. Father had made arrangements with a Latvian who had a horse and wagon to transfer our belongings to the new place. The only thing impeding our move was that we had not received consent from the Russian shoemaker whose house we were to take over. My mother and father were very worried—what could have prevented him from getting in touch with us? Most of the Jews in the neighborhood had already moved out, and we were still in our apartment. "Could our devoted friend have changed his mind and given the house to someone else for a hefty sum of money?" asked my mother; her thoughts made us worry all the more. The shoemaker had no telephone, so we could not call him. Finally, my father decided to go to the ghetto and see what was wrong. Mother decided to accompany him in case he needed to persuade our friend to move out of his house.

When they arrived, the house and yard looked deserted. Father knocked at the door, but nobody responded; they tried to open it and found it unlocked. To their amazement, the house was completely empty; the Russian couple had left without telling us. Father closed the door tightly, and he and Mother headed home, discussing the shoemaker's bizarre disappearance. They could not understand why he had not told us of his moving plans. Maybe something had happened to him, or perhaps they had to move out in a hurry, they thought. I imagined that this poor honest man had become so disgusted about his own problems that he did not care what happened to the house or to his friends. If he had had a telephone, he certainly would have called us, but to travel the long distance to our house was probably too much for him to bear.

As soon as my parents returned home, Father asked the mover to get us out that same day. He wanted to make sure some stranger did not move into the house before we did. As soon as the mover arrived, we hurriedly loaded our belongings on the wagon and were on our way, for better or worse, to a new life. Before our final departure, I went to the vestibule of our building to look at the address board. I saw our names in heavy print: "Kacel, Apartment 30." I said a very sentimental good-bye to the board and left the vestibule doubting I would ever see the building again. I went back to the horse and wagon, where everyone was ready for the long journey. My family followed on foot behind the slow-moving wagon. From a distance, it must have looked like a funeral procession.

The traffic leading to the ghetto was heavy in both directions. You could see people pushing buggies, men carrying all sorts of packages that seemed much too heavy, and horses pulling loaded wagons. The Jews were moving their few belongings into the ghetto, and the gentiles were moving out. After a long walk, we arrived at our new home and quickly unloaded our belongings from the wagon. Father thanked the Latvian mover for a job well-done and paid him for his services. The sun had already set, and everybody in my family was glad we had arrived before dark. We had had a very strenuous day; we had not eaten and were exhausted. We unpacked only what we needed for the night, and after a small bite to eat, my family went to sleep.

The next day, we got up early to see what was going on in the new neighborhood. This was the last day before the gate to the ghetto would be shut, although the Jews would still be able to come and go freely. From a distance, I could see laborers finishing the large entrance gate. The barbed-wire fence around the ghetto was in place. Our small house was located on the main street, called Ludzas, near the corner of Daugavpils Street. On the corner stood the fire station, which had recently been vacated for the erection of the ghetto; according to gestapo policy, we did not need a fire station. Between the fire station and our house was the large yard that served as a vegetable garden in the summer. Across the street was the well-known Jewish Maternity Hospital of Riga, called Lenas Hacedek, which now served as a general hospital for the residents of the ghetto.

My mother was very pleased with our new home, and we were fortunate that the Russian shoemaker had given us his house without compensation. It was fairly spacious: It had enough bedrooms for us all, a dining room, and space for the children to play. In essence, we had all the privacy we needed, although the vehicle and pedestrian traffic was very heavy since we were located on the main street. People young and old walked up and down the street: some rushing, some barely strolling, some pulling empty buggies, some pushing buggies filled with belongings. Some had smiling faces, others very sad faces. People were going in all directions. The street looked like an anthill—the ants were busy at work, but little was accomplished. The Germans had evacuated around two thousand gentiles and, in the same space, forcibly settled about thirty-two thousand Jews. No wonder the streets of the ghetto look like a madhouse, I thought to myself.

I stood in front of our house, taking in the strange environment. I could not yet absorb where I was or what I saw—I felt as though I was living in a foreign world. Even the people I knew looked different. Their strained faces and indifferent looks made me wonder who they really were. I wished everything I was seeing were just a dream, but it was real—it was my new life. Today I am still free, but tomorrow I will be a caged man, I thought. Once the ghetto was closed, innocent Jewish men, women, and children would be put in shackles.

As I was observing the surroundings, I noticed the distinguished face of an old man who was sitting on the concrete steps at the entrance of Lenas Hacedek Hospital. He looked very familiar, so I crossed the street to get a closer look; I then recognized his face from pictures in my history books in school. I asked, "Are you Professor Dubnow?" He replied, "Yes, I am." "You have been sitting here for a long time," I said. He answered sadly, "I have no place to go. I dropped off a bundle of my belongings in the basement of this hospital." "I am very sorry, Professor Dubnow, that you do not have a place of your own. I wanted you to know that I was one of the pupils who studied your history books," I told him and ended our conversation; there was nothing I could do to help the world-renowned historian.

My mother was curious about whether her brothers and sisters had secured apartments for their families, and she was able to see each of them. She was glad to learn that everybody had accommodations in the ghetto, although some had found them easily and others had experienced a harder time. Mother told us what she had seen during her visits with her relatives. It was a very sad story of how the lives of our fairly prosperous family members, all of whom had once had bright futures, had suddenly been shattered. Forcibly relocated from their homes, they had lost everything they treasured, both material and spiritual—as they had lost their human rights and freedom of movement as well. I felt very sorry for my Aunt Lydia and her fourteen-year-old daughter, Gitta, who had to share a small apartment with other relatives. Lydia had bravely moved some of her belongings to the ghetto by herself; her husband, Boris, and son, Leiser, had been kidnapped by the Latvian killing squads and never returned.

My Uncle Wulf and Aunt Channa occupied a large apartment with their adult children. Ironically, their unhappy life in the ghetto did solve some of the minor domestic problems that had previously aggravated them. For example, the adult children who lived with them were finicky eaters; their food had to look and taste a certain way. A loaf of bread from the bakery had to have the right shape and be well baked, with a smooth and well-rounded crust. Also, some of the children would only eat the part of the gefilte fish—the traditional Jewish fish—that was cooked on top of the pot. They felt they could distinguish the fish that were on the bottom from the ones that were cooked on top. Now, in the ghetto, they had to eat whatever was available. Of Wulf and Channa's seven children, only three were living with them—Moisey, Chone, and Dora. Their sons Abram and Julius had been kidnapped by Latvian killing squads, and a married daughter, Lisa, lived in Holland. Their oldest daughter, Ljuba, had escaped to the Soviet Union with her husband, Isaak, and three sons, Grischa, Elja, Mischa.

My Uncle Aron and Aunt Berta, their son, Boris, and older daughter, Ljuba, and her baby occupied a small flat on the top floor of a four-story apartment building, one of three "high-rises" in the ghetto. Ljuba's husband had also been kidnapped by the Latvian mobile killing squads and never returned home. Their younger daughter, Frieda, was living in the United States. Aron, a beautiful human being, changed his occupation from paint manufacturer to baby-sitter for his infant grandchild.

My aunt Debora and her husband, Ljova, lived on the edge of the ghetto with their eighteen-year-old daughter, Lucja. Their son, Rafa, had left Riga for the United States just before Stalin's armed forces overran Latvia. They had been living in a gorgeous, roomy apartment in the center of the city but were forced to leave with only the most essential household goods and furniture. Their apartment became the living quarters of a high-ranking German administrator from the occupying forces. Debora adjusted to their new life more easily than Ljova did; the loss of his possessions was difficult for him. He was very knowledgeable, but he made frequent sarcastic remarks that were sometimes unjustified and drove people away. Debora was a doctor, and Ljova became a technician; they had built a very lucrative dental practice together.

The fate of another Uncle Wolf, his wife, Minna, and their four children—Chaim, Tanja, Leiba, and Bella—was unknown. We assumed that they had managed to escape to the Soviet Union. Our relatives also expressed concern for the well-being of two brothers and their families who resided abroad. Chone and his wife, Rachel, and their son, Urchik, lived in Vilna (Vilnius), Poland. Sascha, his wife, Elena, and two children, Frieda and Jefim, resided in Moscow. My mother and the rest of the family were happy for her sister Rebecca and her husband, Herman, who had lived for many years in the United States, known as the "Golden Land." Such stories could be heard in every Jewish household.

The first day the ghetto was closed was very exciting. The Jewish Ghetto Committee, headed by a man named Eliaschow, was in charge of day-to-day life. This administration was organized into various departments—produce, police, sanitation, and housing, with others established as needed. The Produce Department opened produce stores in which the ghetto inhabitants could receive their food rations. The Police Department was the most important in the daily life of the ghetto. Its members tried hard to keep order and to solve the most difficult problems with great restraint. The police wore blue caps with a Star of David emblem. At the ghetto gate, the German police were in charge, and the Jewish police officers were called if needed. The Sanitation Department, which had strict rules, oversaw the cleanliness of the streets and backyards, as well as the proper disposal of garbage. A large laundry was established, where many women found employment. It was sad to see well-known wealthy people involved in such menial activities as sweeping the streets. Plans were drawn for a public bath to be erected; everything possible was done to keep the ghetto residents healthy and conditions sanitary.

The most urgent problem was the shortage of living space for all residents. Many Jews could not find permanent housing, and the Housing Department was required to find living quarters for everyone. They went from house to house, looking for available space; one such space they found was our home. We had soon lost the comfort of living alone in such a spacious house and were forced to accept a family of four. The new family assigned to us was not of the social class we would have chosen, and we did not think we could have a good, lasting relationship with them. They had lived in the neighborhood that now contained the ghetto, but, to their surprise, they discovered that their apartment building was not within the boundaries. As a result, they had missed the opportunity to secure living space. Knowing the circumstances in which we were forced to exist, we made our lives together as pleasant and comfortable as possible.

The new family consisted of a mother and father about my parents' age, a son, Meyer, who was ten years old, and a daughter my age, whose name was Mary. They occupied the rear part of the house, where one large room had been converted into two bedrooms; the other room was now a living room–bedroom combination. We all shared the kitchen and bathroom. Because of the layout of the house, they were able to have privacy. At the rear entrance of the house was a small room, like a mud room or a shed, that had been built later by the shoemaker. The room had two doors: one led to the backyard, the other to the house. The room was not heated and had only one small light, which was strong enough to allow us to see ourselves in the small mirror on the wall. The beautiful backyard was useful because the children could play there safely.

With the passing of time and the need we had for each other during troubled times, we solidified our relationship with this family and became great friends. It was thus that two families settled down in one tiny house to fulfill the new ghetto ordinance: "two square meters per person."

The fence around the ghetto was guarded by the most trusted German collaborators, the Latvian police, whose leader was a well-known anti-Semite named Arrais. Nobody could leave the ghetto without an authorized guide, so when people were finally able to return to work, a guide from their workplace had to pick them up and bring them back. Individual work units were called kolonnes, each of which was headed by a Kolonnenführer; the group would meet at a designated place near the ghetto gate. The Kolonnenführer had to make sure all of the laborers showed up; he was notified if somebody was unable to go to work. The

Kolonnenführer did not generally work on the job site but acted as the liaison between the Jewish workers and the German employers. If any grievances occurred on the job, he was the person who settled the complaint. A person in such a position was necessary and very helpful to both the Germans and the Jews. When the unarmed German guides arrived at the gate, they would call on him to lead his men out from the ghetto; as he did so, the guards would count how many were leaving so they could be sure the same number returned.

We tried to make the best of our unpredictable situation by keeping the hope of a better future foremost in our minds. It is said that every beginning is hard, and so it was with ours. I was a young man in a world of terrible destruction who was facing a very different, difficult life in the ghetto.

The Riga Jews were in the ghetto, but the Latvian assaults did not stop. The armed police, in their military uniforms with green armbands, were the sole guardians of the ghetto perimeter; we called them "Bendeldike," the Yiddish word for one who wears an armband. Within the first two days, casualties had occurred as a result of conflict between the Jews and the police. On one side of the ghetto, a fence was erected next to a sidewalk within the ghetto proper. Some people were walking "too close" to the barbed-wire fence, so the Bendeldike decided to shoot at them. Although the gate was supervised by the German police, the Bendeldike manned the order and would often beat and injure Jewish workers returning from work. Some unpleasantness always seemed to stem from unwarranted behavior by the Latvian police. The ghetto inhabitants protected themselves by keeping their distance. The Ghetto Committee decided to make openings in the existing wooden fences, erected by the previous owners to protect their private property, so pedestrians would not have to use the dangerous sidewalk next to the fence. Thus, the tragic incidents at the fence ended. Still, I would periodically hear gunshots late at night and sometimes during the day. I often wondered why the guards would shoot into the air and waste bullets, but I concluded that they enjoyed intimidating the Jews on one side of the fence and scaring the gentiles on the other.

After the closing of the ghetto, Father remained in contact with the female shoemaker. He would show up at the fence, where she could see him from her second-floor apartment; when the guards were not in the vicinity, she would throw over some packages—usually meat, butter, and other valuable provisions that were unavailable to us. The understanding was that she would sell some of our belongings she was keeping for us to purchase these provisions. This arranged trade-off lasted for a time until the guards became drunk one night and, in a rage, fired their weapons unmercifully all night long. People both inside and outside of the ghetto could not sleep. The next day, Father took his usual walk to get the shoemaker's attention. She came empty-handed and said to Father, "I am very scared. I cannot help you anymore" and left. My father was very upset and could not keep from trying again, so he returned to the fence a few days later, hoping she had changed her mind. She noticed him through her window, shook her head, and waved one hand as if to say "good-bye." She disappeared from the window, thus ending the long relationship between my father and his devoted Russian friend.

Our family slowly adapted to life in the ghetto. We had enough flour, beans, and canned and dried food to last a long while, but we were short of meat, dairy products, and fresh vegetables and fruits. My mother knew how to adjust her household chores and put together meager menus.

The ghetto was soon in turmoil again. An order came from the German administration that the Jews had to surrender any gold jewelry, coins, and foreign currency in their possession; they also had to register any property owned abroad. The ghetto population received this distressing news in an uproar, for almost every Jew had some kind of gold jewelry, even if only a wedding ring. Father and I had to hide all of our gold, since we had no intention of surrendering it to the Germans. My father, who had learned valuable lessons from his experiences in World War I, had bought gold in various forms for future needs; he knew everything could be bought for gold, including one's life.

We were fortunate to have our own backyard in which we could bury our valuables; few people had such a luxury. Late at night, I dug two deep holes along the wall adjoining the empty firehouse. Mother decided that all of the crystal was to be hidden as well, and she wrapped each of our beautiful vases, dishes, and other pieces we had brought with us. Before Mother took the last piece, I tapped it with my finger; a beautiful high-pitched sound filled the room—a sound I could not forget. Father packed all of the gold pieces, and I carefully laid the crystal in one hole and the gold in the other. Father and I covered the holes with dirt and made two markings on the wall of the fire station to indicate the location of our buried treasure.

After this strenuous burial procedure, which seemed like a funeral, we went back into the house. My parents were very sad because such beautiful objects had been buried in dirt. In a low and sad voice, Father said to Mother, "God knows if we will live to see our jewelry and crystal again." She added, "God knows if I will ever wear my wedding band again." I, too, felt very sad that I had participated in hiding our most treasured possessions, including the rings my mother wore every day. I still remember how my mother had labored so hard to preserve the lustrous look of the crystal pieces. The sun used to penetrate the windows of the dining room and shine on the large crystal dish that stood on the buffet, creating a colorful rainbow. It was a beautiful phenomenon.

The following day, my Uncle Ljova came to our house with a worried look. After a short conversation, he asked my father, "Abrasha, can you do me a favor?" "If I can, I certainly will, Ljova," replied Father. "I have gold jewelry I would like you to bury in your yard. I live in an apartment and have no place to hide it. I do not want to give it to the Germans." With no hesitation Father agreed to do this, so when night fell Ljova returned with a well-wrapped package containing his and Debora's gold jewelry. When he had handed it over, he was prepared to leave, but Father asked him to stay so they could bury it together. My uncle refused and said, "Abrasha, I trust you—otherwise I would not come to you." Father wished him well, saying, "Let us hope we will see the time when you will enjoy your gold and I mine." After Ljova left, Father buried the package in another hole and made a third marking on the firehouse wall.

The winter of 1941 arrived in early November with severe frost and lots of snow. Many homes had heating problems, but we were fortunate because the shoemaker had left enough wood in the shed to last the entire winter. It felt good to be in a warm house, although others were cold. People were forced to tear down wooden fences for heating fuel to keep their apartments warm, since all of the buildings in the ghetto were heated with wood and coal. Father began to look for work. He could have had a job in the ghetto, but he was determined to seek work on the outside to get away from the daily unpleasantness of the ghetto. Everybody was yearning for the outside air, for we all felt as though we lived in a pressure cooker. Working in the city would also give him the opportunity to bring home additional produce.

Good news finally arrived: A new kolonne of eighty people was being created to work for the Deutsche Reichsbahn (the German railroad). I joined my father, along with my cousins Moisey, Uncle Wulf's son, and Boris, Uncle Aron's son. We met at the ghetto gate early one frosty morning. A representative named Weinberg introduced himself as the appointed Kolonnenführer. He checked the attendance list the ghetto employment office had provided; when everything seemed to be in order, a man in a Reichsbahn uniform arrived to pick us up, and we were en route to our new workplace. We walked a long way on the pavement—as always—with the German on the sidewalk. Nobody minded the chilly morning or the mounds of snow on the pavement; it felt so good to be away from the barbed-wire fence. I felt like a bird free of its cage for the day.

The kolonne reached its destination next to the city's slaughterhouse. All of the men were looking forward to working within the compound, where we could obtain some pieces of meat, but we were stopped short of the slaughterhouse facilities. The German guide directed us to the empty boxcars that transported cattle to the slaughterhouse; our job was to clean the floors. In the summer, this job would have been acceptable, but it was winter and below freezing. This made the work very strenuous, as the manure and straw froze together to create a concretelike substance. Every worker received a pick or, as we called it, a kirke, which was made of hardened steel about two feet long, with one flat side and one pointed side and a three-foot handle through the center. With this heavy tool, we had to loosen the three- to six-inch-thick frozen manure from the boxcar floors. Six men were assigned to every car. Our kolonne had to clean all of the dirty boxcars on the track; each group had to clean three cars a day, which took a great amount of hard work. The task was beyond the strength of some of the men, and some others did not feel like working up to their capacity, which meant somebody else had to work much harder as a result. It took an all-consuming effort to break up the frozen manure piece by piece.

A conflict arose when some men objected to working with those who had less physical strength. This problem was eventually solved when some of the men decided that individual groups should pick their own co-workers. The less capable laborers had a hard time joining a group. One of these men was my cousin Moisey, who was so clumsy with the kirke that he became a laughingstock in our kolonne. I understood him well, since I knew his background; he had never done any physical work in his life. As a jewelry repairman, the heaviest object he had ever lifted was a watch, so lifting the heavy steel kirke and breaking off pieces of frozen manure were beyond his strength. Father, my cousin Boris, and I felt sorry for him, so we decided to let him join our group. Among the three of us, we could make up for his lost time. We taught him how to use the kirke, and in time his performance improved. Moisey had a habit that often made us angry: He would chew the sandwich from his lunch all day. Every few minutes he would take a bite and chew it as if it were gum. One day I told him, "Stop chewing your bread. Eat the way we all do. You know, Moisey, you are like a cow in the pasture—your mouth does not stop for a minute. You probably have two stomachs like a cow." He did not say a word, for he recognized his weaknesses and rarely responded to criticism. Moisey understood that he was among friends who were willing to help and protect him.

I remember a rough and very powerful man in our kolonne whose real name I have forgotten; we called him Toothless. He had only two teeth, so he had to dip solid food into a liquid to make it soft enough to swallow. He was used to heavy physical labor since he made his living as a mover; he owned a two-wheel pushcart and delivered freight to various commercial customers. In Riga, very few goods were delivered by trucks; most "truckings" were done by horse and wagon or by pushcarts such as his. For Toothless, cleaning the boxcars was an easy job—he could do it in no time. He was always ahead of his group in cleaning his portion of the floor. To him, the heavy kirke was like a walking cane—he picked it up with ease and smashed the frozen manure like it was cheesecake. Pieces would break off and fly all around him. He used such force that he had to remove his heavy winter coat and then continue to chisel off the icy floor.

No guards supervised us, and I soon noticed that Toothless disappeared every morning and returned with a small can of milk. One day I asked him, "Where do you get the milk?" He did not hesitate to tell me he was milking the cows that were in the boxcars on one of the side tracks. I decided to do the same, but I needed some instructions on how to milk a cow since I had never done so. I asked Toothless if he would tell me how to safely approach the cow and do the milking. He was not happy to hear of my intentions and was unwilling to help me at first, since he was afraid there might not be enough milk for us both. He knew the cattle were milked by professionals before they were brought to the slaughterhouse, so by the time they reached us their udders contained little milk. Nonetheless, a few days later he came to me with a bottle in his hand. On the neck of the bottle he showed me how to milk a cow by squeezing and pulling the teats at the same time.

I practiced for a while and then was ready for my task. All of the men in my work group were excited about my daring undertaking. I prepared a can with a wide opening so no milk would spill, and at an appropriate time I went to look for the boxcars that held the cows. First and foremost, I had to make sure none of the Latvian or German railroad workers saw me near the cattle train. When I reached the boxcars, the doors were shut tight. I had to pry open the big sliding door enough to get through. Some of the doors were frozen so tightly that I could not open them. After a time, I did manage to open a few, but I still had quite a climb to get into the car since the door was high above the ground. Finally, I successfully overcame all of the obstacles and gained access to the cows. When I first saw one eye-to-eye, I was rather scared, for I had never been near a cow before. I followed the instructions I had been given and slowly came closer and closer until I could bend down and put my can under the cow's udder. I started to squeeze and pull one teat at a time, just as I had been taught on the bottle, but no milk cane out. I went to another cow and then another, and still no milk came out. I was so determined to come back with some milk that I tried a few more of the boxcars. I soon had to give up and return to my workplace with only a few drops of milk. I felt very bad because my mission had not been accomplished.

I remember a kind and mild-speaking elderly man in our kolonne named Kirshenberg who had some problems with his co-workers. To my youthful eyes, he seemed to be the oldest person in our kolonne, although the circumstances may have made him look old. He lacked the strength to perform the required work; therefore, nobody was willing to work with him, because he would be a burden to the others in his group. The other men quietly requested that Kolonnenführer Weinberg replace him with a more able-bodied man. Weinberg, an accommodating and good-natured person, solved this problem to everybody's satisfaction. He made Kirshenberg work with a different group each day, so the burden would be carried not by only a few individual laborers but by all the men in the kolonne. Nobody objected to such a fair decision, and harmony and friendship prevailed in our group. We got to know each other very well, and everybody was willing to help others in times of need. At times we argued, at times we laughed, but everything was done in a conciliatory and friendly way, for we were like one big family.

The situation in the ghetto worsened, and some people began to experience shortages of food. At some workplaces, the Jews were able to obtain small quantities of food and bring them into the ghetto, but everyone was searched at the entrance gate. In many cases, the unauthorized potatoes or the like were found and taken away, then the guilty parties were severely beaten. To make the frisking more thorough, the Germans built another gate in front of the existing one so the Jewish workers would have to go through two gates. Thus, the Latvian guards and their German superiors could search and physically abuse the exhausted returning workers twice before they even reached the ghetto.

The inhabitants of the ghetto slowly began to get their lives and thoughts together and lived with the hope that they would be able to overcome this difficult life. We all dreamed that someday the German expansion on all fighting fronts would stop, and the Soviet Army would gain the upper hand. We also hoped we would be able to live normal lives and that our children could grow up in a more tolerant society. At the time, however, they were unfulfillable dreams and empty thoughts, since the Nazi armies were advancing rapidly on all fronts. On the streets of Riga as we went to work every morning, our kommando met with hundreds of prisoners of war (POWs) held captive by the Germans. Their starving, puffy faces, bulging eyes, and worn-out military garments proved one thing to me—they had a long and difficult road ahead. These young men of different nationalities found themselves prisoners in a strange country; their survival in these abusive conditions seemed very unlikely.

Slowly, my family also became used to its new life in the ghetto. My mother did an excellent job of taking care of our small living quarters, and she knew how to feed the family with the little food she could get; nobody ever left the table hungry. The Jewish Ghetto Committee was planning to open a school for the children, which would be a great help to my brother and sisters. Everything looked as promising as possible, considering the circumstances under which we lived. People often spent their few free Sundays strolling down Ludzas Street, discussing their problems or the situation on the front. I used to stand in front of our house and watch everyone pass by, and I would sometimes meet with friends and chat.

One Sunday I noticed a man walking toward me. I did not want to believe what I saw: It was the well-known Captain Cukurs, who I had admired for many years. He became the national hero of Latvia when he flew a single-engine plane from Riga to Gambia, Africa, in the early 1930s. In those days, that was a great achievement in the history of aviation. Cukurs was an officer in the air force and had received many decorations in the line of duty. He was dressed in a green military uniform with a wooden pistol pouch hanging at his left side. When he passed, I wondered what such a noble Latvian officer was doing in the ghetto. He walked to the end of Ludzas Street and returned on the other side of the street, observing the surroundings. His presence lingered in my mind for a long time, and it took several years to find out why he had been there. He was one of the most important Latvian participants in the liquidation of the Riga ghetto. He became a well-known Nazi collaborator and one of Himmler's top henchmen; after the war, Cukurs was recognized as a war criminal and was sought all over the world. It was traumatic for me to realize that the flyer I had idolized had felt such vicious animosity toward the Jewish people. Cukurs successfully escaped to Argentina and hid there for many years. In 1965, according to the *Jewish Press* (March 19, 1965, p. 3), he came to Uruguay from Brazil and was found murdered in a beach house in Montevideo.

In the ghetto, we were considered one of the fortunate families, privileged enough to escape the atrocities committed by the Latvian killing squads. My family survived to stay together, cry together, and laugh together. The only thing left was to be freed together, and we lived with that wish from day to day. As time passed, I developed a cordial relationship with the family that shared our house. In the evenings, Mary and I would sometimes talk about our past social experiences and school activities. We slowly developed a very close friendship, and I began to really like her. She was an intelligent girl, but what attracted me most was her beautiful face: She had dark eyes, brunette hair, small white teeth, and a cute little nose.

After a while, we became uncomfortable talking in the presence of our parents or the other children. We decided to shift our meeting place from the crowded dining room to the cold, secluded back room, which had a wooden bench wide enough to accommodate us both. The little light on the ceiling made this neglected space rather romantic. We could not spend much of our free time in this unheated room, but we began to visit there every evening. We always had something to talk about; I soon felt comfortable enough to confide my innermost feelings to Mary, and she did the same. It was an emotional relief to be with her after a hard day's work with no compensation or kind word for a job well-done. By being together each evening, we were able to forget the harsh living conditions in our ghetto—we were in our own imaginary world. It did not take long for sexual feelings to arise. We embraced and kissed each other as if there were no tomorrow. We forgot all about our troubled days, and every night when we departed we looked forward to the next evening's date. Eventually, we declared our love for each other; we pushed aside all of our present problems and spoke only about our future and how we could have a normal, happy life together.

For several days in November, we experienced peace and tranquillity in the ghetto. The wild shooting subsided, fewer people were frisked and beaten at the entrance gate, and everyone went about their business more calmly than before. Everybody thought the gestapo High Command, which was in charge of the ghetto, had begun to have a less discriminating attitude toward the inhabitants.

Thursday, November 27, 1941, began like any other working day but did not end as such. When all of the workers had left for the day, a bulletin was issued throughout the ghetto that stated: "The ghetto will be liquidated and all people will be removed by Sunday, November 30, 1941." In the evening, when our kolonne returned from work, I noticed the sad faces of the Jewish police at the gate. We realized that something had happened during our absence, for the behavior of the policemen always served as an indicator of what had occurred during the day. All of the men in our kolonne rushed to get home to find out what was wrong.

The entire family was waiting impatiently for us to arrive. They were very happy to see we were safe, and Mother immediately told us about the pending order. Father and I were shocked and amazed to hear such unbelievably sad news, and we were at a loss about what the family should do next. Everyone was in the same predicament, not knowing what to do. A tiny part of the ghetto was evacuated immediately; people living there were chased out hurriedly and could take only their most essential belongings. A wire fence was erected to divide this section from the rest of the ghetto, people were in a complete panic, and all kinds of rumors spread. Nobody could comprehend, until it was too late, the two very important words mentioned in the order: "liquidate" and "remove." No one in the ghetto had made any moves, since we were waiting for further instructions from the gestapo. The following day—Friday, November 28—our kolonne gathered at the gate and went to work as usual. When we returned home, we were told of the new directives for the liquidation of the ghetto: All men belonging to a work kolonne were being evacuated to a newly created work camp, which became known as the Little Ghetto.

Our kolonne decided to make this move with the intention of living together. Many workers were hesitant to leave their families and decided not to go to the new quarters at that time, although eventually everyone did go. The next morning, which was the last day of the evacuation, Father and I packed our most essential belongings and walked over to the Little Ghetto to see what was going on. The entire area was in an uproar—it looked like a mass exodus to the promised land. People were going in and out of the area; they also wanted to see the living conditions in the newly created camp. We saw unbelievably disturbing scenes— people were stampeding, and chaos prevailed. The Little Ghetto consisted of small, shabby houses that would be hard-pressed to accommodate hundreds of working men. People wanted to live with their friends or relatives, but the shortage of space often prevented this. Arguments flared up; even an occasional fistfight occurred. I saw intelligent people go berserk trying to find a space.

Father and I went through several houses before we found our coworkers in a little house facing the large ghetto. Some of them had already moved in and had saved the entire house for those in our kolonne. We were told we had to move in immediately, or they might not be able to keep the space they had reserved for us. Father thanked the men for their concern and told them he was leaving to pick up our belongings from our old house and would return right away. When we got home he called to Mother, "Bora and I have to leave immediately—there is a shortage of space in the Little Ghetto." He caught his breath and continued, "Dear Fanja, you would not believe what is going on there. People are fighting for space, and our co-workers are holding a small room just for us. If we do not go now, we might wind up sleeping on the floor somewhere."

Mother agreed that we should leave immediately, so we grabbed our bags and the pillows and blankets she gave us. Before we left, we told her and the children, "Tomorrow is Sunday, and we will not be working, so we will come back and have breakfast together." The family accompanied us to the street; I was so confused and in such a hurry that I hardly kissed my family good-bye. As we walked away, we kept looking behind us until we lost sight of our dear ones; I was convinced I would see them again the next day. We walked as fast as we could. When we arrived at the small house, the only living space that remained was the little room saved for us by our devoted co-workers.

3

Life in the Little Ghetto

My father and I were very grateful to our co-workers for securing the tiny room, which had just enough space for both of us. It contained a double bed and two small chairs that had been left by the previous occupant. We immediately threw all of our clothes, pillows, and blankets on the bed to indicate to others that the room was already taken. I liked this tiny room, which was separate from the other rooms in the house, so we had privacy. It had a window facing the large ghetto that looked through the newly erected dividing fence. The room had one door that led to the kitchen and another that led to the dining room, which had been converted to a large bedroom. We made ourselves as comfortable as we could. The house looked like a public place; it was overflowing with people looking for living space, although our kolonne had filled it to capacity. As soon as someone walked in, he would see how crowded it was and walk right out.

We were very concerned about the absence of my cousin Boris, who was supposed to share this space with us. It was late in the afternoon; at five o'clock the gates of the work camps would be closed. He did eventually show up, but he had nowhere to go; every bed was occupied by one of our co-workers. Since we wanted to live together, we had to solve the problem of finding Boris accommodations in a full house. My father figured that if we could find a child's bed or a narrow, collapsible bed, the problem would be solved. My cousin was short and slightly built, so he would fit into such a bed, which could then be squeezed in between the wall and the foot of our double bed. All three of us went from house to house in the Little Ghetto, asking people if they had or knew of somebody who had an extra small bed. After trying several places, we finally found an old collapsible bed; it fit in our room perfectly. The tiny bedroom was occupied beyond capacity, and there was no room to move around, but we were all glad that our efforts had been not wasted. My cousin thanked Father for his "genius mind" for coming up with such an idea.

After we had settled down, a co-worker told me, to my surprise, "While you were gone, your little sister Ljuba came to the fence at your bedroom window and asked for you. I told her you had gone to find another bed for your cousin. She waited for a while and then left." "Oh my," I replied, "I am very sorry I missed her. We have a special love for each other—she is a very devoted sister. Most likely, she came here to see for herself how our accommodations are in the new living quarters." I thought to myself that we had been gone only a few hours and she missed us already. "She is a beautiful little girl and was very brave to come here on such a turbulent day," said my co-worker. I was puzzled as to how Ljuba had found our house and my window. Then I remembered that I had described the location of our house to my mother, including the fact that we had a window facing the large ghetto. Ljuba was present during our conversation and must have listened carefully, figuring out exactly where we must be. Her love for us was so great that nothing could stop her from seeing her brother and father again, as if she somehow knew she would never see us again.

The sun set slowly on the horizon, and the highly emotional day came to an end. At five o'clock sharp, the gate to our work camp was shut—nobody could get in or out—and a detachment of the Latvian Einsatzkommando was on guard. The men in our house were exhausted from the day's activities, and they prepared for the first night without their families. Father, Boris, and I went to sleep having had nothing to eat, so I was looking forward to going home the following morning and enjoying my mother's breakfast. I immediately fell into a sleep so deep that sporadic gunshots during the night did not wake me. I was used to this familiar senseless shooting and brushed it off, thinking the drunken Latvian guards were humoring themselves on a freezing winter night. When I awoke the next day, however, I realized that the situation had been different than I had thought. Many of my co-workers had not slept all night. They told me something was going on in the large ghetto, for they could hear groaning sounds and crying voices from a distance. The men in our house thought evil forces were at work—that the Latvian guards were not shooting into the air but were aiming at the people in the ghetto. I looked out my window but could not see anything; the condensation on the window had frozen during the night, and the window was covered with ice.

Everyone was in a panic; some of our group went to the gate to try to get into the large ghetto and see what was going on there, but they were turned away by heavily armed watch guards. By late morning, we all learned that the forced ghetto evacuation had taken place during the night and had continued into the early morning. Each of us heard all kinds of rumors that could not be substantiated. We still saw people walking around in the ghetto, so I thought my family might have been spared. What disturbed me most was that I would not be able to have breakfast or, for that matter, any other meal with my mother and siblings. Father and I were obsessed with finding out what had happened to our family. I felt guilty because I had not stayed home to help Mother with the evacuation. Sunday, November 30, 1941, was a devastating day for me, as I could not stop thinking about the fate of my loved ones.

The following day was our day of judgment, and the camp was still under curfew. Nobody could leave, even to go to work; we were also not permitted to talk to or see anyone who remained in the large ghetto. A few men were able to get out; they returned with gruesome news about our families. They gave eyewitness accounts of what had occurred in the ghetto while we were locked in the work camp. Saturday night, under cover of darkness, hordes of Latvian Einsatzkommandos, led by German SS officers, had stormed the ghetto and entered every house. They notified the inhabitants that they had to be out within minutes because they were being evacuated. The people were taken completely by surprise and were therefore unprepared. Some had barely enough time to put on their coats and boots before they were pushed out of their houses. The evacuation started on the end of the large ghetto that was farthest from our camp; since our house was located midway, my mother had extra time to get dressed and gather what she needed. The Latvian SS units searched every home, from basement to attic, ensuring that nobody could escape.

Anyone found hiding was shot immediately, with no questions asked. People who were slow in leaving their houses were thrown into the street;

those who walked outdoors slowly were beaten. Some disabled people, who could not walk in the deep snow, were shot on the spot, and the patients from Lenas Hacedek Hospital were dragged down to buses that were waiting on the street. Those who were shot were left to die on the snow-covered pavement, and many bodies were discovered later in the houses and other buildings. It was chaos; helplessness and fright permeated every home. I could not imagine the atmosphere in my house or what Mother was thinking about her children and about us in the camp. I was told that the evacuation was planned ahead of time and was conducted in a hurry. Along with their regular weapons, the soldiers had carried sticks and whips, which they used frequently to speed up the mass movement of men, women, and children of all ages. The Jews were led through the streets in long lines and watched closely by large detachments of armed Latvian and German soldiers. Some gentiles who lived on upper floors of buildings probably saw the murderous and inhuman evacuation process in the street below. The relocation of half of the ghetto population lasted from Saturday night until Sunday morning. The people who remained in the large ghetto were not allowed in the section that had been evacuated, which was patrolled constantly by SS Einsatzkommando soldiers.

Monday was "funeral day" for the Jews in the large ghetto; it was time to clean out all of the abandoned corpses lying in the streets, covered with fresh snow. The frozen bodies were brought to the old Jewish cemetery, which was close to the ghetto; it was already filled, so the bodies were buried on top of old graves. Special work units were organized in the camp for this cleanup duty; they were the only ones permitted to cross over to the ghetto and were under strict German supervision. At noon on Tuesday, under the pretense that we were workers in a cleanup unit, Father and I left the camp. We could roam freely in the occupied section of the ghetto; the danger would be in getting into the evacuated area, where not a soul was in sight. Our aim was to reach our house and look for any clues that might lead us to where our family had been transferred; we might also discover what they had taken with them and what they had left behind. It was a very daring undertaking; if we were apprehended by the guards, we would surely be killed, but nothing, not even death, could stop us from entering our house. The fact that we were able to look for our family was gratifying for me and my father; I would never have been able to forgive myself later if I had not done so, no matter what the risk.

We cleared the frightened thoughts from our minds and started to run down Ludzas Street toward our house. The once busy area now looked like a ghost town, with large piles of debris and red patches of blood on the otherwise pure white snow. Most of the house doors were open, and the ransacked rooms were visible from outside. The abandoned street, destruction, bloodstains, and loose, swinging doors passed through my mind without impact; I could focus only on reaching my home and could only imagine the condition in which I would find it. When we finally arrived, we saw that the small fence gate was wide open. The front door was swinging loosely in the cold winter wind, just like all the others throughout the empty ghetto. As we walked into the house, cold air seeped in and penetrated all of the rooms, making it as cold inside as it was outside. A deep, lonesome silence dominated the air, and I felt surrounded by a gruesome and frightful stillness. Everybody was gone. Everything stood in its regular place—nothing had been touched or taken away. It looked as though Mother had merely taken the children for a walk and would return at any moment, but I knew better. My loved ones were gone forever, and nobody could ever take their place.

We knew we had only a few minutes to spend in the house, so Father and I quickly checked every shelf and drawer. Everything seemed in order, and nothing was missing, except for the family's winter clothes and boots. It comforted me to know they were wearing the proper clothing for the extremely cold weather. We walked into the dining room, where the scene was less calm. On the dinner table stood four bowls of unfinished bean soup, with spoons still in them. It seemed Mother and the children did not have time to finish their supper; the intruders must have come into the house unexpectedly and forced them to leave in a hurry. Perhaps they had even been driven out of the house, since they had not taken any additional clothes or other items. What a horrible, frightful feeling they must have endured, I thought. I could not comprehend the state of mind they must have been in when they had to leave the house.

My mother would not normally have left the front door unlocked, but she had done so on this occasion. In desperation, she had been concerned less about the contents of the house than about the safety and well-being of her children. My terrible thoughts about my family brought tears to my eyes. I wanted to spend more time in the house, absorbing everything, since I knew this would be our last visit. Father reminded me several times how dangerous it was to stay, calling, "We have to go—we have to go." It was hard for me to depart, although I knew that if the guards found us they would accuse us of looting our own belongings, which would lead to our demise. My love for those I had lost meant so much to me that even in the empty house I threw kisses and said farewell to their invisible faces.

The fact that we were able to get to the abandoned ghetto to look for our dear family made my father and me feel much better; we would never forget that experience. Father asked me to take some winter clothes and a few other necessary items, but I was more interested in taking our family picture album. I looked all over for it but finally gave up my search, figuring my mother had taken it. The album was the only item missing and was the only thing Mother took with her on her journey to the unknown. Her love for us was so great that she could not leave our images; food and other possessions did not matter to her as much as the heavy picture album.

I stuffed what few belongings I had retrieved into a pillowcase, and Father did the same. In addition to some clothes, he took two special pairs of shoes that meant a lot to us and that later proved to be particularly valuable. Before we left the house, we looked around to see whether any watch guards were visible; we saw none, so we tiptoed slowly out of the house, as though we were trying not to wake somebody who was sleeping. I cautiously shut the door and closed the small fence gate, as if to give notice to the ghostly ghetto that this beautiful little house was still occupied. We had been forced to abandon a fully furnished home with many drawers and closets filled with clothes and pantry shelves filled with food. We rushed desperately to reach our "safe house," where, in contrast, our only furniture was a bed and two old chairs, and the closets and pantry shelves were empty.

Within minutes we reached the populated area of the large ghetto and felt comfortable; here we did not have to worry about somebody seeing us. Unexpectedly, we met my Uncle Aron on the street, holding his grandchild. He and his family were the last of our relatives left in the ghetto. They seemed fine and were to be evacuated at a later date; he told us his belongings were already packed. My father asked him to join us and his son Boris in the camp. His reply was very short: "I cannot leave Ljuba alone with the baby. She will need me when the evacuation comes." Ljuba was his younger daughter, who had been on her own since her husband was kidnapped by the Latvian killing squads. Aron wanted to know what we had seen in the evacuated section of the ghetto, so Father explained everything briefly, since we were anxious to bring our loot to our new living quarters.

Our co-workers were waiting eagerly to hear what was happening in the rest of the ghetto. We were overwhelmed by all of the men in our house, who asked many questions. Father did not feel like talking much, since he was so distressed by what he had seen in our abandoned house. Our friends noticed my father's emotional state, and most soon left our room. We sat down on the bed to regain our composure. I said, "My mama is gone," and tears filled my eyes. "My Fanja and the children are gone," my father said chokingly; he was about to cry. He continued, "Now we are left alone, my dear Borinka," as tears fell down his cheeks; this was the first time I had ever seen my father cry. We embraced and comforted each other.

My cousin Boris tried to comfort us by telling us that the families had probably been sent to a safe place and would be fine. Then he said, "Don't feel bad, Abrasha. My family—Aron and Berta and my sister, Ljuba, and the baby—do not object to the evacuation. They are ready for it; it will not be as bad as you might think." The few men who remained in our room agreed with my cousin. Father was relieved and was now able to tell in more detail what he had seen in the abandoned part of the ghetto. He spoke of the ghostly streets and the bloodstains on the snow and how enraged he had become when he saw the unfinished bean soup on the table in our house. He told how hurried the family must have been, for they had not taken any blankets, pillows, or other necessities. He described the dreadful circumstances of their evacuation, as well as the mistreatment they had probably had to endure. Nobody could guess why they had been evacuated so brutally. After a lengthy exchange of opinions, each man went to his own space to think about the fates of his families and friends.

For the next several days, I was not in a very positive frame of mind. I was filled with intense rage over the way the evacuation had taken place; the manner in which the women, children, and elderly people had been handled was horrible and inhuman. I could not imagine how I could live without Mother, but as great as my loss was, Father had lost a caring wife and three beautiful children. Gone, too, were my evening dates with Mary; all of our dreams had been shattered, and I had only pleasant memories. I was prepared to do whatever it took to find out where my dear ones had been sent; no obstacles, whether oceans or mountains, could stop me from finding out what had happened to Mother and the children. I knew it might take some time, but someday, as a free man, I would find out what had happened to them. I pledged to God Almighty that I would not rest without learning their fate.

We lived in the camp under a cloud of uncertainty. Our kolonne did not go to work; the guide would appear at the gate, only to be told that he could not have his men. When the guides asked when the men would be available, they received no definite answer. Some German military institutions depended so heavily on the free Jewish help that they became very unhappy and complained to the gestapo, which governed the ghetto.

My cousin and I shared a first name, so I was called Bora and my cousin was Boris. Boris called my father by his first name, Abrasha. For some reason, all of the other men in the house were called by their last names. The inhabitants never really felt as though they were in a labor camp; it was more like a continuation of the ghetto, except that our families were missing. As the days passed, many rumors spread in the Little Ghetto about the evacuation of our friends and relatives. Except for discussions about when we would go back to work, that was the main topic of conversation.

The following Sunday, December 7, 1941, one week after the first evacuation, those in the house spent another sleepless night. I heard loud noises and conversations, but I could not make out the words. There was sporadic shooting in the occupied area of the large ghetto, and I knew this time that the Latvian soldiers were not shooting aimlessly into the air. It was obvious that the final evacuation of the ghetto was taking place. The Germans were using the same methods as before: Armed Latvian soldiers, under the supervision of gestapo officers, were chasing people out of their houses and into the streets. Then, under heavy guard, the Jews were marched out of the ghetto; again, those who were too slow or unable to walk were shot.

The evacuation seemed to proceed according to plan, with precise

German timing. So many armed military people participated that nobody had a chance to escape. The second evacuation went more smoothly
for the people in the large ghetto, who were more physically and mentally prepared for the march than those in the first evacuation had been.
The activities occurred much closer to the Little Ghetto than the previous time; at times, I could clearly hear the people groaning and the Latvian
Nazi henchmen screaming, "Heraus, heraus¼ schnell, schnell [out, out¼
fast, fast]!" These nerve-racking disturbances lasted all night and into
the early morning; it was an agonizing night for us all, as I knew every
shot fired meant a casualty for the evacuated Jews. I tried to think of how
I could help the evacuees, but in the end, I realized I was helpless. When
the loud noises and voices had quieted down, I knew the process was
over. About thirty thousand people were uprooted in the two evacuations in a merciless way; this marked the end of Riga's Jewish ghetto,
which had existed for only thirty-seven days.

By midday Monday, December 8, 1941, special work units were
organized to clean up the traces of the messy deeds of the murderous
Latvian and German soldiers. This time the tragedy was even greater
than that of the first evacuation; the casualties in the ghetto were considerably larger. Elderly and handicapped people and small children, none
of whom could follow the fast-moving marchers, were shot right in the
street. Their bodies were left unattended, but the soldiers did not care;
they walked away with smoking guns, as if they were on a hunting trip. I
had no desire to participate in the cleanup work, for it had only been a
week since the first evacuation and I was still in shock. My mind had had
too little time to absorb my own tragedy; I could not endure that of
someone else. I kept thinking about the children and my mother's tender
care and love and still could not comprehend that they were gone. The
scene of the four unfinished bowls of bean soup would not leave my
mind; nor would the tragic loss of the only picture album that reflected
the memories of our family's happy life.

One of our co-workers, Wallenstein, had been my music teacher in
grammar and high school, so we knew each other well. He had the opportunity to join the ghetto cleanup team, and since his wife and child
had been part of the second evacuation, he wanted to see if any clue had
been left regarding their final destination. After a few hours he returned;
his face was white and covered with tears. He cried out in a broken voice,

"They killed my baby—they killed my only child!" Although we tried to comfort him with kind words, his tears were contagious, and each of us began to cry.

After a short while, he calmed down and told us his tragic story. He had been assigned to collect the dead bodies from the streets and load them into a wagon. There were many, and all had been shot at close range. He stumbled onto a child's frozen corpse lying facedown in the blood-soaked snow, picked it up, and recognized it as that of his infant daughter—with a bullet in her head. Wallenstein broke down on the spot; he put his daughter's body gently on the wagon and ran to look for his wife, first on the street and then in their apartment.

The apartment was empty, and his wife was nowhere to be found; she was gone with the rest of the evacuees. He returned to his team, but the wagon with his child's body was gone. He was told it had filled up quickly, and the workers had been ordered to transport the bodies to the old Jewish cemetery. Wallenstein left his work team and ran back to our house—he had to determine the circumstances of his daughter's murder and why she had become the target of the Latvian soldiers. He finally concluded that she must have been in her baby buggy; her mother could not move as fast in the deep snow as the drunken henchmen had wanted. The buggy slowed everyone down, so a Latvian soldier put a bullet in the little girl's head and chased the mother away.

Across the gate of the Little Ghetto stood a three-story building, which had not been in use; suddenly, one day people were there. We discovered that the building was occupied by one hundred Jewish women who had lived in the large ghetto; they were seamstresses working for the gestapo High Command in the city. When the November 27 order came and the liquidation and relocation of the ghetto population were announced, these women were not brought back to the large ghetto after work but were sent to the city jail. The Germans had kept them there until the entire ghetto had been evacuated and then transported them here during the night. They were the only surviving Latvian Jewish women from the ghetto. Their building, which we called the Women's Ghetto, was not part of our Little Ghetto but was conveniently located at our gate.

Our men were faced with the biggest challenge of their lives—finding out where their families had been sent. We had only one clue: After leaving the ghetto gate, they had been led to Maskavas Street, then to the outskirts of Riga and into open prairie. We all hoped that with outside help we could discover the fates of our loved ones and their final destinations.

Within the next few days, every kolonne finally went back to work. The old ghetto leaders had been evacuated, so a new administration had to be created. In charge was a well-known Rigaer named Kelman; the police chief was Wand, and Kassel and Meisel were in charge of employment. New Jewish policemen were recruited, SS Obersturmbannführer Krause became the new German kommandant, and the Latvian Jew-hater Dralle was in charge of the guards. At the gate and around the perimeter of the ghetto were the most trusted guards, a contingent of the Latvian Einsatzkommando. As in the large ghetto, the loyal guardsmen reminded us of their presence by shooting in the air or beating up a Jew at the gate as he returned from work.

The year 1942 was almost upon us, and our employer, German Reichsbahn Repair Works, pleasantly surprised us. Our kolonne was increased from 80 to 120 people and was transferred to a different job assignment. Our strenuous work of removing frozen cattle manure from boxcars ended, and all of the men were sent to the freight car repair shop located nearby; we considered this transfer a lifesaver for many of our people. At the same time, every German institution in Riga began to compete for more Jewish workers. Since many workers had been evacuated from the large ghetto, a shortage of free labor existed. The Germans thought of the Jews as nineteenth-century slaves, so indispensable that any interruption in their work could undermine the function of the institution. Some went so far as to house the workers in or near their workplaces. The jobs that included on-site living quarters or the housing itself were called kasernierung; a few were Lenta, which contained various workshops that served the needs of the gestapo; Quatieramt, a military supply depot; HKP, army repair shops; and the Reichsbahn, the railroad warehouse. Most of the kasernierung consisted of newly erected barracks with the necessary sanitary facilities. Each man had a bed and a locker, was fairly well fed, and did not have to work too hard. They men were fully protected, because their "masters" depended on them. Still, the gestapo had the upper hand, since it was considered sole owner of the working Jews.

The kommandant of the Lenta kasernierung was a high-ranking SS man named Fritz Scherwitz. He treated his Jews well and allowed them to live in a renovated factory building in Riga and provided food and clothing. When the Germans retreated from Riga, my cousin Chone, then kaserniert in Lenta, was not evacuated to Germany with the rest of the Jewish workers but was among the few who were sent to Liepaja, the second-largest city in Latvia, to serve as a protective shield for Kommandant Scherwitz. When the Soviet armed forces approached Liepaja, Chone escaped and was later liberated. Scherwitz successfully escaped to Germany.

Kolonnenführer Weinberg requested a kasernierung for our working men, but the German repair shop administration refused the request because of the lack of space; still, the men were pleased with the new working conditions. Most of the work was done indoors in huge hangars, which were not heated, but at least we were protected from the bitterly cold winter. We could move around freely, since there were no guards at this important military facility. We could speak freely and were in close contact with the Latvian workers in the shop. The German supervisors kept an eye on the relationship between the Jewish and the Latvian workers, but we worked comfortably side-by-side with our gentile co-workers. At times, they were a great help to us; they were the ones who brought us outside information for our broken souls and food for our hungry stomachs. They had access to radios and could obtain information about the situation on the fighting front and all the latest news. We were eager to hear these reports and to convey them to the residents of the ghetto. I approached every gentile worker in the shop to ask whether he had heard about or seen our evacuated families. To my amazement, nobody could give me a satisfactory answer, although they knew the Jews in Riga's ghetto had been evacuated. It was incomprehensible to me that thousands of people could have vanished, leaving no clue as to their whereabouts.

In my conversations with the Latvians, I noticed a change in their attitude and behavior toward me as a Jew. For the first time I heard them complain about the Germans, who they said had come to their country as redeemers but instead became the oppressors. Latvia was in dire economic straits, and everything was rationed and in very short supply. Every practical item, such as food, was shipped to Germany for consumption by its citizens. Young Latvians were drafted into the military to defend and preserve the Third Reich. Although they were thorough in eliminating the Jews, the Latvian people seemed very unappreciative, for they wanted Latvia to be as independent as it had been before the Soviet occupation.

Our kolonne was divided into several work units, each of which was headed by a gentile foreman. Most of our work consisted of repairing boxcars. My father and Boris replaced worn couplings; they also learned how to replace or repair brake shoe linings on the wheels. My father did his assigned work so well that he was considered a specialist, but Boris was less effective and was often assigned with my cousin Moisey to re-move the damaged wooden walls of the boxcars and haul them away for disposal. When I arrived at the railcar repair shop, I remembered the German officer who had praised me some time ago for my excellent electrical repair work; I saw an opportunity and asked to be employed as an electrician. The electrical repair shop foreman accepted me; I got the job and worked with two Latvians. I was very pleased, although I did not know how I would fulfill my duties.

The intensive search for the missing evacuees continued without in-terruption. Some of the kaserniert Jews were assigned to Wehrmacht trucking units, and they drove freely around Riga and its outlying sub-urbs; these workers thus had the opportunity to investigate all of the unconfirmed rumors regarding places to which our families might have been sent. Some German soldiers sympathized with our plight and were actively involved in searching for our missing families, although in some cases the accompanying German officer or driver had to be bribed.

The kaserniert Jews did not give up their search, and their persis-tence eventually paid off. Their findings were not usually encouraging, but good news eventually reached the Little Ghetto. The trucking units drove through the villages of Salaspils, Jumpravmuiza, and others; from a distance they noticed some campsites with women and children of all ages, and they assumed these were the people for whom we were search-ing. Everybody was delighted to hear this encouraging news. I thought to myself, Finally, our people are found. My mind was again filled with thoughts of my mother and siblings: How are their living conditions? Do they have enough food? Are they treated well? Unfortunately, the short-lived jubilation came to a sad end the next time the camp was visited, when it could be seen that these inmates wore only one Star of David on their chests and none on their backs. This meant they were not our Latvian Jews and had probably been brought to this place from a foreign country.

My hopes of seeing my family dimmed further when we learned that carloads of used male, female, and children's clothing had arrived at a gestapo kasernierung, where Jewish workers had been required to sort them. All of the overcoats had front and rear markings of the Star of David, and documents were found that indicated that the owners of these garments were our evacuated Jews, who had perished in an unknown land. Suitcases filled with clothing had also been brought to the gestapo workshops in which Jewish workers had found pictures, jewelry, passports, and other items that had belonged to German Jews. This indicated that they, too, had met with foul play at the hands of the gestapo. The newly discovered Jews around Riga were, therefore, German Jews who had been sent east for resettlement. As if this discouraging news were not enough, we received additional distressing information. Some time ago, Soviet POWs had been seen digging large, deep trenches in the forest near Salaspils, as well as other places. We all initially thought these trenches had been dug to bury massive numbers of POWs who had died of starvation, but our assumption was not correct. The Latvian land had become a killing and burying ground for European Jews, including our own family members and friends.

From various kasernierung the Little Ghetto received atrocious news of mass killings of German Jews in portable gas chambers contained in tightly sealed vans. The so-called resettlement Jews would arrive in Riga by rail with all of their belongings in suitcases, which were taken away from them upon their arrival. Some of the people were sent to different internment camps around the city, but others were guided into the vans; they assumed they would be transported as well, which they were—to the barren land of no return. When the vans were fully loaded and began to move, carbon monoxide exhaust was fed into the rear. These inconspicuous vehicles thus became gas chambers; by the time they arrived at the burial site, the passengers were dead from breathing the poisonous fumes. Many of the newly arrived Jews were loaded into military trucks at the rail terminal and transported to the Bikernieku woods to be shot and buried in the mass graves that had been prepared.

After a long time had passed, we were able to speak to the German Jews, who confirmed that during their presence in various internment camps around Riga they had not seen or heard of our vanished families. Rumors spread that our people had been massacred in the Rumbuli woods, at the very end of Maskavas Street. Such an inhuman undertaking was incomprehensible and unacceptable to me. I knew the Jews were thought to be expendable, but did this warrant killing them? Is this rumor a hoax? I asked myself. Even wild animals would be treated with more gentleness than these innocent and defenseless human beings have been, I thought. My mother lived in my memory, as I kept thinking of her and my siblings. I could not accept the idea that they were gone forever. I told myself that the killings were only rumors; I kept hoping—where there is hope there is also life. I felt devastated and had little incentive to carry out my daily chores.

With the arrival of the German Jews in the abandoned large ghetto, my young, confused mind slowly began to accept the undeniable fate of my dear ones, and my hopes of finding them were slowly dashed. The persistent rumors eventually became a bitter reality, substantiating the fact that the ghetto Jews had not been resettled somewhere, as we had been told by the Germans, but had been massacred in the Rumbuli woods. This was another clever Nazi ploy to separate me and other able-bodied men from our families so there would be no resistance to their murderous undertakings. The members of the gestapo High Command, dressed in their highly polished boots and immaculate uniforms with the skull's-head emblem, had proved once more that they were cowards. These high-ranking SS officers would rather fight the Jews and receive rewards for their deeds than fight for their fatherland on the front lines and possibly be killed.

By mid-December 1941, the first German Jews had moved into the large ghetto. The first transport came from the city of Köln, followed by transports from Hannover, Bielefeld, Hamburg, Berlin, and other cities; Jews from Cologne, Vienna, Austria, and Czechoslovakia arrived later. They all wore yellow Stars of David with the word "Jude" (Jew) in the center over their chests. The new arrivals were of all ages and included families with children. They had left their hometowns assuming that they would be able to live normal lives in the east. They were permitted to take some belongings in suitcases and wooden boxes, but when they arrived at their destination, these items were taken away without explanation. Before they came to our ghetto, these Jews had lived in various internment camps around Riga, the most notorious of which were Salaspils and Jumpravmuiza. When those who had survived the inhuman ordeals in the camps finally reached the ghetto, they were hungry and were improperly dressed for the extremely cold winter of 1942.

I felt very sorry for them; at the same time, I disliked them until I found out who they were. Only then did I realize that my negative thoughts were unjustified. At first, I thought of them as intruders in our abandoned ghetto; my yearning and love for my family was so great that their occupation of our old house was too much for me to accept, even if they were also persecuted Jews. I resented the fact that Mother had been sent away and perhaps killed and an unknown Jewish woman had taken her place. I watched the newly arrived Jewish women through the barbed-wire fence and compared them to my mother—which was agonizing. I observed the ghetto during my leisure time, as if my mother's image might appear at any time. At first, the area looked like a ghost town, with squeaking gates that swayed back and forth and open front doors on every house. Debris blew all over the streets and sidewalks. Eventually, though, this place abandoned by God was occupied by newly arrived German Jews, and within weeks, our old ghetto had become a crowded living area for the resettled German and other Jews.

By this time, I was convinced that all of these evacuations and other horrible proceedings were part of the systematic implementation of Hitler's anti-Semitic ideologies. The action of the Nazis under the code name *Beseitigen* (to eliminate) was not a local undertaking, as was initially believed, but an overall plan to exterminate the European Jewry. Rumors soon spread that three women had miraculously saved themselves from the mass murder; the number was later changed from three to two survivors out of more than thirty thousand people. Nobody knew the names or whereabouts of these women; I had lived in the United States for more than thirty-eight years before I learned the name of one of them. I also discovered in detail—by sheer coincidence—how the massacre of Riga's Jewish community had taken place.

I was president of a B'nai B'rith lodge in Chicago and, as such, received a variety of materials from the district office. Among them was a small catalog of the most recent books published on Jewish subjects; I would then inform the members of their availability. I noticed one called *I Survived Rumbuli.* This is one of the mystery women for whom I have been searching all these years, I thought to myself. I immediately ordered the book; when I received it I could not put it down until I found out how the massacres of my mother, brother, and two sisters had taken place those many years ago. In the book the sole survivor of the massacre, Frida Michelson, describes in great detail how the killings were done, who did them, exactly where they took place, and how she escaped and survived. The long-standing rumor about a second female survivor still remained a mystery. In 1963, against everybody's advice, I felt compelled to visit Riga to see the Rumbuli woods, where the massacre had taken place. The combination of this rewarding book and my experience at Rumbuli allowed my weeping soul to rest in peace, for I now knew the final resting place of my mother, my sisters Dora and Ljuba, and my little brother, Leiba. I had now fulfilled the oath I had taken many years ago; I could finally say, "I am here with you—rest in peace, my dear ones. I will miss you all to the very end of my life."

The year 1942 was upon us, and the battles still raged on the fighting front. The German blitzkrieg offensive had been slowed and, in some places, stopped by the Soviet armed forces. Our new ghetto administration was serving the people well; the Jewish police consisted of the brightest young men, who knew how to handle the Latvian guards and their German superiors. The labor department was able to perform the difficult task of organizing and handling individual kolonnes for outside work. The Little Ghetto was under the leadership of Obersturmbannführer Krause; Obersturmbannführer Lange was in charge of the German Ghetto, an individual entity separated from us by a barbed-wire fence. That ghetto had its own administration and police, as well as its own work kolonnes and a different service gate, and the people lived in individual sections according to their hometowns. The relationship between the two ghettos was cool; with its numerous directives, the gestapo tried to disrupt, rather than unite, the areas, which led to distrust between the two.

One of the orders was that there was to be no conversation at the dividing fence and no visits to the other ghetto. The Latvian Jews began to call the German Jews "yeke." I knew neither the origin nor the meaning of the word, but people with great knowledge of Yiddish interpreted it to mean a German. The German Jews did not consider the word offensive; on the contrary, they found it very humorous, and many jokes were created around it. As time passed, the Latvian and German Jews began to work at the same places. The relationship between the two groups improved considerably, and our men began to visit the other ghetto regularly, even though they would have been severely punished if they had been caught. In fact, the German Jewish police did apprehend some of our people; luckily, after lengthy negotiations they were released and were not turned over to the German authorities. In time, love affairs even took place between some of our men and the female yekes. Some couples were so madly in love that they supported each other as husband and wife in their daily struggle for food and survival.

There is an old Jewish saying that "the one who exists must live." I accepted this thought, for I had to live and survive despite the overwhelming odds against me. A year of sorrow and degradation was behind me, but more suffering lay ahead; I understood that I had entered a new era. I felt comfortable living in the little frame house; I was under my father's devoted guidance and got along so well with my cousin Boris that he became like an older brother. I was lucky to be surrounded by kind people. We knew much more about each other than do newlyweds after their wedding. This unique group was made up of men from all walks of life, and our camaraderie was strong; in essence, I felt as if we were all drawn together. We lived in such close quarters that we had almost no privacy, but the men respected each other's behavior, habits, and desires; most of all, we were honest with each other. No arguments or fights occurred among the nine men, although each was experiencing a very turbulent and tragic time in his life. Order and understanding prevailed among these brave men.

The two Adelson brothers had lost family members in the liquidation of the large ghetto. Before the war, they had worked together in the lumber business; they were specialists in sorting timber before it was shipped to the sawmills. Both were soft-spoken, always willing to help others, pleasant to talk to, and neatly dressed at all times. Their brother-in-law, Klempner, a rough-looking individual with a deep, harsh voice, was the opposite in regard to neatness. He was a bachelor and had been a dock worker at the Riga port. He told us he had worked very hard all of his life, and he was proud of that fact. He frequently related his unusual experiences during his many years of working at the docks, which he claimed was more difficult than his work under the German occupation.

Klempner was never neatly groomed. He did not drink alcohol but was a compulsive smoker. Since regular tobacco was not available, he would use any grass that would produce smoke. He made his own tobacco by taking all kinds of leaves and drying them until they were crisp; when he was ready to smoke, he mulched them in his palm and wrapped the end product in a small piece of newspaper. When he lit his makeshift cigarette, a heavy odor and smoke appeared, forcing him to keep his eyes shut and his nose closed. His addiction to smoking was so great that at times he would give up his last piece of bread to get a small amount of any kind of tobacco.

Klempner also had an unusual eating habit: When he received his bread ration he would eat it immediately, without thinking about what he would have for his next meal. We used to ask him, "Why not leave some bread for tomorrow the way we all do?" Klempner always had a justification for his behavior. "I want to know how it feels to chew a mouthful of food. If you men wanted to experience such a delightful feeling, you would do the same." After Klempner had eaten his meal, he would walk around holding his hand on his belly and saying, "Oh, it feels so, so good—I was looking forward to this moment all day." These thoughts helped him overcome the misery of the hunger we all felt.

Another man in our house, Viselevsky, was a former traveling salesman who was slim and soft-spoken. He suffered from chronic asthma; to help with his breathing, Viselevsky frequently smoked medicated cigarettes. He and his gentile wife had no children; she remained in the city and supplied him with the cigarettes he needed. During the war, cigarettes were scarce although for a high price they could be obtained on the black market. His wife would sometimes come to the ghetto gate and follow our kolonne from a distance; other times, she would come to see him at our place of work. When they met they looked at each other but did not engage in any conversation, for they could not let anybody notice their meetings. Viselevsky could write well, so he kept a diary about himself and everything that occurred in the Little Ghetto. Every week he would meet his wife at a prearranged spot, pick up his medicated cigarettes, and drop off his writings. Mrs. Viselevsky possessed an important and exciting diary about life in the ghetto; I wonder now, many years later, if she made good use of this historical document.

One of the better-educated men in our group was Wallenstein, my old music teacher, who had graduated from the Music Conservatory of Riga. He was a mild-spoken but very energetic person, and we all held him in high regard. At first, he spoke often about the loss of his wife and child, who he had found dead in the snow, but as time passed he stopped talking about them, since he noticed our reluctance to listen. His story was but one of many we had heard repeatedly from others, and we had our own tragedies to address. In the evenings, we had nothing to keep us occupied or entertained; we were forbidden to have radios or newspapers, books were unavailable, and television did not yet exist. Wallenstein came up with the idea of having a "katzenjammer [cat-humming] orchestra" that had no instruments; each person hummed the melody of a given song. He determined whether a man had a high- or a low-pitched voice. He would hum a popular melody and our humming voices followed him. We did not sound very good in the beginning, but with time we improved and enjoyed participating.

As our choir became more harmonious, homemade instruments were added, such as pots and pans and other items that made noise. I still vividly remember that Lifshitz was a good tenor and Klempner was our best bass. Wallenstein said to me, "Boris, I remember that your voice did not qualify for the school choir." "You still remember that?" I replied. "Oh yes, I remember that you were a kid whose mind was not on singing," he said. "You are right—I preferred playing football to going to choir rehearsals," I replied. "The passing of years has not changed your poor-sounding voice, so I ask you to hum only the tunes your ear can absorb," Wallenstein finally said to me. I thought to myself, Now I have all the time in the world for rehearsals—I do not have to play football anymore. I am no longer a free young man who can go wherever he wants.

One of the most carefree men was Lifshitz—a tall, slim man with a constant smile. He was a neat-looking person who liked to give and receive compliments from others. In addition to leading our tenor section, he was our comedian; he never took things too seriously, no matter how unpleasant. He had also lost his family in the evacuation of the large ghetto, but he seldom spoke about them. Before the war, Lifshitz had been a salesman in a textile store; as such, he had heard many stories and jokes, which he now had an opportunity to share.

Our "ghetto family" of nine men would not be complete without mention of the "troika": Abrasha, Bora, and Boris, as we were called. We were known as a troika (trio) because we were always together and had a uniquely close relationship; the three of us did and shared things equally. Some wondered how we managed to live together; my father was essential to this, for he had the will to keep all three of us together under these difficult circumstances. He was the eldest in the troika, so whatever he said was considered law. By profession, Boris was a chemical engineer who had graduated from Prague University in Czechoslovakia. He was not married and knew little about housekeeping or cooking; he had lived with his parents and had not needed to know these things. Housework in our ghetto was an important undertaking, because we had little food that had to go a long way. The cramped living space we occupied had to be kept clean and sanitary at all times to prevent disease. Boris, like me, was inexperienced in living this way. Neither of us could imagine how we would have been able to live without my father. He never ordered but always asked us to do things around the house; most of the time, he would do them first.

Everybody in the house admired the way my father handled us and kept things harmonious. He became our food supplier, and I never knew he was such an excellent cook. Once a week we received our meager food ration, which consisted of a piece of horsemeat, a small pat of margarine, a small piece of liver or blood sausage, and one loaf of army bread for two people. During the week, we were given an additional ration of bread and a few potatoes, carrots, or some cabbage. Every time we received our food ration, the men were confronted with a serious dilemma—how to divide the loaf, which had to serve two people and arrived uncut. I asked myself, How does one cut an uneven square loaf of bread for hungry people, when every crumb counts, without a scale or a proper knife? After many arguments, Lifshitz was entrusted with cutting bread for everybody. To make his job easier and more precise, he invented a scale made of strings and small sticks, which became so popular in the neighborhood that all of our neighbors made similar ones for themselves.

Another problem arose over what to do with the rationed horsemeat, which nobody ever ate or knew how to prepare. The unappetizing meat was tough and had a slight odor, and everybody threw it out except my father. He did not dispose of any food, no matter how bad it tasted or looked, but always found a way to make it edible. He tried several methods of preparation and eventually became the expert horsemeat cook: out of our three rations Father managed to prepare three steaks and some hamburgers. To make the meat tender, he flattened it with a bottle; then he ground the hamburger several times and added the ingredients that were available. After lengthy and careful preparation, our troika was ready to dine on a "gourmet dinner" served on our bed, which was the only available space in our room.

Another "delicacy" created by my father was the potato-peel kugel. During the weekdays, our troika collected potato peels; by Sunday Father had enough to prepare an extra dish for us. He would wash the peels thoroughly and cook them in a big pot for a while; then they were mashed, and additional ingredients were added. The substance was poured into a flat cooking pan and put in the oven to bake; the not-so-appetizing ingredients soon became a delicious potato-peel cake or, as the Jewish people call it, kugel. Everyone in our house tasted my father's specialty; all of the men were delighted with the taste, and some tried to imitate it, but the taste was never as good. Almost every week we had a kugel party in our house, thanks to my father's ingenuity; this was another source of entertainment. My father taught us all the art of living in a communal environment.

In the large ghetto I had felt fenced in, but here I was truly caged. A human being can adapt to any circumstances, though, and I was no exception. I slowly got used to my new environment and was comfortable among the other men in our little house. I tried to concentrate on my primary goal—survival. All of our possessions remained in our house in the large ghetto, since we had been forcibly settled here with very few belongings; we treasured most the two pairs of boots we had brought from the other house to secure our survival if the need should arise. In spring of 1941, the Soviet authorities rounded up those considered enemies of the Soviet Union to be sent away to Siberia. My father made sure he was ready for this long voyage if necessary; in addition to preparing clothes and produce, he also obtained proper footwear.

I was with him when he selected two pairs of boots in his shoe store; each was purposefully different in style and durability. One was heavily constructed and was water repellent. It was a very popular style, commonly used by farmers and laborers. The second pair was one of a kind, made of fine, soft leather with wide, expandable rubber bands on the sides. This pair had been custom-made for my grandfather Schleime and could not be bought in stores. Father had put the returned pair on the shelf in the store, but they were never sold. These shoes were intended to hide old Russian Czar Nicholas II ten-ruble gold coins, the size of an American quarter in their heels.

I helped Father take the heels off both pairs of shoes, then he carved out each heel. In the heel of one water-repellent shoe he put five gold coins, in the other a small family picture. In one of the other boots he put another five gold coins, and he placed Mother's small passport picture in the other. The boots, with the gold coins and pictures, helped us during our gravest days in a foreign land. Later, thanks to my father's foresight, he and I were able to survive when others perished. To this day, that picture of my mother is the only one I possess. We kept both pairs of shoes hidden under our bed. Cousin Boris knew about the hidden shoes but never found out about the treasure in the heels.

The gestapo put us all in the cramped ghetto to face a slow starvation, but they misjudged the ability of the Jewish people to fight for survival. We could not sustain ourselves with the food ration we received twice a week, so an outside source had to be created to subsidize our nourishment so starvation could be kept at bay. The urgent need for food caused us to become something resembling ancient commodity traders; we bartered and exchanged everything we possessed with the gentile population of Riga. Some of our people worked in places where they had no access to gentiles with whom they could barter but where they had access to abandoned supplies of clothing, shoes, and consumer goods. Workers would risk their lives to try to fight off their hunger by "organizing," which was ghetto slang for stealing. No matter what the cost, survival was key in the ghetto.

Few consumer goods were manufactured during the war, which created great demand for a variety of household and clothing items. The ghetto workers who were employed in civilian establishments had the chance to organize goods to be brought into the Little Ghetto, where an artificial merchandise exchange market was created; the asking price was dependent upon supply and demand. There were even middlemen who linked the supply work units, which brought the stolen merchandise into the ghetto, with the units that could dispose of the stolen goods at their place of work. These trades represented a free enterprise market in its purest form. The Little Ghetto had a flourishing economy without cash, for all trades occurred on an honor system, using only food as currency. For example, the price for a good, fluffy towel was five potatoes and a one-centimeter slice of bread; we then sold the towel to a civilian for ten potatoes and half a loaf of bread. For a nice pair of pants, the price was half a loaf of bread and a quarter kilogram of butter; they were then sold for one loaf of bread and half a kilogram of butter or bacon. The best profit could be made on army boots, because the supply was very limited and the demand was great. Our kolonne had the ideal workplace through which to barter organized merchandise because many Latvians and other workers at our railcar repair shop were eager to deal with us. We were thus able to obtain enough potatoes, bread, and other edibles to feed our troika.

Happily, we had good relationships with our gentile co-workers. The work most of our people did was very dirty but rewarding in that nobody was rushed, we were allowed to walk around relatively freely on the premises of the large shop, and the German and Latvian supervisors were kind. I was the helper to a well-qualified Latvian electrician; there were two more Latvians in the shop, but I was the only Jew. I got along fairly well with them all. When I started, we were very busy replacing and repairing old electrical wiring in the huge railroad hangar. The work was finished fairly quickly, because it did not take long to replace all the damaged wiring. The only thing left for us to do was to maintain the existing electrical equipment in the shop. My supervisor would get nervous if some of us had nothing to do. One day he asked me apologetically to walk around with my small toolbox and a pipe on my shoulder, as if I were doing some work; he was afraid the German superintendent might see me idle. In other words, he wanted me to pretend I was busy. He was not protecting me as much as himself; he wanted to secure his job as supervisor of the electrical shop.

My moving around in the shop gave me an opportunity to approach the gentile workers and barter my merchandise. The Latvian electrician to whom I was assigned was a bachelor from the rural part of the country; his entire family still lived on their farm. He was a very kind and understanding young man, and we got along very well. I spoke to him about politics, and he responded very favorably. Eventually, he became my most reliable customer; I supplied him with various pieces of clothing for himself and his family. They had a generous supply of potatoes, bread, butter, and other dairy products on their farm, and he supplied me with the produce I wanted. Our friendship grew to such an extent that he introduced me to his younger brother, who had been drafted into the Latvian SS brigade and who sometimes brought the provisions from his parents' farm to pay me.

Our close friendship could not be exposed to our supervisor or to other gentile workers in the shop; therefore, whenever we wanted to have an intimate conversation or discussion, we had to find a secluded place. Since I was his helper and we were working together most of the time, this was easy. In some instances we pretended we were doing some work when we were actually engaged in friendly conversation. Everybody knew we were partners, so such activity did not raise the suspicions of the German or Latvian supervisors in the shop. We always protected each other. My knowledge of electrical work was very minimal, which he knew but revealed to no one. Instead, he taught me the trade. He demonstrated how to bend and handle electrical pipe and other materials and showed me different pieces of equipment and how they should be repaired in case of a breakdown. I admired this young Latvian man, who was not only my friend but also my teacher. The knowledge I gained of the electrical trade gave me the strength and ability to survive my years of work.

My father and Boris did rather well in their bartering arrangements with the shop workers, although Father did most of the bartering. In many cases the worker took some clothing and gave nothing for it or gave only part of the prearranged amount of food. Father was unwillingly forced to accept the buyer's excuses for not fulfilling a verbal obligation. He knew some gentile workers took advantage of us, but he could not say or do anything. After a while, the same untrustworthy men had the chutzpah (nerve) to ask for more garments, knowing they had not fulfilled previous verbal agreements. Since Father was desperate for food, he bartered with them as though nothing had happened, hoping he would be more successful with the trade this time. The gentiles knew we Jews had too little food and that their support would go a long way to ease our hunger. A day seldom passed that one of our troika did not have something to bring to the ghetto, so we had enough basic food items to keep our energy levels high.

Once we had received the bartered food at the workplace, though, we faced a much greater challenge—how could we bring all the food into the ghetto through the well-guarded entrance gate? We had to cut what little food we had received into smaller pieces so it would not be noticeable, then we put it in our pockets or around our waists and hid potatoes under our shirts with our belts holding them in place; heavy winter coats made the hidden food less obvious. The behavior of the German and Latvian guards at the gate changed daily, so the Jewish police who were also present gave the approaching kolonnes a hint of what to expect through their own behavior. As we came closer to the ghetto gate, Kolonnenführer Weinberg was always the first to reach the entrance; he could see how the attitudes of the Jewish police reflected the mood of the SS guards. If the Jews were talkative and happy, we knew passage through the gate would occur without problems. If Weinberg saw the opposite behavior, we could expect some problems.

Some days the German and Latvian guards were ordered to search every worker returning home. In this case, Weinberg gave the password *oblave,* which meant an intensive search was proceeding at the gate. Our men then prepared to get rid of all of the hard-earned provisions and threw them on the sandy ground before reaching the gate. After the kolonne had passed through, the Jewish police would clean the road before the Germans noticed the food on the ground; they were truly our devoted protectors. If Krause, our kommandant, had ever learned how much food was illegally obtained outside the ghetto, everyone, including our police, could have been severely punished for defying the standing gestapo policy to weaken the Jews through hunger.

One day on our return from work, our kolonne was searched thoroughly. All of the men emptied their pockets before reaching the gate, but the kolonne was moving so fast that my father did not have enough time to empty his completely; two potatoes remained and were found by a German SS guard. He made my father throw them out and then began to beat him mercilessly over the head with a wooden bar as Father kept moving through the gate. When he got into the ghetto, his head and nose were bleeding, so our men grabbed him and brought him to the house. I was very concerned about the bleeding, but it finally stopped after cold water had been applied. It took a few days for my father to recuperate and go back to work; he would have been killed if he had not been wearing a heavily padded winter cap. The beating left him with a permanent mark—a growth in the middle of his scalp that grew larger every year.

The winter of 1941–1942 was very cold—the temperature reached far below zero—and there was a great deal of snow. It took a lot of effort for our kolonne to get to work, as we had to walk on pavement that was covered with a deep layer of snow or slush. About a mile from our workplace, we took a shortcut through an empty field, where we had to make a path in the deep snow; we were undernourished, so this was quite a task. Although we were dressed in warm, heavy clothes, the sub-zero temperatures were merciless. Our outerwear was old, dirty, and oily because of the type of work we were doing at the rail repair shop. Nobody would come too close to us, and we felt degraded wearing such shabby clothing, but we had no choice. No provisions were made for us to wash up and change clothes at of work, whereas the gentile workers had their own locker room. Our group walked through the streets of Riga like homeless people with nowhere to turn. No traces were left of our former presentable selves.

Many times I observed that most of the people on the sidewalk paid no attention to us. We barely moved our feet on the snow-covered pavement, and some of them looked at us hatefully, as if to say, "You Jews are getting what you deserve, what you had coming to you." They knew we were Latvian Jews, and some of them may have lived next to us and worked or gone to school with us. Perhaps they had shared happy times with us or had enjoyed friendly dealings with us on a daily basis. Now all at once their attitude toward the Jews had changed. I was convinced that we Jews were under a curse and that the Latvians had a mistaken illusion about themselves, which reminded me of a popular Latvian legend. A very powerful Latvian named Lacplesis was confronted in the woods by a huge bear. To protect himself, he threw the bear down between his feet; with his bare hands, he grabbed the bear's jaws and tore him in half. I saw myself as the huge, defenseless bear and the Latvians as the "heroes" who were ready to tear me in half. The stern, cold faces that looked at us were those of churchgoing people who had forgotten the prayers and sermons about mercy, human compassion, and helping the needy. I often became enraged. I thought to myself, God willing, that when my suffering came to an end, that of the Latvians would begin. They would be so miserable that the Jews would never leave their minds or souls.

To make my long walks more pleasant, I thought about my happy youthful past and laid the groundwork for a successful future. I told my father that after our liberation we would go to Palestine, where we would help build a Jewish state and live among Jewish people. Our walk to and from work was made more bearable when we discussed where we would get our next meal. Father was the spokesperson in our troika; he instructed me and Boris about whom we could approach with our goods and how much we should charge for them. Our minds were always on food—walking to work, working on the job, and going to bed.

On workdays we had a self-imposed routine: We had to get up early in the morning, spend the day on the job, and in the evening if we had some food we ate it or else we went straight to bed. We looked forward to our day off, which was Sunday, when everybody attended to personal cleanliness, repaired torn clothes, cleaned the house, and then prepared a special dinner.

One Sunday in early February 1942, I left the house in the morning with the intention of taking a walk to learn the latest world news from neighbors. I met some unfamiliar, well-dressed men; it was unusual to meet strangers in the morning on the streets of the ghetto. These men wore strange-looking winter caps with earmuffs, which were not worn in Riga, and the yellow stars on their overcoats were shaped differently than ours. I asked myself, Who are they? How and when did they come into the ghetto? I rushed back to our house to see if my father or the others knew anything about them, but nobody could explain who these strange Jewish people were. As we were talking, Boris rushed into the house excitedly. He told us that he had visited Uncle Ljova, whose cousin had recently arrived from the Kovno (Kaunas) Ghetto in Lithuania. In fact, five hundred Jewish men and women had come to our ghetto last night, so the puzzle was solved.

These people had been forcibly loaded into boxcars and told they would be shipped to Riga—for what purpose nobody knew. Upon arrival, the men and women were separated. The former found their quarters in our ghetto, the latter in the Women's Ghetto, which consisted only of the isolated three-story building next to our gate. I thought to myself, We already have German, Austrian, Czechoslovakian, and now

Lithuanian Jews. Who will arrive next in boxcars like cattle for extermination? I wondered whether Riga was the dumping ground for the European Jews—the thought boggled my young mind. It was easy for the ghetto administration to accommodate the new arrivals, since many of our people had moved out to become kaserniert at their places of work. The Lithuanian Jews told us of the traumatic events that had transpired in the Kovno Ghetto, horror stories of how they were treated by the German SS troops and their Lithuanian collaborators; the tales were almost identical to what our own Jews had experienced. They also told us that thousands of Jews had been massacred in Kovno's Ninth Fort.

From the start, I had an affinity for these people and enjoyed speaking Yiddish with them. The Riga and Kovno Jews quickly found common denominators and soon developed a friendly relationship. I was sorry such camaraderie did not exist with the German Jews, although we were only separated by a barbed-wire fence; a certain coolness and mistrust prevailed, and no common understanding existed between the two ghettos. The Lithuanian Jews brought a new vibrancy to our Little Ghetto. Some were tradesmen and could find work in the ghetto, although most of them joined other kolonnes and went to work outside. They worked in places where they could organize some articles of clothing that could be bartered in the ghetto for food. The newcomers were unable to trade their goods directly with the gentiles, since they did not know the Latvian language, but the trading business was soon booming. The Kovno Jews were very aggressive and went from home to home offering their articles. From time to time, some of the kaserniert Jews—honestly or sometimes with a false pretense—came to visit; they considered the Little Ghetto their home away from home. These men also came to purchase items that were unobtainable in the city. One of the main topics of conversation among the men in the ghetto concerned their ability to steal and deal at their workplaces. All of these undertakings were done in desperation to provide enough food for survival.

Riga's Little Ghetto became a somewhat flourishing Jewish community, despite the daily atrocities inflicted by the gestapo High Command. The Germans tried hard to divert our attention from self-preservation, but we did not allow that to happen. Little did we know that our future had already been determined. After the war, we found out that the chief of the Nazi SS special police force, Reinhard

Heydrich, had met with fifteen high German government officials on January 20, 1942, at a villa, Am Grossen Wannsee No. 56, overlooking Lake Wannsee. It took them less than two hours to reach the agreement they declared to be "the final solution" to the Jewish "problem" in Europe. They worked out a very detailed plan for identifying, rounding up, transporting, and eliminating every Jew in their occupied countries. It was said Heydrich was so pleased with this successful meeting that he had a toast with a glass of brandy and then lit a cigar. The gestapo, with its powerful SS Einsatzkommando units and all of the necessary government resources, cared more about annihilating the Jewish people than it did about winning the war against the Allied forces. Hitler's fanatical hatred of European Jewry was never assuaged; nor was victory ever won on the front.

Slowly, spring of 1942 approached, and the deep snow turned into a mushy, watery substance that was hard on our old footwear. The slush in the fields and the streets of Riga slowed my walk to and from work, and my feet and baggy pants were always soaked. When I returned from work, my prime concern was drying the shoes for the next day, because we had no sanitary facilities to keep ourselves clean and dry. The sweaty, wet shoes of the men in our house assaulted my nose, as the foot odors permeated every corner of our house.

Most of the men, myself included, wore no socks. I improvised with a 2'x2' square of cloth, preferably white, which I wrapped around my foot before putting on my shoes. The perspiration, soiled shoes, and wetness discolored this piece of fabric and gave it a peculiar, unpleasant odor. I always walked with damp shoes because they never dried out overnight. They were very uncomfortable, but my father would not permit me to wear the ones hidden under our bed. He kept saying, "On a very crucial day, we will wear these." I was angry at him at times, but in the end he was right. It was not long before that day was upon us.

The men in our house were more concerned about their health than they were about the condition of their shoes. We could not afford to be ill, even with the slightest cold. Miraculously, none of us ever became sick. I suppose a strong will and the need to survive overcame all of the obstacles our bodies had to endure. This immunity gave us the physical and mental strength to go on with our difficult daily lives.

Whereas the Latvian Jews lived serene lives and could provide enough food for their meager existence, the lives of the German Jews were completely different. They occupied the area of the ghetto that was empty following the evacuation of the Latvian Jews. Only a barbed-wire fence divided our small Latvian ghetto from the large German one, and strict orders were given regarding the separation of the two. Because of the language barrier, the German Jews lacked the capacity to develop a close relationship with the gentiles at their workplaces, which meant they could not barter for food and were very dependent on the food rationed to them. I must admit that I had no interest in learning more about their living conditions, since my mind was always on finding ways to support my own existence. Our close-knit troika thought only of self-preservation and cared very little about what was going on with others. Such an attitude was normal under our living conditions.

Our ghetto kommandant, Krause, and the kommandant of the German Ghetto, Lange, were always ready to introduce new hardships, killings, and unpleasant directives. If they were not acting upon one ghetto, they were certain to do so on the other. Such was the case in the German Ghetto in January 1942, when about a thousand people were sent to work in a labor camp in Salaspils that was liquidated within a few months. Very few people returned alive, for the Jews had perished there from malnutrition. At about the same time Lange, with the help of Latvian storm troopers, transported several hundred elderly German Jews, allegedly to work in a fish-canning factory in Denamunde. Nothing was heard from them for a long time, but the report eventually reached the ghetto that they had been massacred in the Bikernieku woods. When this tragic news reached us, we were sorry and very disturbed. The entire ghetto was alarmed by such a cowardly, cold-blooded slaughter of elderly men and women. The morale of the people in our ghetto was very low, but time is the best healer; before spring was in full bloom, everything was forgotten. In a way, it had to be, because we always faced new, life-threatening challenges. We had to stay strong and preserve our physical and mental strength to fight them all.

4

My New Lease on Life

The spring of 1942 came like a blessing from heaven, and the severe winter days became nothing more than a topic of conversation—we had survived them. Colorful wildflowers began to bloom in the rough, uncultivated field through which our kolonne walked to work, and it was refreshing to smell the air. I named this the Path of Desperation, as it was created out of the desperation to shorten the walking distance to the workplace. With the arrival of spring came the annual cleaning of our huge railcar repair hangars. The shop administration requested Jewish women from the German Ghetto to do some of the work, so a kommando of twenty women was created. To make it easier for everybody, they were attached to our kommando. We met the women outside the ghetto gate and went to and from work together under the watchful guide of a German railroad worker.

We did not mind this new attachment; the women were fairly young, good-looking, and very conversational. A close friendship developed between us and the new female workers, which was delightful for all of the men in the kolonne. In no time my cousin Boris had befriended a lady from Prague, and Wallenstein soon had a similar attachment. I met a girl about my age who was from Berlin. Boris, who had graduated from Prague University, could speak with his friend in her native tongue, Czech, and I could converse with my acquaintance in German. It was refreshing to be in the company of a young lady, for I now had a pleasant companion with whom I could conduct enjoyable conversations on various subjects on the way to and from work. She was tall, with a distinctive, sexy walking style that would entice most young men; her cherry-shaped eyes and small pointy nose would lure most males; her beautifully shaped lips and nicely arranged white teeth would attract young or old.

We talked mostly of our past, our schooling, and the social life in our respective countries. She often invited me to her house in the German Ghetto, where she lived with her mother, but I refused. My deep love for Mary had not diminished; I felt sad that our short, meaningful acquaintance had ended abruptly, and I did not want to build a friendship with a new girl in uncertain times. At that time many men of all ages had serious relationships. I did not want to have a girlfriend in the German Ghetto while my father stayed alone in the background; I did not know he secretly wanted to befriend one of the ladies in our group. Perhaps I was selfish, but I could not see him in the company of a strange woman. The image of my mother's face always appeared before me, and I preferred to sacrifice my delightful companion rather than encourage him to betray his love for my mother.

On our daily walks, my Berliner friend told me about her hometown and how she walked with her parents or with a date on the well-known boulevard in her neighborhood, the Kurfürstendamm. I told her that Riga had not always been the grim city filled with hatred and suffering that she saw now. It had a beautiful canal where one could rent a rowboat, and students would serenade their dates on these boats and view the surrounding park. The opera, the theater, and other cultural institutions were greatly enjoyed by the Jewish population of Riga. The young people made good use of the attractive boulevards and parks for recreation and dates. She was interested in hearing what Riga had been like when I was a free young man. I told her that on our days off from school, students would congregate at noon to see the impressive changing of the guards at the Latvian Freedom Monument. At the top of the monument stood a woman holding a cluster of three stars that were supposed to represent the three provinces of Latvia. When one looked up at the monument she appeared to be naked, so we had nicknamed the monument "the naked lady."

I would often pick some wildflowers and give the little bouquet to my new friend. She was happy to keep it while we walked through the streets; she knew she would have to throw it away at the ghetto gate, for no flowers—wild or cultivated—were permitted inside. I had to admit that in this young Berliner girl I found all I could expect to find in the girl of my dreams. We expressed the hope that we would survive the Nazi ordeal and be able to enjoy life to the fullest. We even set up an advance date—I told her I would meet her after the war in Berlin on Kurfürstendamm Boulevard.

Cousin Boris carried on a very intimate friendship with his girl-friend from Prague. They would hold hands while walking in the kolonne, and I found them passionately embracing in more secluded places. He sometimes visited her in the German Ghetto, although it was against the standing orders of the kommandant. Father and I did not mind what he was doing, as long as it did not interfere with our bartering at work. At one point Boris went too far, and it threatened to break up our troika. He felt sorry for his girlfriend and bartered some of her apparel to the same gentile worker with whom we were dealing. My father became furious and reproached him; Boris did not like his remarks, and an argument ensued. Father gave Boris the choice of remaining in our communal relationship or being on his own and continuing to help his girlfriend as he wished. In the end, I was happy that Boris gave in and decided to stay with our troika, so our energies could again be devoted to our mutual survival.

Wallenstein was completely devoted to his girlfriend. They bartered together and had their meals together at work; they walked arm in arm as passionately as newlyweds. Many times their inappropriate behavior was called to their attention, but it did not help. On days off, Wallenstein was not seen in our house; he spent the day in the German Ghetto at his girlfriend's house. The men did not appreciate his absence, since he neglected his house duties. Just a few months before, he had lost his wife and found his infant daughter dead; he had been so heartbroken that he was ready to end his own life. My father and others reminded him of how quickly he had abandoned the memories of his family and become involved with a much younger girl. Wallenstein had his answer prepared: "Life is short. We do not know what tomorrow will bring, so I want to enjoy it now while I can." I considered him to be an intelligent person, but I was very disappointed with his behavior.

Our repair shop also underwent a thorough outdoor spring cleaning; for this purpose, a group of Soviet prisoners of war were brought to our workplace. They were malnourished, worked very slowly, and congregated on the lawn next to our electrical shop during their rest period.

Although they were guarded, I could have short conversations with them. After several days, I became acquainted with a middle-aged Ukrainian prisoner, who told me he had lived in a kolchoz (a communal farm) with his wife and two small daughters until he was drafted into the army. With very little training, he was sent to the front against the well-trained German Wehrmacht, and his unit quickly disintegrated. He was happy to be alive, even though he was a prisoner. He missed his family very much and was doubtful that he would ever see them again.

This man was very creative: He would make miniature toys from small scraps of iron, then try to barter his creations for a piece of bread or a potato. I was afraid to have any dealings with him, since I considered him a stranger who, through his desperation, could have been a participant in a gestapo ploy to hurt me or others. Jews at the workshop were strictly forbidden to have any contact with the Soviet prisoners, many of whom disliked the Jews and would do anything to improve their own poor living conditions. About that time a Soviet army general named Vlasov gave himself up to the Germans and became their admirer. He began to recruit prisoners of war to become soldiers for a new anti-Soviet army; I was told that the majority of these recruits were Ukrainians who deeply sympathized with the Nazi ideology regarding the Jewish people.

Since my new acquaintance was Ukrainian, I was somewhat frightened of him and tried to stay away as much as possible, but he approached me as his trusted friend. One day he showed me his newest creation: a little contemporary figurine made of pieces of wire. I liked it very much and obtained it for a piece of bread, intending to give it to my Latvian foreman as a gift. At an appropriate time when we were alone in the shop, I tried to give it to him, but he knew it had been crafted by one of the Soviets. Although he liked it, he would not accept my gift. He said nervously, "Oh no, no, no—I will not take this. Get this figurine out of here immediately." He became very excited and his face turned red, so I calmly put the miniature in my pocket. I could not understand why my usually friendly foreman had become so enraged, but he later told me the figurine had terrified him because if they found it, his German superiors could accuse him of collaborating with the Soviet prisoners and supporting Communist sympathizers. I finally understood why he never engaged in lengthy conversations with me: The Germans could have accused him of being too friendly with the Jewish workers in his shop.

The inflammatory anti-Semitic speeches given by Nazi leaders in 1941 and 1942 were reminiscent of the 1930s speeches I had listened to on the radio in the comfort of my old home. Unfortunately, radio and newspapers were not permitted in the ghetto, but many of our Jewish workers had access to them at work. I knew these people and was eager to meet them as often as time permitted. We drew our own interpretations of the one-sided Nazi information, and everyone was convinced that our destinies would be determined by the outcome of the fighting on the bloody battlefields of Europe. The intensified anti-Jewish sentiments of Hitler, Goebbels, and others did not bother the ghetto Jews, as we were used to such hateful speeches. Many times the rhetoric was merely repetition in an attempt to mentally brainwash the Germans' and other people's minds in the occupied lands.

During the disastrous Soviet retreat in 1941, when more than five hundred thousand square miles of the Soviet Union were occupied by the German armed forces, the Soviet Army confronted the Wehrmacht along an immense front extending from the Barents Sea in the north to the Black Sea in the south. That same year Japan attacked Pearl Harbor, and the United States declared war on Japan, which successfully advanced across Southeast Asia and the western Pacific. On the Soviet front, Leningrad was besieged, Moscow was threatened, Sevastopol was seized, and Stalingrad was sealed off by the German troops. I still remember the very sad day when I heard that Hitler had announced triumphantly on the radio that "die Russen sind tot [the Russians are dead]." The führer knew little of what the Allied forces had in store for the Third Reich. By the end of 1942, the Soviet forces had undertaken limited counteroffensives, and the Allied leaders were discussing opening the Second Front. The invasion of French North Africa was undertaken; in the Pacific, the United States began to recover from the Japanese attack.

When the discouraging news from the front reached the ghetto, the Jews were faced with disturbing experiences. I observed that the members of the ghetto administration were nervous. Kommandant Krause, with his group of henchmen, began to visit the ghetto more often. They must have had a reason for doing so; past experience had shown that Krause's presence in the ghetto brought only hardships or unfavorable consequences for the people. Eventually, his intentions were made clear;

on the last Friday of October 1942, he ordered all of the inhabitants of the ghetto to appear before him. Everyone was disturbed by this unexpected order, and I feared the worst—the partial or complete liquidation of the Jews in the ghetto. All kinds of rumors persisted within the Little Ghetto, but we had no substantial evidence. Only one thing was clear: Something serious was in the works. Everybody was anxious to leave the ghetto for work as soon as possible, and Kolonnenführer Weinberg was concerned about his men. He summoned all of the kolonne workers to meet at the gate early in the morning; he was going to attempt to guide our work unit out.

The following day, at six o'clock in the morning, we stood shivering at the gate to learn the outcome of Weinberg's intention. His plan was a good one, but he was not the only one who had that brilliant idea. When I arrived at the gate, a crowd had already congregated to leave the ghetto. Among the men were some who were employed inside the ghetto but who were trying to sneak into an outside work unit. Near our group I observed a gathering of our ghetto police, who had also received an order to appear in full force before the kommandant. They were well dressed, their clothes were clean and freshly pressed, and their boots were highly polished. The young men's faces showed concern, and some nervously tapped their feet on the ground. Their conversations were muted; occasionally, one of them would say something funny and the men nearby would burst into loud but quick laughter.

I enjoyed watching them, since I knew many of them from my days on the soccer team in high school. Many of them had attended private schools and belonged to high school fraternities; they were part of the Jewish youth intelligentsia of Riga. I envied them for the work they had volunteered to do in the ghetto; I would have liked to have been among them to do their noble work of helping the people of the ghetto. As I stood next to my father and other co-workers, I soon realized I was lost in thoughts of yesteryear's activities—wishful thoughts that would do me no good. The only thing that mattered was getting out of the ghetto rather than admiring one special group of people. Our kolonne was very anxious to leave, but we were not allowed to do so. Weinberg tried several times to convince the officials to let us out, but he always returned with a negative answer.

Finally, our German guide became impatient waiting for us on the other side of the gate and spoke out on our behalf. He tried to explain that we were essential to the welfare of the Reichsbahn. He emphasized that many damaged boxcars received from the front lines needed to be repaired immediately, which could not be done on time without the help of the ghetto workers. After a lengthy conversation, he finally persuaded the gate guards to let our unit leave. We were relieved of the agony of being in the ghetto and facing Krause in a lineup; still, we were concerned about those who remained. As it turned out, all those who had congregated were free to go after we left for work. No reason was ever given for the order.

The following day, Saturday, October 31, our work kolonne was picked up, and we were ready to start another day at the rail repair shop. Our mood remained tense; we felt something was awaiting us, but nobody knew what it was. During our walk to work, we all thought of the destinies of those we had left behind. The next day, we were supposed to have a day off, but our frightened men decided to go to work. We thought we would be better off away from the ghetto so if something occurred we would not be present. Our Kolonnenführer notified the workshop that we were willing to work on our day off; the shop officials were happy to let us do so, since they would benefit without incurring any expense. Saturday was a day on which my work was disturbed by thoughts of the people we had left in the ghetto. I could not block out the memory of the horrific things I had seen when the large ghetto was liquidated; I hoped I would not find such scenes upon my return to the Little Ghetto.

When the working day was over and we returned to the house, we had to face the tragedy that had taken place during the day. Our Jewish police force, the forty-one brave young men I had admired the previous day, had been mercilessly gunned down by the gestapo SS military unit. Accusations without substantial evidence spread that they had in some way conspired with the gestapo against the Latvian Jews. We were told that an order had come from the kommandant that the entire police force and its chief, Wand, were to appear before him. Wand was then taken out of the lineup, and the rest were told to march toward the German Ghetto. As they approached the open square called the Blechplatz, they were surrounded by SS soldiers with machine guns; the policemen ran for cover in an attempt to save themselves. All but two were gunned down; within a few days, the escapees were caught and shot. The ghetto

population did not understand why the police chief's life was spared—
it remains a mystery to this day. The official reason given for the brutal
murders of our police was that they were involved in a conspiracy against
the German administration and were not fulfilling their duties in the
ghetto.

Following this murderous act, Kommandant Krause gave a new di-
rective: The German Ghetto administration would now have overall ju-
risdiction of the Little Ghetto. The ghetto population now had no
self-management privileges, and the tension between the German Ghetto
and ours was very strong, with no hope of resolution. Our fairly quiet
life had changed overnight to something horrible, and 1942 ended with
a bleak outlook for me and my fellow ghetto Jews.

In January 1943, the kommandant was relieved of his duties; Krause's
gruesome era came to an end, but it had been only a prelude to what was
in store for me and other Jews in the Little Ghetto. Everybody was in a
joyful mood; people were happy that we were finally rid of a notorious
German sadist. We all learned very soon, however, that the new
kommandant, Obersturmbannführer Eduard Roschman, fulfilled his
duties to the German Reich as thoroughly and conscientiously as Krause
had. Our jubilation ended, and the ghetto remained in a state of unrest.
Roschman spent more time in the ghetto than had any previous
kommandant; I suppose he had to prove to his superiors in the gestapo
that he was doing a good job in handling the Jews. New rounds of searches
and sporadic arrests took place, and the gestapo discovered various weapons hidden throughout the ghetto. A plot was unfolded: Our people had
unsuccessfully attempted to build a resistance organization against the
murderous Nazis in case they tried to liquidate the Little Ghetto. A
curfew was declared, and many people were implicated in this resistance;
several Jews were arrested and taken away, never to be seen again. The
ghetto had lost its most heroic men, whose memories remain with us
forever.

When our underground leaders were gone, the situation in the ghetto
was truly desperate. We were in complete disarray and did not know
what precautionary measures to take. What kinds of punishment would
the ghetto population have to endure from the gestapo soldiers? Each
man was ready to assume responsibility for his own protection but did
not know what to do; with our great leaders gone, the helpless men faced

a grim future. This was the beginning of the end of our Latvian Jewish ghetto, as the gestapo High Command began to transfer groups of workers to an unknown, newly built concentration camp called Kaiserwald just outside Riga. The inhabitants of the ghetto quickly learned about the horrible conditions there.

News reached us that a special work kolonne, consisting primarily of sick and handicapped men, had been created in Kaiserwald under the code name *Stutzpunkt;* as punishment for not obeying rules, some healthy men were also included. These kommando groups were sent out weekly from the concentration camp to an unknown place; nobody ever returned to tell what kind of work they were doing. After a few months, the secret place was unofficially revealed: The Stutzpunkt kommando was being sent to Rumbuli woods to dig up and burn the buried corpses from the massacre of the large ghetto in 1941. My mother and siblings were buried there. These kommandos may also have been sent to other places, but nobody could verify that.

When the unfortunate men arrived at their workplace, they were chained to each other to prevent escape. The gestapo considered their work to be top secret, but we knew about it. The purpose of unearthing the bodies and then burning them was merely to destroy the evidence of the Nazi crime. The Nazi leaders wanted to hide from future generations the proof of their genocide of the innocent Jewish civilian population; this was an ugly Nazi ploy to convince the world of their innocence. When the laborers were exhausted beyond their capacity to work, they were shot, and the next incoming group of men burned their bodies.

Numerous Jews began to consider escaping from the ghetto and finding hiding places among the gentile population, but that would have been almost impossible. The lucky ones who found refuge with sympathetic gentiles were eventually caught or turned over to the gestapo. Rewards were posted for turning in a Jew; according to the gestapo, the escapees had committed such a grave crime that they deserved a bullet in the head. Nonetheless, my father, Boris, and I discussed a possible escape, in spite of all the dangers. Before the war, Boris had lived with his parents in a two-story building owned by the Russian Orthodox Church; the physical church was on the same premises. His parents, my Uncle Aron and Aunt Berta, occupied the second floor, and the church prelate lived in the first-floor apartment. The relationship between Boris' family and the prelate had always been cordial.

The three of us thought we could find a suitable hiding place in either this building or the church. A large, open area surrounded both structures, and all of the grounds were enclosed by a high cast-iron fence. The church was fairly well attended every day, so people were always around. About half a block away was a Latvian police station, which might have been a drawback; at the same time, it could secure our hiding place. Nobody would imagine that three Jews had found a hideout a few hundred feet from a police station. Everything sounded right, and we were ready to undertake the dangerous task. There was one major stumbling block: Would the prelate be willing to hide us? We decided that without his consent, we would not undertake the daring escape and would instead let destiny guide our lives.

We had to find a way to contact the Russian prelate. Boris suggested that this could be accomplished through a Russian maid who had served their family for many years. Her name was Fenja, and she was known to everyone as a very devoted and trusted woman. She knew the prelate, for she lived in the same building and regularly attended his church. We paid a gentile man from the rail repair shop to get in touch with her and bring her to work, where Boris could discuss our escape plans with her. To our amazement she had moved out of her apartment, and the man could not find her; he said he would need more time to learn her new address. We did not have time to spare, since the evacuation of the ghetto was forthcoming, so we told him we had no further need of his services. We were desperate to find a way to avoid being transported to Kaiserwald. To keep their Jewish workers, many German institutions were speeding up the process of kasernieren, so many men were leaving the ghetto to live at their place of work. Our troika was fortunate to discover that a new kolonne was to be created for the Ilgeciem Cement Factory, whose workers would be kaserniert on the factory's premises. All three of us registered immediately; our dreams of escape from the ghetto were thus realized. We were prepared to leave our unpleasant surroundings and our devoted group in the little house, although some of our co-workers joined the kolonne as well.

Within a few days, a work force of two hundred men had been assembled, and we were on our way to the next opportunity to save our lives. For the present, we were safe from being sent to the treacherous concentration camp. We kept wondering whether we had done the right thing, but we decided only time would tell. To us, the fall of the Third Reich was clearly imminent; it was only a question of time. We had to do everything possible to gain time to overcome our present difficult life. With a new kasernierung secured, we prepared for our departure, and our troika packed our few belongings. "Now is the right time to wear our boots," said my father. He put on my grandfather's, and I wore the ordinary working boots with soft, new army socks. They were so comfortable and looked so good that I could not take my eyes off them. Unfortunately, they also looked too new and shiny, so we had to apply mud to them to make them look dull and somewhat old. We had to say farewell to our only other living relatives, Uncle Ljova in the Little Ghetto and cousin Moisey, who remained with our old kolonne; his brother Chone was kaserniert in the city with Lenta. When our departure arrived, it was a very sad day, for I had to say a final good-bye to the most devoted friends I had ever had. Even before I left I missed the little house to which I had grown so accustomed; through all of our troubled times, it was my only home. It was here that I had grown up too soon and become old before I was young.

5

My Kasernierung at Ilgeciem Cement Factory

The long-awaited spring of 1943 was upon us. Ordinarily, people rejoice at the start of nature's annual blooming cycle; the snow-covered landscape turns into a colorful pasture in which nature shows off its beautiful blooms, the animals come out of hibernation, and people rid themselves of their heavy winter garments. Birds were once again everywhere, but we did not notice them in the Little Ghetto, for this was not a place sparrows flew over or made restful stops. No daisies were to be found; even the yellow crabgrass dandelions did not appear in our midst. All one saw was a God-forsaken piece of land in which the only inhabitants were the lonely Jews. As Mother Nature was sprouting from a deep winter's sleep, we had to concentrate on just the opposite: We had to find a way to hibernate in an underground shelter until the Nazi hordes had left our land.

One beautiful April morning, our kasernierung work unit of two hundred men met at the ghetto gate to be transported to our new workplace and living quarters: the Ilgeciem Cement Factory. Father and I had all of our worldly goods under our arms; on our feet we wore the boots that contained the hidden treasures. We stood next to Boris among the waiting men, and the appointed Kolonnenführer introduced himself as Kagan; after brief formalities and the counting of the men, we left the Little Ghetto in rows of five under heavily armed guard. I passed the gate filled with grief and uncertainty, and we left our house behind without knowing when or if we would return. I knew I would miss that house, for it was inhabited by people I loved; my new quarters were hastily assembled barracks that were barely livable.

As I walked through the city I could not take my eyes off my sur-roundings. Everything looked different, as if I had been gone forever, when, in fact, I had only been away from this familiar area for about two years. Within that short time, my image of the buildings and the entire area had changed considerably. My thoughts quickly reconstructed my past; I could not help thinking of all the happy and sad things that had happened to me on these streets.

We were led through the main streets of Riga, and we turned onto Gogola Street, where once had stood the beautiful Gogol synagogue, since burned to the ground by the Nazis while several Jews prayed in-side. Across the street was the corner building where my Aunt Hanna, Uncle Wulf, and their family had lived. A few steps below street level was a well-known Jewish bakery; people came from all over town to buy baked goods there. I had thought its special dough was the very best; I called it "Grandfather's bread" because my grandfather had first intro-duced me to it, and he always had it on hand whenever I visited.

Farther down the street, we passed the Russian Orthodox Church in which our troika had planned to seek refuge. A half a block away was Timofejevskaja Street, where my grandparents had lived. From a dis-tance, I could see the second-floor windows from which I used to watch the church. I had enjoyed visiting my grandparents; as a child I had played with the old Russian souvenirs and figurines displayed on a small oval table. On my grandparents' grand piano were pictures of my aunts and uncles; it was through these pictures that I got to know them during my youth. I thought of the traditional gathering at the Passover supper, known as Seder; when my grandmother Chaija was alive, she made the Seder for much of our family. My grandpa Schleime always sat at the head of the table and would lead the prayers in Hebrew. My cousins and I sat to-gether on one side of a large table, along with my parents and other relatives. Each child had a colorful drinking cup with a handle small enough for our fingers. I remembered how we children always asked the four Passover questions, beginning with "Why is this night different from all other nights?"

A visit to my grandparents was never complete without a trip to my Uncle Aron's paint factory a few blocks down the street. Aron always greeted me with a smile and kind words, and he would sometimes call on his Russian factory foreman to show me how paint was made. Another pleasant memory drifted into my mind. I had once come to see my grand-parents, but my grandfather had gone to study the Holy Scriptures at the Gogol synagogue. After a short visit with my grandma, I decided to go to his shul, where I found my grandfather in a small building attached to the main sanctuary. This building contained study rooms and a small synagogue, the Bet Hamidrash, which was used for daily services. I was glad to see my grandpa among other elderly men who were busy with their discussions. I did not stay long but was introduced to the other men as a favorite grandson.

Our tightly guarded kolonne kept moving, and I continued to think of yesteryear. We walked under a viaduct, over which the railroad tracks led to the numerous resort places along the Gulf of Riga, which was part of the Baltic Sea. Farther away I could see the Dwinsky Vokzal, the once-bustling train station off busy Marijas Street. Opposite stood three pavilions with cupola-shaped roofs; these were part of the Central Food Market. My mouth watered when I thought of the tremendous selection and varieties of cheeses and other dairy products, fish in cans and by the barrel, breads and other baked goods, fresh fruits and vegetables, honey, mustard, horseradish, and a variety of fresh flowers every day. All of this was long past, however—now I had to risk my life just to get an extra piece of bread or a few potatoes because I am a hungry Jew.

We were moving faster, and I did not have time to admire every passing structure. We passed the familiar Prefecture, which brought sad memories of the night my father had spent in that torture chamber. I looked at this monumental structure as long as I could, knowing he could have lost his life there. Not far away was the Opera House, with its beautiful flower garden, and there was a little bridge to the recreational canal where I had spent many hours rowing a rented boat. Farther along I could see high in the sky "the naked lady," the statue on top of the Latvian Freedom Monument. I was reminded of the many pleasant dates I had enjoyed at the foot of this beautiful monument.

Although we were moving quickly, I still took time to look at the people on the sidewalk, and I became enraged and bitter at what I saw: Nobody paid any attention to us. These free people were inured to seeing long lines of shabby people with armed guards. Hundreds of Soviet war prisoners were sent from one war-torn place to another, so people on the street were jaded. I kept thinking, You people know who we are—

we are not foreigners; not so long ago we were your neighbors. Have you already forgotten us? I lived my whole life next to you, I went to school here and had the same education you did, and now you look at this as punishment I deserved. I do not expect you to cry for me, but at least wink an eye or show some sympathy for my unfortunate life. I wanted to cry out in a loud, furious voice, "Of all the people on earth, you are the most evil and uncaring—you are happy to witness my tragedy unfolding in front of you. Your dream of a free and independent Latvian state has not been fulfilled. No rewards were handed out to you by the Nazis for laying the groundwork and then fully participating in the genocide of the Jewish population throughout Latvia."

I noticed that my feet were moving faster than the deep thoughts in my disturbed mind. As I walked and looked around, I could not help but see that some children were holding on to their mothers and fathers. I thought, My siblings, and hundreds of other Jewish boys and girls, were deprived of such a close family relationship. Instead, the children's small bodies were scattered in large mass graves; one day, history will take note of these events. I only hope these young people will not simply follow in their parents' footsteps but will wisely find their own road in life. I hope they will enrich themselves with the Judeo-Christian teachings and build a new and more tolerant society in which understanding and compassion will prevail among all people. Father, who walked next to me, interrupted my thoughts and asked, "Bora, you are so quiet. What are you thinking?" I replied, "I am dreaming of a better world."

We soon entered the narrow streets of the old section of Riga, known as Vecpilseta. These buildings seemed to have aged considerably since I had last seen them. Riga was founded in 1201 by Bishop Albert, who was one of the crusaders, and it rapidly became an important trading center in the Baltic. Some of these monumental old buildings had been built in the sixteenth and seventeenth centuries by the Swedes and later by Peter the Great, the Russian czar. The buildings stood close together, yet each had its own architectural characteristics—different heights and shapes. The old, famous Peter shul was still standing in full glory; it was the only synagogue not burned to the ground. Because of the narrow proximity of the adjoining structures, if this place of worship had been set on fire, the entire neighborhood would have been engulfed in flames. In the distance I could see the few narrow streets that made up the red-light district, where, as a mischievous teenager, I used to come with friends to tease the prostitutes. We would start a conversation with them with the intent of arranging sexual favors and would then back out, causing the women to become extremely angry and to swear at us, using the most vulgar language I had ever heard.

As our kolonne was about to leave the narrow, winding streets of the old city, I was faced with open space and a bright, clear sky. We were near the shores of the Daugava River, and we soon found ourselves at the river's dock. A ferryboat was waiting to transport us to the other side of the river, where the Ilgeciem Cement Factory was located. Before we boarded we stopped for a head count, and it was refreshing to spend a few minutes at the beautiful riverbank. From a distance I could see the Presidential Palace and the floating pontoon bridge, with its attached swimming pool, which brought back many pleasant memories. As a young-ster I had visited this pool often, since it was the only one available in town. My first swimming lessons had occurred here, sponsored by the local Red Cross chapter.

Farther away was another steel bridge on which noisy steam loco-motives pulled their trains over the river. In the summer they brought me and thousands of other city dwellers to the beautiful resorts, called the Riga Jurmala, along the Gulf of Riga, where my family spent many vaca-tions. The resorts were surrounded by a forest of pine trees, and there were abundant blueberries and mushrooms for everyone to pick. The unforgettable dunes and beautiful, well-kept beaches were other delights on hot summer days.

Our kolonne was the only one on the regularly scheduled ferryboat that carried people over the Daugava River. It was a large boat and could have accommodated more passengers, but to my amazement nobody else was allowed to board; they had to wait until the "human cargo" was unloaded. I supposed this was the case so the rest of the civilian passen-gers would not be "contaminated" by our breath or be bothered by being around us. Whatever the reason, our ride alone did not bother me. As the boat reached the middle of the river, I was watching the beautiful skyline of Riga when I noticed that a familiar landmark was missing—the steeple of St. Peter's Church, with its wrought-iron rooster weathervane. I later discovered that the church had been hit by a German artillery shell and was severely damaged, so the beautiful steeple would have to be rebuilt. The closer we got to the factory, the more upset I became; I was ready to cry, "God, why did You make my beautiful Riga such an unforgettably evil city?"

Our ride soon ended, and factory representatives were waiting for us. We left the ferryboat, and another head count took place, as if we were an irreplaceable commodity. Maybe they thought some of us had jumped off the boat to save ourselves. This would have been impossible; the river and shore were infested with traps set by "human sharks" who had laid bait to catch Jewish escapees and receive a handsome monetary reward from the gestapo.

The newly appointed kommandant, a lieutenant in the SS Einsatzkommando, was the first to reign over us. Before we could enter our quarters, he ordered our camp elder, Kagan, to take a head count. Our men tried to put on a good showing like well-trained soldiers of misfortune. We lifted our heads, straightened our bodies, and lined up four in a row, for easy counting. Kagan quickly went through the lines and gave the count to the lieutenant, who then finally allowed us to enter the factory premises. We were guided straight to our new quarters, which consisted of two barracks surrounded by a high barbed-wire fence with an entrance gate in the middle. I became terrified and distressed as our kolonne approached the labor camp. I walked through the gate not knowing what to expect.

All two hundred men proceeded slowly into the barracks in an orderly fashion and laid claim to their bunk beds. Ever the trio, Father, Boris, and I put our little satchels down on bunks to let others know they were taken; the rest of the men did the same. Father felt very bad that at this point in his life he had to live in barracks and sleep on a straw bed. His first remarks to me were in Yiddish, as if they were a secret: "Nu, mein zun, wie gefelt dir? [Now, my son, how do you like it?]" He meant to convey that he was sorry he could not provide me with more comfortable living conditions. In a way, he wanted to apologize for the circumstances under which we all found ourselves, perhaps feeling I blamed him. With the same Yiddish words, he approached some other men, and they understood as well. Every man was occupied with his inner thoughts; on every face I saw the concern: "Let us see what time will bring us in this new place."

The factory administration did not waste time; after a short rest we were called to appear on the plant grounds, since the open space between the fence and our barracks was too small for all of the men to assemble. Our appearance before the factory representatives was to divide the men into small work groups. I told our superiors that my last job had been as an electrician. They told me politely that they did not need an electrician since the plant already had its own, but they were pleased to have me among the newly arrived workforce. I was promised that if they ever needed an additional electrician, I would be called; in the meantime, I was assigned to a group of three men. After the assignments had been made, we were given a tour of the entire cement factory, and the specific locations at which each group would work were pointed out. We were told to report to our workstations at eight o'clock the next morning and were then sent to our living quarters; thus began our Ilgeciem Cement Factory kasernierung.

Each of us had been received cordially by the administration. We had not expected to be treated like the regular workers, but these people were polite and well behaved. I wondered whether these Latvians had finally come to their senses and forsworn Nazi ideologies. Whatever the reason, they left us with a positive impression, and everyone in the barracks was happy. My father asked me again in Yiddish how I liked the way things were going, but his face was no longer fearful; he was smiling, as if he was pleased with this gathering of the Latvian factory administrators. The sad expressions on the men's faces were also gone; everyone was in a more relaxed, happier state of mind. I was very pleased to be in this kasernierung instead of within the walls of Kaiserwald Concentration Camp. So far so good, and let us hope the pleasantness of the first day will continue, I thought to myself. None of us had eaten all day, and another unexpected pleasantry was a supper with bread, which brought our first day to an end. Most of the men were exhausted and immediately went to sleep.

After breakfast the next morning, we assembled outside the entrance gate, and Kagan and the kommandant took a head count; when everything seemed to be in order, we were released to go to our assigned places of work. There was a guard at the gate and a few guards were located around the perimeter of the plant, but to my amazement no guards were assigned to us. My group's workplace was on the second floor of the factory in an open structure where the cement-making process began.

Large lime boulders were lifted up to us in a big wooden crate; my co-workers and I threw them into a hopper that crushed them into smaller pieces. A conveyor belt transferred the crushed limestone to the crew below for the next step; they, in turn, threw the pieces into a more refined crusher. So the manufacturing process continued until a powdery binding substance was created that was packed in sacks and loaded onto barges on the Daugava River.

Every worker received heavy-duty canvas gloves to make the job easier and less painful; the limestones themselves were not heavy, but toward the end of the day they felt heavier and heavier. A Latvian foreman supervised our work and watched for any breakdowns in production, but none of us was ever rushed or harassed by the supervising staff. Every man in our workforce knew his obligation and made sure the conveyors constantly supplied the necessary raw materials for the final production of Portland cement. I was pleased that my job was within my physical capabilities and that I could handle it without feeling hurried. In a way, I enjoyed this work, as I stood on an open platform on the second floor and could admire the open countryside from above during the summer. Few people had the opportunity to work at that height and enjoy nature's beauty, which served as mental rehabilitation from our actual surroundings.

Our conditions were generally good; during working hours we had a few rest periods, and we received enough food for our needs. Our job sites were constantly covered with a heavy layer of dust, but we often received clean underwear and work clothes, as well as sufficient amounts of work gloves and other materials. All of us had excellent relationships with our superiors, but Kagan often committed irrational and spontaneous acts in an attempt to earn recognition from the German kommandant; he wanted to prove he was worthy of the title of camp elder. One of these outrageous incidents involved my father. At a morning head count one day, Father was the last to leave the barracks. As he approached the formation, Kagan ran up to him and, with full force, kicked him from behind. Father lost his balance and was in excruciating pain; knowing the severe consequences of not appearing for the head count, he pulled himself together and, limping, joined the other men in the column. He was in pain for many days and one day asked Kagan why he had kicked him so hard. The reply was that the kommandant had been watching Father and saw that he was late; Kagan said it was better to receive punishment from him than from the SS officer. The kommandant was probably pleased with what he saw, but the camp elder never expressed any regret for the pain he had caused.

One morning during work I noticed a large group of men in the distance, coming toward our factory and guided by heavily armed guards. As they came closer, I could see they were Jewish men dressed in shabby clothes. Their jackets had a wide white *X* painted front and back, and the pants had a white stripe down the side. From a distance, they looked as if they were participants in some kind of carnival celebration, had it not been for the presence of the SS guards. I did not have time to leave my place of work to see them at closer proximity, so the next day I arranged for my co-workers to take over for me if they appeared again so I could go down to see them. At the same morning hour, the ragged-looking kolonne appeared. I rushed down and stood on the side of the road, waiting for them to pass by. The group consisted of about five hundred people from the Kaiserwald Concentration Camp on their way to work at nearby Spilve Airport. I recognized some of the Jewish workers; they noticed me standing on the side of the road and recognized me as one of their own. I waved, and they slowly responded. Many pointed a finger at their mouths, a familiar sign that meant they were hungry and in need of food.

The kolonne moved slowly, and I tried to see if I could find a good friend or relative among them. I noticed that a man in the middle of a row was waving at me and pointing to his mouth. At first I did not recognize the slim, worn-out face; in those clothes he was unfamiliar, but with a closer look I recognized him as my Uncle Ljova, to whom I had said farewell in the ghetto not long ago. I waved at him and called out his name to make sure it was he. I had enough time to acknowledge his pantomime of needing food before several of the armed guards ordered me to go away. Seeing my uncle in that condition, I concluded that after I had left the ghetto his kolonne had been dissolved, and all the men had been sent to Kaiserwald. In the camp he had been reassigned to a new kolonne that was working at the airport building additional runways. It seemed all Kaiserwald inmates' clothes had been painted for easy recognition and to prevent escapes. I was shocked to see these innocent people subjected to such inhuman branding.

When I returned to my platform, my co-workers were bewildered by my emotional expression, but when I told them who and what I had seen, they understood my feelings. At the end of the workday, I told my story to Father and Boris; they, too, were amazed to hear about the Kaiserwald kolonne and how Ljova was asking for food. Our trio recognized how blessed we had been when we were accepted for this kasernierung; I told Father, "Mother in heaven watches over us." That same evening we prepared two liverwurst sandwiches and wrapped them individually so they would be easier for me to throw and for Ljova to catch. The next morning I stood on the side of the road and watched the long, slow-moving lines. I was ready for my mission—to find Ljova among all of those people. Soon I noticed his row of men approaching, so I ran toward him to the closest point and threw him the two sandwiches. The guard ran toward me viciously, pointed his loaded rifle, and warned me to stay away from the kolonne. I ran away but had enough time to see that Ljova was able to catch one sandwich and somebody else the other. I left praying the SS guards would not take the sandwiches from the men, as they often did.

The physical appearance of the Spilve kolonne shook every man in our kasernierung. The following day everybody was willing to give up some of their food ration, and the men who could leave their workplace at the time the Kaiserwald people passed our factory would throw pieces of bread to them. Since my job site overlooked the entire area, I became the self-appointed observation man. When I saw the Spilve men approach, I called out the signal and all those who were able came to the road with pieces of bread in their hands. At the right moment, they threw the bread to the passersby. To the hungry men in the kolonne, it must have been manna from heaven. The entire undertaking took less than a minute, but the participants' gratification lingered for hours.

Everyone was happy to help our own unfortunate people. I was happy that I could help not only my uncle but others as well. The only people who were disturbed were the SS guards, whose orders had not been obeyed; they were helpless to prevent our humanitarian undertaking. I did not care, as long as the small pieces of bread reached the men who so desperately needed them. We were concerned that our acts of charity would be reported to our kommandant, but for the next several days a few men were always willing to risk their own safety and appear at the roadside with food for the concentration camp Jews. I wanted my help to reach Uncle Ljova specifically. At times, the bread I threw did not reach him. To make my undertaking more successful and to avoid the harassment of the powerful guards, Boris and I arranged a more precise delivery: He became a decoy.

When I was ready to throw the bread to Ljova, Boris would appear at the roadside, which would cause the guards to chase him away. This distraction would allow me to get near the row of men that included Ljova and deliver the much-needed nourishment. I was gratified that I had the means and the opportunity to ease my uncle's hunger. Our new approach worked every time, and Ljova received the bread with a smile. It was strange to see him in such a condition; he was known as a proud, self-reliant person who would not seek help if he could avoid it. Now he was fighting for a piece of bread to satisfy his hunger. Day after day, at about ten o'clock in the morning, Boris and I, and at times Father, made sure Ljova got a small piece of bread, which we sometimes spread with margarine, marmalade, or a meat product we received in our weekly food rations. One day the Spilve kolonne stopped passing our factory, so we thought something had happened to them. To our sorrow, I later found out they were being led to the airport by a different route, away from the road that ran near us to avoid the factory buildings. The SS had gotten their way, and I lost the opportunity for a daily rendezvous with Uncle Ljova. That was the last time I saw him, for he vanished without a trace.

The longer we were in Ilgeciem, the more we appreciated this place of work. In this kasernierung, unlike the Little Ghetto, we did not have to engage in intensive wheeling, dealing, and trading with our gentile co-workers to secure an additional piece of bread or a few potatoes to satisfy empty stomachs. We did not have to worry about having a roof over our heads or keeping warm and dry, and we were not beaten at the entrance gate or shot near the fence, as we had been in the ghetto. We knew the work was within our capabilities and felt a degree of responsibility toward the factory. Last but certainly not least, we knew we would not go to bed hungry and that we would be treated as human beings. I did not think I would mind spending the rest of my days in confinement right here until freedom came. When Sunday, our day off, arrived, we had enough time to relax and fulfill our personal hygiene needs. I could take a comfortable walk within the premises of the plant, and the guards would look at me but never cause any harm.

In the barracks, camaraderie prevailed. In our midst was a cantor named Sorenson, a likable man with a sparkling tenor voice who always had a melody on his lips and a smile on his face. He slept in my barracks, and I got to know him very well. In the evenings and on our days off, he was our voluntary entertainer; he loved to perform a variety of cantorial melodies or an assortment of arias from different operas. At times, when people were not in the mood to listen, he would ask me whether I had a request. Sorenson was so likable that nobody could be angry with him. Some men did not care for him, but his songs and encouraging words made our lonesome lives more pleasant.

We closely followed the latest military updates on the battlefields and were pleased to hear the encouraging news from the fighting fronts. The German Army had retreated in some places, and the domination of the Nazis was slowly being reduced. We hoped to see a complete containment of the German armed forces with a final Allied victory. It was not pleasant to live in such confinement, where one's human rights were completely lacking, but I could not complain about being in this kasernierung since I knew many of my co-religionists lived in much more dreadful places. Everyone in our barracks had one common dream: to become free men again and to see our geula (salvation); of all places, the Ilgeciem Cement Factory could be the site of this wish. We hoped our extravagant dream, which kept us all in a healthy state of mind, would prevail.

The days were slowly passing, and the warm summer would soon be behind us. The leaves had already started to turn; I saw no trees or greenery around our living quarters, but the wind would bring yellow leaves from distant places. The men in our kasernierung were prepared to spend the winter here, but to everybody's amazement we were told in September 1943 that our time at the Ilgeciem Cement Factory would soon come to an end and that all of us would be transferred to Kaiserwald Concentration Camp. This unexpected and frightening announcement hit me like a shock wave that threw my mind off balance. I knew what Kaiserwald would mean for me, Father, and the others in our two-hundred-man family. It seemed Ilgeciem was not meant to be our salvation, as we had dreamed.

A date was set for our departure; we were to leave at the end of our workday. On the last day, before I left my job site, I said good-bye to my best partner, which had served me well and given me no problems—my steel hopper, which had crushed my limestone uninterruptedly and without fail. I left my heavy work gloves on top of the hopper, like a devoted pallbearer at a friend's funeral. Before the final head count took place, each man was handed a double ration of bread; we took this as an expression of thanks for a job well-done. The kaserniert men then walked to the ferryboat for the final ride on the Daugava. I was very sad, and I knew my short stay at the Ilgeciem Cement Factory would remain in my mind for a long time. The men stood in the boat like lonely orphans; everybody was in a deep silence, for we knew very well what we could expect in Kaiserwald. On the other side of the river, canvas-covered trucks waited for us; before we boarded we were told that because of the late hour they would take us to the Little Ghetto for the night. We could occupy our old quarters and continue to Kaiserwald the next morning.

Upon our arrival at the ghetto gate, two hundred people dispersed in different directions, each to his familiar home. Father, Boris, and I, with a few others, went to our old place. On the way we met no one; the entire ghetto seemed to have been evacuated. We reached our little house, but nobody was there, and everything inside stood just as we had left it a few months ago. We looked around and called out some names, but nobody responded. Our troika could now sleep in any bed, but we chose our old arrangement: Father and I in the double bed, with Boris next to us on the small one. We were tired and disappointed by the day's activities, but I took time to drink some water and eat half of the bread I had received before leaving the factory.

Before we went to bed, Father and I stepped into the backyard for some fresh air. Not a sound was heard, and it was darker than I had ever seen; even the moon did not appear over the horizon. I felt as if I had been abandoned by heaven above, for the next day I had to face a new destiny and renew the struggle for survival. We embraced and tried to console each other, mentally preparing for the difficult days ahead. We agreed that my father would wear Grandfather's boots, as they were commonly worn by elderly people and he thus might be able to sneak them into the concentration camp; I would wear the other pair. The coins in the heels would serve as emergency life support, and the pictures were the everlasting memories of our dear ones that gave us the moral support to continue fighting for our lives. After a short stay outdoors, we went to bed for a good night's rest.

6

Kaiserwald, the First Concentration Camp

It felt good to sleep in my old, comfortable bed, to rest my head on a soft down pillow, and to lay my bruised body on a comfortable mattress. My father, Boris, and the others also had a restful night. I got up early, and the first thing I did was to eat the leftover bread from the previous day to make sure it wound up in my stomach instead of in the hands of the gate guards. I was pleased that the day had started off well. Our trio, with the rest of the men, packed our belongings in small bundles. We left the house with great sadness, knowing this time that we would never return. We walked to the ghetto gate, where our people were congregating. At exactly eight o'clock, we went through the familiar head count, which determined that all two hundred men were present. The head of the SS guards ordered us onto the canvas-covered trucks; I was one of the last to board, as I wanted to be closer to the open rear end so I could see out the back. To my disappointment, the entire rear was occupied by German guards, and I could barely see the road we traveled. In no time the trucks started to move, and we were on our way to the mysterious place called Kaiserwald.

On the way, I wondered why the gestapo had picked Kaiserwald, of all of the Riga suburbs, as a site for a concentration camp. Why was it so suited for this purpose, except for the fact that it had a German-sounding name? My questions were unanswerable; it was impossible to understand the workings of the Nazi mind. In the winter, I had taken the Kaiserwald streetcar to go skiing; the area consisted of both summer and year-round homes with wooded areas and greenery. Only wealthy people could afford to live there, and it was considered an affluent suburb. I tried to figure out where the concentration camp could have been built; the sub-urb was well-known among the people of Riga, and to my knowledge there was not enough vacant land to build a large camp. I knew of one empty field located in the middle of a wooded area, for our high school class used to play soccer there; perhaps this was the location to which we were headed. The truck moved quickly and did not stop at intersections; I guessed that the Germans wanted to keep the people on the street from seeing us. I supposed that the Nazis considered us as good as dead, and they wanted to prove to the local population that Riga was Judenrein (cleansed of Jews).

I tried to peek through the back, between the SS guards, but I could see very little. Still, I noticed that we had left the city limits and were on the highway that would lead us to Kaiserwald. Suddenly, the trucks slowed considerably, and I assumed we were approaching the campsite; the truck convoy soon stopped. The high wooden gate opened onto the entrance of the grounds, and the attendant on the watchtower next to the gate ordered us to proceed. Everything had been planned ahead of time, and I could see in the distance that an entire staff was ready to receive the human cargo. Our accompanying guards saw the high-ranking SS offic-ers; they quickly jumped off the trucks and shouted, "Heil Hitler, Heil Hitler!" Their formerly mild behavior changed radically. They ordered us out of the trucks, "Heraus, heraus; schnell, schnell, schnell [Out, out; fast, fast, fast]!" These military men were suddenly playing a role for their superiors. One by one, we stepped down from the trucks.

When everybody was on the ground, our group was led to a large barracks, the "reception hall" for the newcomers in the camp. There was a receiving "committee," consisting of SS officers and a few Jewish but mostly gentile inmates. They waited eagerly for their next group of inno-cent targets; they seemed ready to eat someone alive. One at a time, we had to approach the tables that had been lined up, where we were asked whether we had any gold or other valuables; if so, they had to be turned in. The officers warned us that if any valuables were found in our pockets or sewn into our garments, we would be severely punished. Each super-vising officer had a few prisoner helpers do the actual work; they began by checking our private possessions. Everything was taken from us ex-cept eyeglasses and a razor. All pocket- and wristwatches had to be thrown into a plastic container; as I added mine to the large collection I could see hundreds, some valuable and some plain. After we had been cleared at the tables, we faced a row of barbers, who cut off our hair. Curly and straight hair of all colors lay all over the floor; in the pile was mine, curly and black.

Everything had to be done quickly; we were constantly called upon to move on: "Fast, fast; do not delay—you are holding up the line—fast, fast; keep on going." Next, we were ordered to remove our shoes and throw them into a pile; Father and I were heartbroken, since we were about to lose our last loving memory of our family—the pictures of my mother and the children. We were also about to lose the gold coins that, at the proper time, could have been used to save our lives. For a moment I thought of tearing off the heels and taking the pictures, but I had no time and was being watched on all sides. Father took Grandfather's boots off and put them at the side of the pile, intending to come back and find them right away. I took a piece of gravel and scratched several marks on the upper part of my boots for easy recognition among the similar styles, then I put them down next to Father's.

We were then led to an enclosure where we had to undress and leave our clothes. We were each left with only a razor, shaving soap in a wooden container, and a shaving brush, with which we entered a shower room. A long wall with shower heads attached to it was supposed to be our bath. The water ran constantly, yet it was difficult to get wet. To make the situation worse, the non-Jewish inmates stood there, hurrying us with abusive words: "Move on, move on; make it fast, make it fast." If somebody was too slow, the inmates did not hesitate to push him over or hit him. We were given no time to dry off; instead, we wound up in the clothes storage room, where another group of brutal gentile prisoners threw us underwear, socks, shirts, pants, jackets, and other outerwear. All of the garments were given out at random, regardless of whether they were long or short, narrow or wide; they were picked from a pile without concern for the size. If someone's clothes were too large, he had to keep them; if they were too small, they could be exchanged for a larger set.

The next room was our dressing room; here we were also hurried. It was a chore to put underwear onto a wet body. I was lucky to have received garments that were about my size, which was not true for many men. All we were missing was footwear. I desperately hoped they would send us to retrieve our shoes from the pile on which we had left them, but that was not the case. We were guided to a different pile of shoes that had been left by the previous group of men. I picked a sturdy pair of shoes in my size and was convinced no one would wear our shoes until the next men arrived at the camp; therefore, I still had a chance to recover one or both pairs of boots.

The men in our group were dressed in a variety of colored garments that were in good condition, clean, and even pressed in some cases; the only problem was the sizes. Everything was done with such speed that we had no time to look at ourselves or at others; our only concern was to stay clear of the growling SS men and their helpers, who stood around us at all times. As newcomers to this concentration camp, it was strange to have such a frightful experience. The worst moment came when we had to face the camp "artists." With the stroke of a brush, they painted a wide X on the backs and fronts of our new outer garments and a white stripe on both sides of our pants. A prisoner's identification number printed on a piece of cloth was pinned to our chests, signaling the end of our initiation. We became full-fledged members of the concentration camp society, in which hunger, degradation, hate, and brutality prevailed at all times.

Within hours, my birth name was replaced by a number, 73421, and I was transformed into a two-legged creature. I was now called *häftling* (prisoner), with my corresponding number, and a yellow Star of David had to be worn on my outerwear. All of this meant I was still considered a lonely Jew. In my worst dreams, I could not have imagined the dreadful experience of the first hours following my arrival at Kaiserwald; my options for self-determination were nonexistent. I had submitted to the unscrupulous force of the tyrannical Nazis, and my destiny was now completely in their hands.

When our emotions had settled, we had free time to roam around the campground. We were in a complete state of shock, for it seemed that we had entered a newly created world—a world completely of its own in which decency, kindness, and understanding did not exist; a world in which people became animals. My father, bewildered, said, "The Germans are absolutely crazy—it is unbelievable. Look what they have made out of us." Our group of men gathered together, feeling as though we were carnival clowns or creatures from outer space. We laughingly admired our decorated clothing. Jokingly we said, "You have a beautiful garment—who was your tailor? He made your sleeves too short and the pants too long." Or someone would ask, "Did you buy your suit at a flea market? Who was your clothing salesman? Your jacket hangs over your shoulder—who designed your garment?" Another person might poke fun by saying, "You look like a general with your striped pants—to which raggedy army were you assigned?" We had a few laughs, but bitter tears followed. All of the men soon realized that we were in a dire situation. Before we came to this place, I had only heard about Kaiserwald's inhuman treatment of others; I was now one of the recipients of that treatment.

The Nazis could take away everything but my dreams—they were untouchable. They were dreams of freedom and human dignity for me and other people of the world. History has taught us that before Hitler came to power in Germany, many other tyrants and anti-Semites had set out to destroy the Jewish people. The Babylonians, Greeks, and Romans had all tried and failed—and the Nazis would fail as well. At the last, decisive moment, a miracle from God had always saved us from evil hands. In this generation, we would again gain our freedom with God's help, and the Jewish people would be led into their promised land of Israel. I desperately thought, I must weather this horrible storm—I must survive. The Nazi goal to destroy me must not succeed.

The gentile inmates of Kaiserwald Concentration Camp were hard-core criminals who had been convicted of murder and other major crimes in Germany; the gestapo had transferred these dangerous men here to serve their long-term jail sentences. They wore gray-and-blue-striped prison clothing and were called Zebras, since nobody knew their true names; the leader of this group was a middle-aged man called Mister X. They were rough and cruel, and the gestapo made good use of them in the camp. The convicts were appointed to oversee the Jewish prisoners and had full power over us. They were the barracks elders and the leaders of specific work groups at various workplaces; as such, they had a major influence on camp life. They did not work but received sufficient food for their needs. The Zebras occupied comfortable living quarters adjacent to the Jewish barracks. Many times they took advantage of their unlimited power over the Jews and used brutal force at their will.

The first day in Kaiserwald was almost over. At six o'clock in the evening a bell rang, calling all men to appear for evening roll call in rows of five in front of our barracks. The appointed Zebra, as our barracks elder, took over our group and gave us instructions on how we should greet our camp kommandant, SS Obersturmbannführer Sauer. The Zebra told us when to take off and put on our caps as Sauer passed by, which had to be done instantaneously. We also had to follow the kommandant with our eyes when he passed. After the count we were dismissed, and the inmates went to their barracks to receive their daily ration of bread and coffee. After the meager meal, we were directed to our bunks. Our trio was able to remain together again. There were two-story bunk beds with some space between them; Father took the lower bunk and I the top, and Boris occupied the lower bunk opposite Father. Each bed had a straw mattress, a pillow, and a blanket and was already made when we entered the barrack. At a certain hour, we all had to be in our bunks. A dim light fixture hung from the ceiling, but it did not bother us; everyone was too tired from our unpleasant experiences and overall treatment.

At the crack of dawn the following morning, the barracks elder and his helpers appeared in our barracks and ordered everyone to get up, wash, and dress. This was easier said than done, for the morning rush was underway. I could hear voices on all sides: "Get up, get up; fast, fast." Every Zebra was holding an object in his hand—a rope with a nut on the end, a rubber hose, or a wooden club. They used them frequently on the backs of the Jewish inmates; those who were slow to leave their bunks were beaten up, so I got out of bed as quickly as possible. I could barely get dressed, as one of the Zebras was already after me with an outstretched arm, ready to hurt me. We were told to leave the bunks in the same orderly fashion as we had found them, but to do so would have required time we did not have. Some inmates slept in their clothes to gain time and avoid a beating. I made sure my pillow, mattress, and blanket were evenly spread and neatly tucked away before I left the bunk.

As if this rush were not enough, we were hurried even more in the washroom. I could barely soap my hand and wipe my face before the Zebras took positions in the washroom. Again I could hear orders: "Wash up; faster, faster; keep on going; go get your coffee." There were too few sinks to allow everyone to wash in an orderly fashion. At the door stood another Zebra who pushed the men out of the washroom. To avoid being hit, many men shoved each other out of the way; others did not go to the washroom at all. Using the toilet was not much easier, and I saw many swinging clubs and whips there over the backs of my friends.

The morning procedure resembled a busy anthill. With great strength I managed to push myself out of the washroom and get to the line where I could get coffee. My father and Boris were with me; we got our coffee and, with the leftover bread from the previous night's ration, we had our first breakfast in this "friendly" concentration camp. Before I could finish my small piece of bread, I was forced to leave the barracks for the morning roll call. The slower inmates were chased out and beaten by the Zebras. At the Appelplatz, a large area used specifically for roll call, the usual head count took place and we were dismissed, but the harassment of the inmates did not end. Several men were called back to the barracks, where they were beaten for having not made their beds properly or because a speck of dirt was found under their bunk. The innocent inmates were forced to remake their beds many times until the Zebra in charge was satisfied.

After roll, the majority of old inmates went to their jobs; some worked within the grounds of the camp, whereas others left to work in the city under guard. The newcomers stood around in the open yard. I roamed around to get better acquainted with the camp's surroundings. As I approached another barracks, which was also occupied by Jewish inmates, I noticed two people sitting on the barracks steps. Their faces looked familiar, so I went over to them; it was the Adelson brothers, with whom I had lived in the house in the Little Ghetto and worked at the rail repair shop. They were part of my family of friends in the ghetto, and they were happy to see me as well. I told them that our troika had arrived in Kaiserwald the previous day. I inquired about our co-workers who had not joined us in the Ilgeciem Cement Factory kasernierung. The Adelsons told me all of our friends had been transported to this camp when Weinberg's kolonne was dissolved shortly after I left. Most of the men were presently at work, but some were part of the Stutzpunkt, the work kommando sent to the Rumbuli woods to dig up and burn the bodies from the 1941 Riga massacre. The Kaiserwald inmates were put in chains while they did this work; they were then shot, and their bodies were burned by others. I was very sad to hear that my cousin Moisey had been among these unfortunate laborers.

The Adelson brothers were in poor physical condition; they were too weak to work and, therefore, stayed in the camp. The older brother's face and feet were swollen, and he was so undernourished that his bones were visible through his skin. They were sitting on the steps because they lacked the strength to stand, let alone to walk around. Only a few months before, they had been robust and strong enough to do any work required of them; compared to them, I looked like a healthy giant. I considered how blessed I had been to have found myself in the generous hands of the people at the Ilgeciem Cement Factory. After a lengthy conversation I left, but I promised to visit them again. The following morning I decided to go see them, so I went to their barracks, but they were not there. I was later told by one of the inmates that the brothers had been sent to the Stutzpunkt. I felt very sad that the two brothers faced such a horrible death, for they were two of the nicest people I had ever met.

My grandfather's shoes were still on my mind, but the shoes and gold coins did not matter as much to me as my mother's picture, hidden in one of the heels. I looked constantly at the other prisoners' shoes, for I thought I might be lucky enough to find one of the two pairs. I sometimes leaned down in front of an inmate to look for the scratch mark that would identify my shoe. I was much less concerned about the other pair, as that style of boot was seldom worn and could easily be recognized from a distance. Day after day I stared at people's feet, with no result. I told Father we would probably never find our old shoes and that Mother's picture would be lost forever. He tried to reassure me that if we were freed from the Nazi yoke, we would find our family pictures somewhere. I was persistent in my aim, which finally paid off. One day a young inmate passed me, and I immediately noticed he was wearing my grandfather's boots. I was so excited that I did not know what to do next or how I should approach him without raising suspicion. I had to decide quickly, since I did not know whether I would ever see this man again. He had already passed by, and I was so completely confused that I was still undecided, so I thought I had missed the opportunity to retrieve our shoes.

Suddenly, I knew I had to have my mother's picture in my possession. I ran after the inmate, who was now fairly far away. I caught up with him and politely said hello; he replied the same with a smile. Then I asked gently, "I like your shoes. Would you be willing to exchange them for mine? I am here with my father, and he has trouble lacing his shoes. With yours, he will not have any problem putting them on or taking them off." He looked at me sternly and replied that he was comfortable with these shoes and had no desire to replace them. I was very angry and disappointed, since I had been sure he would agree to exchange them. I asked him again, "Do you not think my shoes look sturdier than yours? I would not propose to exchange them if it were not for my father's sake." He did not reply but merely walked away. I could see that his thoughts were not on the shoes but on something else that bothered him deeply. I followed him to see where he lived, and he walked into my own barracks. He was one of the new inmates that had arrived after us, and I had not had a chance to meet him. As soon as possible I told my father about my sad experience, and he assured me that he would speak to the man. The following morning Father politely tried to explain the difficulties he had in lacing his shoes, but the man insisted he had the same problem and was not willing to give the shoes up. After a lengthy conversation, we parted, but Father kept looking for an opportunity to get the shoes.

One day, all of the inmates from our barracks had to take a bath, which amounted to a quick, lukewarm shower. A German SS officer always presided over such gatherings, and Father went up to him after the shower. He stood at attention and removed his cap, then told the officer in German, "One of our men mistakenly took my shoes, and his shoes do not fit me." "Who is this prisoner?" asked the officer. Father pointed to the inmate who wore grandfather's shoes. "That one," he replied. The officer ordered the young man to give the shoes to Father, then he slapped him several times, giving a verbal warning that he should watch himself next time and not take somebody else's shoes.

When the officer had left, Father apologized to the innocent inmate. "My son and I asked you several times to exchange shoes, and you were unwilling to do so. If you had agreed, you would have avoided receiving those painful slaps from the SS officer." The stranger did not say a word but walked away with an angry face. I was intrigued by the way my father had handled this matter, for he did not mean to hurt another Jewish inmate. The young man may have had a reason for wanting to keep the shoes, but we also had reasons for needing them. The incident would not have taken place if there had not been such a strong need for self-preservation. The gold coins were for future emergencies, and my mother's picture supplied spiritual support through an everlasting memory. In years to come, this picture would be the only available printed image of my mother, one I cherish to this day. I continued searching for the other pair of shoes, but I could not find them. To my sorrow they were lost forever, as were the family picture and the five gold coins.

During the day the camp inmates could not congregate in the barracks, which were meant only for sleeping and for receiving our watery potato soup and rationed bread, so we had no choice but to be outdoors roaming around the empty campgrounds. Every few days the Zebras appointed some of us to wash the floors in the sleeping area of the barracks; others had to do cleanup work in the washrooms. These jobs would not have been so bad had it not been for the brutal behavior of the Zebras. We were rushed through the cleaning, but they expected a very thorough job. Several of them supervised this work with whips in hand and hollered loudly at the workers, "Fast, fast, fast; keep on going; do not waste any time." To scare us they would swing their whips against the floor or the wall. Once, when I had finished washing the barracks floor, the supervisor called me back and pointed to a spot I had missed. I had to wash the entire floor again, and I received several whippings on my back when I was done. My cousin Boris also had an unpleasant experience with the Zebras. After morning roll call one day, he was called back into the barracks, where one of these vicious men was pointing to a few specks of dust under his bunk. As he picked up the tiny pieces, the Zebra hit him with his belt buckle. Boris was fortunate to be able to pick himself up and run out of the barracks.

We experienced similar individual harassment and beatings every day. The most gruesome event occurred early one morning, when all of the prisoners were mercilessly beaten. A horde of Zebras, headed by Mister X, quietly entered our barracks while everyone was still asleep and locked the two exit doors. Then, for no reason, they began to beat the helpless inmates in their bunks. Our men, including myself, were panicked and shocked at what was happening. I heard screams from my fellow inmates and the harsh voices of the Zebras. Our trio and a few other men got up, grabbed our clothes, and ran to the door but found it locked; there was no way for us to get out, since all escape routes were blocked. In desperation, we were forced to break the window and jump to the ground one at a time. With each of us helping the others, we managed to get out unharmed. While our escape was in progress, the barbaric behavior of the Zebras raged in full force; they beat up everyone who was asleep or in their way.

Eventually, the other windows and both doors were smashed by the furious, frightened inmates. At the narrow doors, where only two could pass at a time, a tremendous amount of shoving and pushing took place. Many men found themselves on the floor, stampeded by other inmates, and others were hurt by the broken glass of the windows; this was in addition to those injured by the attacks themselves. During the turmoil, the Zebras behaved as though this was the biggest entertainment of the year; they laughed with every stroke of their strong arms. After things had cooled off, they were asked why they had behaved in such a manner, and they answered simply, "We wanted to have some fun with our Jews." Their reply made no sense to me—how could someone be entertained by beating up weak, unprotected, sleeping people? I supposed I had my logic and the psychotic Zebras had theirs. The rest of that morning was spent outdoors; after the morning roll call we were called into the barracks to clean up the mess. Camp maintenance men repaired the structural damage that had been done to the barracks. It appeared that the camp leaders fully approved of the previous night's turmoil.

After being at Kaiserwald for a few days, I concluded that everything I had learned, everything my parents and teachers had taught me, was completely worthless in a place like this, because you must begin anew if you want to survive. I found myself in the midst of people who acted on animal instincts, in a world in which the strongest win and the weakest perish; people became frustrated, and violent criminal tendencies arose. The morals and customs were different in a way someone who had not been there could never comprehend. We all became strange, inhuman creatures. The word *mercy* was erased from the dictionary, and the words *love* and *man* were replaced with *hate* and *beast*. In this place, degradation and suffering prevailed, and fundamental human rights were discarded. In this strange environment, we were driven only by fear and the will to live. I had to learn these new concentration camp rules and play by them if I wanted to live. Part of that education was learning the concentration camp slang, which consisted of words like *nachschlag* (receiving additional food), *muselman* (an inmate who had become thin like a skeleton), *entlausung* (a lice cleansing), *capo* (a Jewish foreman on the job site), and *scheishaus* (toilet). This strange place, in which thousands of Jewish people were confined and many lost their lives, was called Kaiserwald. This name, well-known by thousands of people, has taken a prominent place in history.

Two weeks had passed, and I was eager to be assigned to a work group. The weather had slowly changed, and the chill of nippy fall days began to invade my undernourished body. I did not want to spend my leisure time around the barracks, since that would mean being exposed to the unpredictable, cruel behavior of the Zebras. I roamed around the grounds like a sleepwalking ghost with no place to go. Some of the men stood clustered together in little groups to keep themselves warm. During my third week at Kaiserwald, a rumor spread that a large work group would soon be created, and I was looking forward to being assigned to that group. One very cold day after morning roll call, all of the inmates dispersed as usual, and those who had jobs went to their workplaces. The rest of us walked freely on the grounds or congregated on a corner protected from the wind. I was about to take my daily walk around the campgrounds when SS guards appeared from all sides; it looked as though something terrible was about to happen. They were rounding up all of the idle inmates who were standing around, as they would animals in an open pasture. The group included Father, Boris, and me, and we were driven into an empty barracks.

A few minutes later I learned this was the way a new work group was organized in the camp; true to the rumors, a large working kolonne was indeed being created. Five hundred people were to be sent away to a new workplace, but some of those chosen tried to run away because they did not want to be separated from relatives or friends who were already at work. It did not matter to me—our trio was mentally prepared to leave Kaiserwald. We knew we could be hurt by the Zebras if we stayed, and our chances for survival would be considerably diminished. All three of us were determined to get out of the camp while we were still in good physical shape and were capable of doing a variety of tasks.

Within a few hours the SS had their five hundred Latvian and German Jews. Each of us received a scarf, gloves, a winter coat with a warm hat, and a blanket; as the day passed we got our watery soup and a large piece of bread. Before the sun had set, we were herded into boxcars like cattle, and we were concerned about our destination. Only now, at this juncture in my life, can I fully comprehend the agony of the thousands of Africans who, two centuries earlier, were rounded up and shipped into bondage in a foreign land. They were transported from freedom, however, whereas I was pleased to leave this fearful place called Kaiserwald, the largest concentration camp for the Jews in the Baltic states.

The only Kacel family photograph in the author's possession, Riga, 1932. *From left:* Leiba, age 2; Abram, author's father; Dora, age 7; Boris, age 10; Ljuba, age 3; Fanja, author's mother.

Chaija and Schleime Lidowsky, the author's maternal grandparents, who lived in Riga and died of natural causes.

Rachel and Kusiel Kacel, author's paternal grandparents, who died during the 900-day German siege of Leningrad.

Abram, author's father, with two of his friends at college, 1919, in Riga.

This photo (actual size) of the author's mother was hidden in his shoe from 1941 to 1945.

Boris, after the liberation, 1945, taken in a coin-operated photo machine in Berlin.

Passport and badge issued by HIAS (Hebrew Immigrant Aid Society).

HEBREW IMMIGRANT AID SOCIETY		IMMIGRATION STATUS	
HEADQUARTERS GERMANY and AUSTRIA APO 757 MUNICH Möhlstr. 37		Office Registered	HIAS-Munich
This is to certify that			18. Feb. 1947
Mr. Mrs. KATZEL, Boris		Destination	
is under the protection and sponsorship of the HEBREW IMMIGRANT AID SOCIETY. Any courtesey extended to the above named will be appreciated.		Visa recd.	
		Staging area	März 5. 1947
		Embarked S. S.	ERNIE PYLE MRZ 10. 1947
ABE GROSSMAN Director of Hias Project in Germany and Austria		Admitted HIAS Pier Service	
		Remarks	Ind. Affid.

MUZEUM

STUTTHOF

W SZTUTOWIE

82-110 Sztutowo
woj. Elbląskie
tel. 83 53
fax 83 58
Oddział Muzeum Stutthof
81-703 Sopot
ul. Kościuszki 63
tel. 51-29-87

¹⁹ 94 04. ᵈⁿⁱᵃ 25.

L.dz.1278/223/94

Pan

Boris KACEL
4020 North Shore Ave.
LINCOLNWOOD, ILLINOIS 60646

Państwowe Muzeum Stutthof w Sztutowie stwierdza,
że w materiałach dokumentalnych tutejszego Archiwum są następujące dane o niżej wymienonym więźniu b. obozu koncentracyjnego
w Stutthofie:

KATZEL Boris ur. 11.3.1921r. w Rydze, dostarczony został do KL
Stutthof w dniu 23.8.1944r. przez Sipo Ryga. W obozie oznaczony
numerem 73 421. Dnia 3.11.1944r. przeniesiony został do KL
Buchenwald.

Innych danych o w/w Muzeum nie posiada.
PODSTAWA informacji: I-III-39 330 Karta personalna więźnia.
                    I-IIE-14 Księga ewidencyjna więźniów.

/ka/

D Y R E K T O R
mgr Janina Grabowska-Chałka

Letter providing information about the author from German records.

Abram in front of Soviet memorial, Rumbuli; inscription: "These are the fallen people from fascism, 1941–1945." This granite memorial was erected by the Soviet authorities.

The very first wooden memorial erected in Rumbuli by unidentified Jews despite objections by the Soviet government.

Boris Lidowsky, the author's cousin.

7

The Journey to Estonia

It was a chilly October evening in 1944, and many stars shone in the dark, cloudless sky. Our group of five hundred men stood in individual rows of five in front of a freight train. All around us I could see armed SS soldiers. We were divided into groups of fifty men each and ordered to climb into the boxcars. Loose straw covered the floors, and a big bucket, which served as the toilet, stood in one corner. The car had only two small windows on either side, both of which were located all the way up the wall near the ceiling, so they were unreachable; on the outside they were covered with barbed wire. They were not meant to serve as observation windows but as ventilation for cattle during transportation. It was a tight fit, but everyone could lie down flat on the floor. Our trio occupied the corner farthest from the bucket; I felt sorry for the people who were near it. I rarely used this homemade toilet, since it was easier for me to urinate through the split opening in the wood floor. As I looked around, I noticed that many of the men were too physically weak to undertake any manual work, let alone to be confined in a cold boxcar for an extended journey.

After all the inmates had boarded, the SS guards shut the doors tightly from the outside. At the end of the train was a caboose car that was the travel quarters for several guards. This was the first time in my life I had been forced to rest for the night on the cold, straw-covered floor of a cattle car. I did not know how to deal with it and was bewildered to find myself a passenger in such a vehicle. Boris and my father were my moral support; I cannot imagine what I would have done if they had not been beside me. During the night the train moved very fast, and its steel wheels were noisy; as I lay on the floor, I could feel every point at which we connected with the track. Nevertheless, I, as well as every other man in the car, was soon in a deep sleep because of the previous day's exhaustion.

At sunrise we were awakened by the loud conversation of our guards. With great difficulty several of them managed to slide open the heavy door. The sudden opening of the door caused the cold autumn air to rush into our car; it felt good to breathe fresh air again, but at the same time the sudden change in temperature sent a cold chill through my body. I pulled the thin blanket over my head and could see my breath steaming from my mouth. The guards set a bucket of drinking water on the ground and called us to come and drink; we gladly accepted their generous offer, since we were all very thirsty. Those who were able jumped off the car, grabbed the large ladle submerged in the bucket, and took a few gulps of cold water. Many of the men were unable to jump out of the car, so I picked up the bucket so they could enjoy the fresh drinking water. All of this was done under the strict supervision of several young SS men. After everybody had consumed his share of water, one of the men was ordered to empty the toilet bucket near the tracks. I saw the ill effects of the night's travel on the faces of many inmates. A few of us who were outside stretched our legs next to our boxcar until the guard shouted, "All on board—we are leaving." I returned to my car, and the soldiers rushed to slide the heavy door on its track, pulled the lock, and went back to their comfortable caboose. The locomotive engineer gave the last whistle signal, and the train proceeded on its journey.

The slow-moving train soon shifted into high speed, which caused the terrible friction noises to begin again. The men were either lying flat on their backs or sitting up, filled with emotions and thoughts. Little conversation was heard, although one could hear a few whispered words at times. At about noon the train stopped again, although I did not know why. I looked through the open barbed-wire window to see whether any signs or markings indicated where we were. Father and Boris picked me up, and to my amazement I saw a sign that told me we were in Valka, the border town between Latvia and Estonia. I reported this to the rest of the men; a few were anxious to see the sign, and I helped lift them up to the small window. Now we knew the direction in which we were headed—the train was going to Estonia. After a short stop at the station, the train proceeded again at full speed; during this time I was raised up to the window several times. Sure enough, all signs indicated that we were traveling north through Estonia.

In the afternoon the train made a short stop in an open field. Each man received a piece of bread with hot coffee, and a bucket of drinking water was prepared for us. Few drank the cold water, for we were all eager to have something warm, and the coffee was fine. Again, the toilet bucket from the car was emptied at the side of the train. The people in our transport had not received food for an entire day, and we were all very hungry and cold. Although we had been given warm clothes, they were inadequate; traveling north, the weather had changed considerably, and it was already winter in this part of the country. I was cold and unsure as to how long I could last locked in a cattle car with so little food, but the hot coffee and stale army bread helped everybody's hunger and gave us strength to continue our journey. After the men had received the bread and coffee, the heavy sliding door was pushed back into the locked position, and the train continued on its course.

I was one of the privileged few to have my father at my side to comfort me. His concern for me never abated, and he was always asking me how I was. Once in a while he would put his arms around me or share his blanket with me to make sure I was warm enough. He wanted to help me in any way he could, and I tried hard to do the same for him. To make him feel good, even if I did not always succeed, I always told him I was fine and that the cold air did not bother me, but, in truth, the drafty air that penetrated the loose boards of the boxcar bothered me, as well as others. We were all on the floor next to each other, so our bodies kept us all fairly warm. Nobody felt like standing up, as doing so would dissipate our energy and allow cold air to pass across our bodies, so I got up only when I wanted to peek through the window to see the passing landscape, towns, and villages. At times, I had a hard time convincing anybody to get up off the floor and lift me up to the window.

During our feeding periods the young elite SS guards stood around us. There were several of them, perhaps even an entire army unit. At the time I thought to myself, These young Germans could be the best fighting soldiers on the front, but instead they are guarding unarmed, helpless, tired Jews on the way to some meaningless labor camp. It did not occur to me that these guards in the Einsatzkommando unit were only a few of the many that were the backbone and protector of the Nazi regime in Germany and the occupied territories.

The second day was almost over, for I could see the sunset through the small windows. It looked as though we would spend another night within the stifling walls of the smelly cattle car. The air had become unbearably stuffy, as the windows did not sufficiently ventilate our car. Some people were complaining about the lack of food and the very cold air. Everyone had the same questions: How far will the train bring us? When will they let us out of here? What is our destination? We had embarked on a seemingly endless odyssey of frustration and misery that, at times, became a panicky situation because nobody could give us answers. Slowly, we settled down for another night on the cold, straw-covered floor. During the night the train made a few more stops, but nobody thought of us—the human cargo in the locked-up boxcar. At some stops we could hear the steam locomotive being maintained with fuel and water, but we were not offered the same maintenance of food, water, and warm clothing.

The second night passed, and the physical condition of the men in our car had declined. Some were already too weak to get up; others were so cold they could not talk. Early the next morning the door opened, and the guards gave us bread and hot coffee. That morning fewer people were able to jump out to get to the coffee, so several men lifted the heavy coffeepot into the car so everybody could have a generous amount. To make it easier to chew the stale bread, we soaked it in our coffee. This meal, our only one of the day, quickly disappeared. On this third day of our journey, the guards tried to stay away from us when they opened the door; the smell in the boxcar was so strong and unpleasant that they held their noses. The primary odor came from the toilet bucket, which had only been emptied, never washed or rinsed.

We were on the road for another night, traveling farther north. The weather had become steadily colder—it had changed considerably since our departure from Kaiserwald, and we now faced freezing temperatures. Finally, late in the afternoon of the fourth day, the train stopped for good, and the steam locomotive was uncoupled and taken from the train. The boxcars with the five hundred men and their guards were in an open field that was covered with a light blanket of snow. A cold northern wind made the air feel colder than it was. We had arrived at the end of our journey. The sliding doors were opened, and all of the men were ordered to leave the cars. Many who had experienced no difficulty getting on the train only four days earlier could no longer get off by themselves. I left my odorous shelter without regret; thankfully, the members of our trio were some of the healthiest men in the group. Sadly, I looked at my new surroundings, the weak, undernourished men, and the wild, snow-covered wasteland that stretched as far as I could see.

I was seized with fear and became very emotional about ending up in such a remote place. My body was trembling from the severe cold, and I silently wept. I pretended I felt fine, since I did not want to upset my father or Boris, although I knew their physical condition was the same as mine. I was certain I would soon face many hardships in my new environment. Terrifying thoughts arose: Was my ride from Riga only a prelude to the "final solution" in a foreign land? Was this a final stop for the train or an end to my existence? I prayed, "O gracious and compassionate God of mine in heaven and on earth, is this my day of judgment? I seek mercy for myself and others around me; help us to survive our ordeal in this no-man's land."

The German SS men had a difficult time getting the slow-moving men lined up in rows of five. The guards became shepherds trying to get their flocks of sheep together, with no concern that one of them might vanish, for they knew there was no place to which one might escape. It took some time to empty the boxcars and count our people; this was done to make sure all of the men were present at the delivery point, regardless of how they might feel. After our long journey we were all hungry, thirsty, and, most of all, cold from the fast-shifting wind. No one was properly dressed for the harsh northern Estonian climate, or, as this region was called, the "Estonian Siberia," and we were dirty and our hygiene had been neglected. It was not pleasant to look at the people around me, for everyone had suffered severe weight loss. My strength had diminished considerably, as in the last four days I had been fed only a few pieces of stale army bread, hot coffee, and drinking water. I was glad to see that Boris and my father were in fairly good physical condition; they could move around on their own, whereas others could not do so and were forced to hold on to their friends. To protect ourselves from the cold, we all pulled our blankets over our heads; only our drawn faces were visible, and we looked like creatures from another planet. Nobody spoke in a clear or recognizable voice; enervated from cold and hunger, we could only mumble. Everybody's mind was in disarray, and we were unable to comprehend our destiny.

Finally, the five-hundred-man kolonne was on its way, and the German guards were leading us on a seemingly endless march on a country road alongside the tracks. The newly fallen snow made the road muddy and very slippery, so we had to hold on to each other to continue to move forward. At some points our feet sank into the mud, which stuck to our shoes as we lifted them. The farther we walked, the heavier our mud-covered shoes became; some men became so exhausted that they were ready to drop. A large part of this transport consisted of people in very poor health. When we were selected, the Kaiserwald SS men had rounded people up indiscriminately, with no attention to their physical condition or age. The aim was merely to fulfill the order of their superiors: get five hundred prisoners who could still walk and breathe. We walked around our new surroundings for several hours and, except for us, not a living soul was in sight. It seemed as if we were in a land without civilization.

After a long time I noticed a bright campfire in the distance, near several barracks. As our kolonne approached this isolated camp, the bonfire became much clearer, and it looked as though a large barbecue wood pit was burning. The wishful thoughts of a hungry man went through my mind: Maybe our new "host" was preparing barbecued beef for the new arrivals. I later found out this had indeed been a large bonfire; however, they were not roasting beef but were burning the bodies of inmates who had died in this camp. Our kolonne arrived as the evening head count of current inmates was about to be taken. The German SS guards turned us over to the waiting Estonian unit, and we joined the other Jewish inmates on the Appelplatz. I learned from them that this new labor camp was called Vaivare.

8

My Fight for Survival in Vaivare

The odyssey to the new labor camp had finally ended, and I stood among the other inmates at the Appelplatz, awaiting the familiar head count. I surveyed my new surroundings. This was an isolated, tundra-filled region in the northernmost part of Estonia, and no civilization was in sight. It seemed a barren land, with low-lying shrubs all around, and I questioned how useful or significant this labor camp could be in such a wasteland. When I began to work I learned the answer: A few miles from our campsite was a strategically important railway junction with maintenance facilities for the steam-driven locomotives that were still in use.

After a quick head count we were led to the barracks. At the entrance each inmate received a piece of bread, some margarine, and a bowl of hot, watery soup. We walked into a long, dimly lit barracks, about one hundred and fifty feet long and fifty feet wide, part of which was already occupied. On both sides were continuous rows of two-story bunks with individual straw sacks packed tightly next to each other; the arrangement resembled two long shelves. The only way to reach one's sleeping space was to crawl in from the front. The barracks had two small cast-iron, coal-burning stoves with chimneys through the roof, but they were a poor source of heat for such a large space. In the middle of the building were a few long tables and benches where the inmates had their meals or could spend social time together. The only natural light came from two small windows at each end of the room. There was never enough light, so the electric lights were on at all times.

The few inmates who already resided in our barracks tried to be friendly and make us comfortable. They were eager to find out where we came from. The city of Riga was familiar to them, since most of them were from Poland. They had been forcibly rounded up in the Vilna Ghetto and transported to Vaivare; some had even participated in building the camp. They informed us that this barracks had been fully occupied until a few days ago, when the former occupants had been sent to a newly erected camp, Nerete, about twelve miles away. The inmates wanted to keep up the conversation, but none of our men felt able to continue. We were all glad our transport ordeal had ended and that we were finally in a warm place. Most of our hungry men were busy enjoying their hot soup and the soft, edible bread, but some were so weak they barely ate the meager rations. We congregated around the stoves to warm our cold bodies and then chose our bunks. Our trio managed to stay together again; Father and I picked a lower bunk for easier accessibility, and Boris took the one above us. There were no partitions between the straw sacks; each of us lay right next to the other. Every morning we would wrap our straw sack with our blanket to mark our sleeping area.

I slept between Father and a middle-aged man who was so weak he could barely crawl into his bunk. His tired, worn-out face and skinny body looked familiar, but I could not recall where I had seen him. I felt very sorry for him, and I knew he was too exhausted to attend to himself, since he still had his rationed bread. He desperately needed help, so I went to get him some water. When I returned I asked him, "How do you feel? Why don't you eat your bread? I have some water for you." In a low, stuttering voice he replied, "I don't feel like eating; I am too exhausted. I just need to rest." I tried to feed him his bread, as I knew that if he did not finish it somebody would take it from him while he was asleep. With many kind words I convinced him to eat his bread with a cup of water. It felt good to help a fellow Jew in dire need. I covered myself with the thin, gray blanket and fell into a deep sleep in no time.

When the sun was barely up I heard loud voices shouting, "Everybody up, up, up; everybody up from your nares." *Nares,* I found out, was the camp slang for bunks. The voices were those of the barracks' Jewish elders and their helpers. They were in charge of waking us and keeping the barracks in order. I was barely able to get up. My father, as always, was ahead of everyone, up and on guard for the next move. He called, "Bora, get up; it is time to get up." My cousin Boris was also slow to get out of bed, so Father climbed to the top bunk and told him to do so right away. Father was ready to start his first day in this new labor camp. He started to give out his first orders of the day: "Boris, Bora, let's go wash up; let's go get our coffee while it is still available; we have to hurry to be ready for the morning roll call." Boris and I had barely finished in the adjoining washroom when Father was ready to guide us to the hot, black coffee one of the orderlies poured into our metal cups. Our trio sat at one of the tables nearest the hot stove. The piece of bread from our previous night's ration and the hot coffee constituted our first meal of the day.

The barracks became very crowded, since all of the inmates had left their bunks at around the same time. The men tried to speak as little as possible, but it was still fairly noisy. We tried to clean our muddy clothes from yesterday's relentless march. Everybody was in a rush to finish the coffee, which, for some, was the only hot meal they would receive until their daily ration in the evening. I noticed that we were like most of the inmates in saving a small piece of bread for breakfast.

The most difficult part of getting ready in the morning was getting dressed and putting on shoes, because the barracks were very crowded and much shoving and pushing took place. I was accustomed to such a situation, thanks to my experience in Kaiserwald, and had become a graduate student in the school of concentration camp life. The older inmates acted as though they were the superiors in the barracks and were, therefore, able to overpower the newcomers, so we had to let them have their way.

When I left my bunk that first morning, the man next to me was still asleep. I had pushed him to wake him up and then left the bunk to follow Father and Boris. As we were about to leave the barracks, I noticed that he was still lying in his nare. I pushed him again, but he did not respond, so I pulled down the blanket that was over his head. His body was motionless, his eyes were closed, and his face had no expression. My body shook as I realized I had slept next to a dead man. He had died in his sleep, and I never knew. Everybody was ready to leave the barracks for the morning roll, so I quickly notified one of the orderlies that there was a man dead in his bunk. Unconcerned, the orderly replied, "I will take care of the body after everybody leaves for work." My emotional voice did not bother this seasoned inmate; he was accustomed to seeing and taking care of the dead.

I left the comparatively warm barracks for the subzero temperatures outdoors. A light snow covered the frozen ground on which we were lined up for the morning roll. I noticed that in addition to the men, a large contingent of women was in the camp; they had been brought forcibly from the Vilna Ghetto. Most of them worked indoors, taking care of the German living quarters or working in the camp kitchen or in warehouses. A quick head count was taken by the German SS lagerführer and the Jewish camp elder, and the several hundred camp inmates were dismissed. The old inmates left for work in organized groups headed by a foreman, and the newly arrived prisoners were left standing around in clusters, waiting to be assigned to a work group. I could not avoid seeing the bonfire that served as a makeshift crematorium. The previous night the fire had been glowing and shooting flames high into the sky, but by this morning the odor of burned flesh had diminished. A few Jewish inmates were ready to clean out the old ashes and prepare a pile of wood for the next bonfire. The fire burned full blast every day, and this day was no exception. Several corpses were already visible on the pile of wood that would be lit with gasoline.

The entire camp consisted of two rows of several barracks each that were used for prisoners' living quarters, a kitchen, a small infirmary, and an administrative office. The space between the two rows of barracks served as both the camp's main thoroughfare and its Appelplatz. In the center of the area stood a hand-operated well, which was one of the main sources of water for the camp. The grounds were surrounded by a high barbed-wire fence with a wide gate guarded by Estonian soldiers. The camp administrators were German SS officers, so the guards had little authority over the camp population. They oversaw the security of the camp and the region around it, but the main force in Vaivare was the Todt; its members were found in every work group as foremen and project engineers.

The Todt was a paramilitary organization—an arm of the Nazi Party—whose name came from Dr. Fritz Todt, an outstanding organizer and engineer who died in a plane crash in 1942. He was the builder of Germany's military defensive West Wall, known to most people as the Siegfried Line, which stood on the opposite side of France's well-known fortification the Maginot Line. Todt was in charge of Germany's construction industry and was a devout Nazi Party member. His "Todt

Organization" was responsible for building roads and other facilities in Nazi-occupied countries—the original German forced labor program. Todt members wore green military uniforms with their own insignia but did not carry weapons. I could not determine whether these men had volunteered or had been drafted to help Nazi Germany in the war effort; most were far above the mandatory draft age.

Our transport of five hundred men was divided into several work groups. My father, Boris, and I stood together and became part of a fifty-man kolonne. Under the guidance of a few Todt men, our group left the camp. It was hard for me to walk, since I still had mud stuck to my shoes. I wore my grandfather's boots, which felt good when I had to walk on flat, frozen ground. Less than a mile from the camp gate, we stopped at a railroad track. In the distance I could see a tall building with a water tower next to it; this was the maintenance plant, where all passing steam locomotives stopped for refills of water for their engines. On the tracks stood several flat railcars loaded with large pieces of steel beams brought from the Soviet Union as the Germans dismantled and stripped the Soviet manufacturing plants. We were divided into groups of ten men to a car. Each piece of steel was ten to twenty feet long and weighed several tons. The heavy cargo had to be unloaded and dropped into the open field. One man could not undertake this task alone; since no tools were available, everything had to be done manually. This difficult job called for a coordinated effort among all ten men. The Todt man in charge left the job site without telling us how to unload the beams.

After waiting to no avail for the supervisor to return, Father decided to take over and to figure out how to accomplish the job. He wanted to be on good terms with his new German master, if it was possible for a Jew to be on good terms with a Nazi. He directed the men to various positions along the heavy steel beam; when everyone had taken his place, Father called out when to pick up, when to stop, and when to move. All movements had to be perfectly synchronized, and each man used his full strength to complete the task successfully. When the heavy object had been lifted off the railcar, additional instructions were given as to when to drop it to the ground. Any slip by even one man could mean disaster or serious injury to some workers, which, in turn, would mean certain death for the men in our labor camp. To avoid such a situation, as we held the heavy piece of steel everyone called out all of the instructions, which enabled each man to understand what he had to do and encouraged the men to be alert and act responsibly. The calls sounded something like this: "Pick up the front; hold the side; pick up the rear; do not let it down; hold it; let's move it; the rear is letting down; pick it up slowly, right side; let it go down; slowly, slowly."

Some men had difficulty adjusting to the physical work, and they often had to be reprimanded for not cooperating responsibly with their fellow workers during the strenuous lifting. For many, the freezing weather and the heavy weight of the steel were too much to handle. The gruesome train ride from Riga to Vaivare had left their undernourished bodies in an unstable condition. I sometimes thought these fine men would probably not survive the rough climate or the harsh camp life. It was sad to accept that those in our troika were among the few healthy men in the group.

Our supervisor, the Todt man, showed up frequently to check our progress. Once in a while he would yell at us when we were too slow in unloading the steel cargo. Although it was freezing outdoors, we perspired from the work. All of the men wanted to be at their best on the first day. At noontime a truck arrived with a large container of watery potato soup. It was little nourishment for hungry men, but it warmed our bodies, and the extended rest period helped us. I felt somewhat stronger after I had eaten my small piece of leftover bread with the hot soup.

That first day I could not absorb or analyze my living and working conditions; I was walking and working in a haze. It felt as if a strange, invisible power had taken over me and was guiding my movements. Before the day was over, my body felt numb. I would have given anything for a warm, peaceful rest. I pushed myself the last few hours of the day so as not to disappoint my father or other co-workers. When the day was over, the rest of the men in our group could not have gone on much longer. At four o'clock we were told to stop working and to congregate in one meeting place. We were glad the day had ended without any injuries to our ambitious, hard-working men.

Under the watchful eyes of the Todt men, the kolonne was guided back to the labor camp, and we were in front of our barracks in less than half an hour. Everyone was ready to warm up around the stove after being in freezing temperatures and handling cold steel all day, but our wishes were denied, and we were forced to stay outdoors for the evening roll call. Only when the SS lagerführer had finished were we permitted to enter the living quarters. Inside, everybody received his daily bread ration with margarine, and hot coffee was available. Now came the hardest part of the day. I was very hungry and ready to eat all of the bread, some of which was meant for the following day, but I knew I must save some. I exercised incredible restraint and divided the bread into three pieces: one to be consumed immediately, one for the next morning, and the third for the next afternoon on the job. Under the supervision of our own elder, my father, we slowly cut up each piece of bread. The pieces not meant for the evening meal were wrapped in a cloth. The cutting and wrapping of the bread had to be done very carefully to avoid making any crumbs.

After we had our evening meal, the men could devote some time to personal hygiene. I tried to keep my grandfather's shoes clean to prolong their life, for I knew I had an obligation to preserve the gold coins and my mother's picture. I kept myself as clean as possible, and every evening I washed my face, hands, and, at times, chest. During the free evening hours, most of the men relaxed on their bunks or went to sleep early; nobody was in the mood to socialize. I felt a certain compassion for my sleeping neighbor who had passed away. I later realized he had looked familiar to me because he was a very well-dressed gentleman I had often admired on my way to high school, although I never spoke to him. I admired his custom-made suits, the variety of beautiful ties, and the colorful cufflinks that adorned his sleeves. He must have been an attorney, since he always carried a briefcase and was on his way to the central part of Riga. It was sad that such a capable person was unable to withstand the harsh living conditions under the Nazi yoke.

That same evening, before my tired body rested, I exchanged a few words with my new bunk neighbor. He felt more comfortable than he had the previous night, when he had not had his own straw sack. There was a shortage of sleeping spaces in our barracks, but in no time all of the men were in a deep sleep, and another day was behind us.

I found out that this camp had a special work crew to take care of the many corpses. Every night, several people expired in their sleep. I developed a daily habit of checking the upper and lower bunks to see how many inmates had not uncovered themselves, and there were some every morning. I became frightened; I was aware that the Nazis were dissecting my young life, but I knew I must sustain the courage and strength to fight this evil. I became a victim of the fanaticism that had gripped the German people. I also knew I had been brought here not for the sake of my free labor, as they claimed, but for my elimination. Our compulsory labor was a false front—in reality, it was part of Hitler's plan to exterminate European Jewry. I had to learn how to survive in the brutal world that surrounded me at Vaivare and slowly learned to deal with my personal trauma.

The days and weeks passed with great difficulty for all of the men. Our numbers were dwindling with every passing day. Our relationship with the old inmates from Poland became strained; those transported from Riga were labeled unwanted guests. Most of the Riga and German Jews were mild-mannered, soft-spoken men with limited ability to per-form the work required in this labor camp. The inmates who had come before us from the Vilna Ghetto were more seasoned and suited to the work, so they found it much easier to adapt to the harsh life. A majority of them had rough manner and talked tough, and they derided us as a "fine and gentle class of Jews," unsuited for the labor camp. They might have been right about us, except for the fact that we performed work unsuited to any human being. The work had to be done without heavy building equipment or tools, but despite the hardships we managed to fulfill our obligations. In conversation, the old inmates expressed a pro-found concern and sympathy for those from Kaiserwald, but some of the inmates in leadership positions did not practice what they preached when it came to assigning the less strenuous jobs. None of our men was ever assigned to indoor or camp work. In the end it would not matter, since we all had to face the same daily problem—the fight for our survival.

On one of our days off, a surprising thing happened: I met an old friend from Riga named Wulja. For many days we had been so absorbed with our own problems that we had not noticed the people around us. I was not aware that he had come to Vaivare with the same Kaiserwald transport as I. Happily, we embraced each other and had enough time to exchange a few words. We agreed that we would try to visit each other in our respective barracks and reminisce about our lives in Riga. Thus the day began on a happy note, and I hoped it would end the same way. An even bigger surprise followed when it was announced that all occupants of our barracks would be transported to a bathhouse. Truckloads of men were sent several miles away to a building that housed a large room with many shower heads, a dressing room, and a waiting room. As we entered, we surrounded our underwear for entlausung and, after we had enjoyed hot showers, we went to the dressing room to receive those unwashed but deloused garments. The rest of our clothes were sprayed with an odorless disinfecting powder. It felt good to be clean again, so it was a very pleasant day.

The following day we resumed routine of the working day. Another heavy load of steel was unloaded and piled on the frozen ground; at four o'clock the exhausted, hungry men were again on the way back to the barracks. We passed through the open gate under the watchful eyes of our Todt men and the two Estonian SS guards. I was bothered most by the never-ending pit of fire with the high flame. I visualized the smoke and the bright red flame reaching to the blue sky, asking the heavens for acceptance. In reality, the hot, smoky flame routinely dissipated in the clear, unpolluted air, with nobody paying any attention to its source. I thought, I am one of the very few who knows the flame has engulfed many innocent, decent human beings; if only the charred corpses could cry out and say to the heavens, "Almighty God, why did You let us suffer so much? Now take us in Your arms and spare the lives of the oppressed people below." I could not escape the thought that someday my naked body might simmer in that towering flame, but I had to overcome such emotional thoughts if I wanted to survive. I had to restrain the fight between mind and body; my life was too precious. This inner struggle was difficult for me. I became moody and depressed; at times, I was ready to give my life up, since I did not see the purpose of continuing. It took me a while, but I finally realized that I had to distance myself from the gruesome vision of flames. With the help of my father and Boris, I was able to pull myself together and bring my mind back to reality.

As time passed, a new phenomenon swept the camp. As a result of malnutrition, the lack of sanitation, and poor hygiene among the inmates, the lice infestation reached such proportions that we had to clean ourselves each night before we could get to sleep. We thus had something new to occupy our time—entlausung. We would try to find all the lice in our clothing and kill them one at a time. They multiplied so quickly that we could never get rid of them all. In the evenings, everybody sat on his bunk, looking for and killing his lice. My father found an easier, more effective way of getting rid of these tiny creatures. We would go to the well in the middle of the campsite, undress halfway, and rub our underwear against the ice that was encrusted on the well; we also washed our chests and backs with the cold well water. All of this had to be done very quickly, as the outdoor temperature was often below zero. This method was cold and unpleasant, but it was also very effective.

Because of the freezing temperatures, at times I did not feel like leaving the warm barracks and was ready to skip my daily rendezvous with the lice. Father went after me faithfully, and his persuasive words always made me agree to go with him. When we returned to our quarters, I was always glad I had listened to Father. We were the only ones who used this effective method. The lice multiplied so quickly that only icing them daily could keep them under control. The insects could eat us alive, and it took me a while to realize that they were as deadly an enemy as the Nazis. I was sorry that a few of my fellow inmates fell victim to these parasites that lived on human blood. Some days they multiplied so rapidly that we could not see an individual louse but saw only large gray spots made up of several thousand lice. Only scraping them against the ice on the well could dislodge them from our underwear. Although this method was harshly cold, it not only temporarily relieved us from the lice bites but also strengthened our bodies' resistance to the harsh winter climate.

One morning before our kolonne went to work, a few of us were taken from the lineup and sent to another work unit that consisted of about a hundred men and needed additional people. The man in charge of this group was an elderly Todt with a back that was severely curved; he had to use a cane when he walked. This supervisor, whose name we never learned, barely spoke to his men, and the few words he did speak were uttered in a strong, nasty voice. He wore a stern, unpleasant expression that seemed to convey that he wanted no one near him. My impression of this man was verified when I went to work for him.

This work kolonne existed for some time, building roads in the middle of the wasteland. The men in our unit had to level off the ground that would serve as the new road foundation. When we reached our work site, we received shovels with long handles. The supervisor ordered several inmates, including me, to take up digging positions across the full width of the projected road. I worked very slowly, since I lacked the proper knowledge of how to dig frozen ground. The man with the cane constantly surveyed us and checked our progress. If he thought we were working too slowly, he would tell us to shovel faster. I wondered, What is the hurry—where will this road lead to, anyway? This tundralike region is not populated—who will be using this road?

The elderly German let every worker know he could be physically violent. Despite his disability he was on the go all day, checking every group. If he did not feel his harsh words were speeding things up, he would use his cane without hesitation. The unscrupulous man would hit the workers on their heads, backs, and feet. His severe beatings were not limited to one person but would include all of the men in that person's group. At times, he reversed his cane and hit the men with the curved end. Those beatings were painful but did not fully penetrate the heavy, padded winter clothes the inmates wore. Still, some of the men were bruised to such an extent that they were unable to work the next day. The supervisor was so eager to advance his road project that he was willing to shout at and beat his workers. His Nazi beliefs were so strong that he had developed the mentality of a slave owner. I constantly heard his loud voice saying, "Hurry up, hurry up, dig faster; fill your shovels; move your shovels faster!" At times I thought a man his age must have his own family, with children and perhaps grandchildren. How could he gently caress his innocent children's faces with the same hand that had hurt a helpless man? This man was filled with vicious hatred of the Jews and seemed devoid of the natural instinct to be considerate of other human beings. He was a cruel man and very well suited for the Third Reich.

One day, the supervisor was standing on high ground watching his men dig up the ground. He did not seem to like what he saw, as he lost his temper and started to move furiously toward my group. With the help of his cane, his walking speed increased, and he came straight at me. I was very scared and did not know what to do or to whom I could turn for help. I sent a prayer to heaven: "O Lord, hear my prayer; do not ignore my plea; have pity on me; do not let him hurt me." Before I could utter the last words, he was behind me and began to beat me mercilessly. I received multiple blows on my head and back, and he then turned to the others with his cane raised. While hitting us he shouted, "You dirty bastards—you were moving empty shovels. You tried to fool me. Fill your shovels to the top; keep on digging; faster, faster." I summoned all of my strength and dug as fast as I could. I filled the shovel to capacity with dirt. He watched us for a while and then left to check on the other groups. That was a frightful moment for me. The Todt man had swung his cane with full force but had not hurt me much, since my heavy winter outerwear protected me. I wondered whether somebody in heaven had heard my prayer.

I concluded that I would not last long if I did not learn an easier way to dig. The best teachers were the more seasoned members of the kolonne, so when the supervisor was not around I watched their technique. I noticed that they did not pick up the shovel; instead, they glided it along the sandy ground. A slight turn of the shovel and the dirt slid off to the side of the road. I liked their method, which had two advantages: It required less strength, since the heavy shovel did not have to be picked up, and the shovel was in movement all the time, which pleased the supervisor. After some practice I mastered this new digging process. I was glad when, after several days, I was released from this kolonne and escaped from the ruthless Todt supervisor. I went back to my old job working with the steel beams and was reunited with the rest of my troika. My job transfer occurred because a few men had been hurt by falling beams; this was unfortunate for them but was a big improvement for me.

The Todt supervisors on this job were more tolerant and understanding of human needs than my previous supervisor had been. These men may have hated Jews much less than that particularly nasty overseer; whatever the reason, they did not beat us. The only threat made to this group was verbal, which hurt no one. The only injury we could incur would be a result of the negligence of our own men. As long as everyone kept working within his capacities, no problems were foreseen. Within a few days of my return, though, Father was severely injured when some men lost their grip on a steel beam and it landed on his foot. For several days he was in pain and could barely move, although he continued to go to work and did his best to help the others. Eventually, he recuperated, but he lost one of his toenails.

A few months had passed since my arrival in Vaivare. The cold fall weather had changed to the most severe winter of the decade. That winter of 1944, with subzero temperatures during the day, turned out to be the determining factor in the outcome of the fighting on the eastern front. The city of Leningrad, located sixty-two miles from Vaivare, was under a siege that lasted nine hundred days. Little did I know that as I was fighting for my survival in German bondage, Father's entire family was fighting off famine and cold in Leningrad. During the war my relatives had moved from their native town of Ostrow to Leningrad to seek shelter. The family consisted of my grandparents, Rachael and Kusiel, two uncles, Monja and Mischa, and my Aunt Rebecca. I knew little about them; I remembered only that Father had sent food packages to Ostrow in the early 1930s. Sadly, my grandparents succumbed to the famine that persisted in Leningrad during the German siege and to their exposure to extremely cold weather.

The terrible winter also left its mark on the men in our labor camp. Every morning before I got up, I noticed motionless bodies still covered; men had died during the night from hunger and the freezing temperatures. So many good people were gone who could have served our human race well. The more able-bodied men moved slowly on their job sites, their worn, swollen faces showing weariness. Our work group grew from ten to twenty just to accomplish the same job. My growling stomach, freezing limbs, and parched lips caused me to become progressively weaker. There was no way to obtain additional food, and I thought we had finally reached the stage of becoming objects for destruction. I lived from day to day; each day I drew on my inner strength to enable me to continue my work. I soon became a victim of failing health; I developed a small pimple on the back of my neck that soon became a large, infected boil. It grew to such an extent that it affected my entire neck and head. I sought help at the camp's inefficient infirmary, but the treatment was ineffective, so I decided to treat the boil myself. In the open field I found a white rag that I washed several times at the well. When it had dried I wrapped my neck with it. Every night I washed the cloth and dried it on the stove in the barracks, which gave me a warm, clean bandage in the morning. I soon felt an improvement in my neck, and I eventually managed to heal my own boil. From then on I always wore the ragged piece of cloth around my neck; it was pleasant to at least have a warm scarf in the morning.

The most severe winter of the decade left its mark on the German soldiers in the Leningrad region. Train after train filled with wounded and sick men of all ranks stopped a few hundred feet from our campsite for refueling and maintenance. The soldiers were engaged in the severe fighting on the northernmost front; they were the ones who kept up the long siege of the city of Leningrad. Most had not been injured by bullets but had suffered frostbite. The intense cold created the greatest number of casualties in the German Army; in fact, it was one of the main factors in the downfall of the superb Third Reich Army on many fronts in the Soviet Union. Through the fogged-up windows I could see the bedridden soldiers. Some could move around, but others lay flat on their backs in narrow bunks. Nurses were seen inside and outside the train. The wounded soldiers often sang patriotic military songs in a spirit of victory. Many looked bewildered when they noticed our inmates around the train. I am sure they were wondering who we were and what we were doing in this isolated part of the country. We were happy to see that these evacuated soldiers were wounded and sick, for we viewed their unfortunate destiny as revenge for our sufferings.

These hospital trains had their own kitchens, and when the trains pulled out we often found food on the tracks. I once had a serious argument with my father when one train had left after a lengthy stopover. Our kolonne was on its way to work, and we had to cross several tracks to get to our train. Father picked up a handful of crumbs of bread and other food from the ground; he was very hungry and was ready to eat them. I grabbed his hand and told him he should throw the crumbs back on the ground; I tried to explain that the food could be contaminated with germs from the sick soldiers and that he could get sick if he ate it. Finally, I raised my voice and said, "I always listen to your advice. This time you must listen to mine. Please drop the pieces of food. It is better to be hungry than sick." He did not reply, but he took my advice; he slowly let the crumbs drop to the ground. Apologetically, he said, "I was very hungry—that is why I was keeping them. I still do not think I would get sick from a handful of leftover food." With this, our short misunderstanding ended, and no hard feelings lingered between us. I congratulated myself on having withstood my father's strong will; until now, I had merely lived in his shadow. My decision to challenge and convince Father proved I had matured to adulthood faster than I had thought. I was now seen as a mature son who could make important decisions on his own and whose opinions should be considered.

Our trio's health slowly deteriorated. The subzero temperatures, insufficient food, and ever-increasing lice were fearful concerns. I thought,

I am on a hopeless road to destruction; only a miracle from God could save me. Even the gold coins I kept in my grandfather's boots could not help us. We found ourselves in a completely barren land, with no other humans in sight. At our present job site we had no access to anyone who would accept our gold coins in exchange for a piece of bread or a few raw potatoes. Vaivare was a place for abandoned people like us, but, most of all, it was a place of death. Every day I quietly prayed for a miracle. Every passing day was precious to me and my two loved ones.

One day I heard an announcement that the Todt organization was seeking a few qualified electricians, so I decided to apply for the job. When I arrived to register, a large group of men had already gathered in front of the Todt barracks. The supervisors were surprised to see so many electricians applying for work. Only a few of the men assembled were actually electricians, however; the rest were simply desperate to try a lighter, more pleasant job in an effort to survive. Since the Todts were very suspicious, they decided to screen the applicants by examining each one separately. I was sure I would not pass the exams and that my application for the job would be denied. Among the applicants, I met my good friend Wulja. I knew he had attended the Jewish Trade School in Riga, where students took general education courses and learned electrical and mechanical trades as well. He had knowledge of wiring and electronics, so I asked him whether he would help me if necessary. He agreed to do so but told me he did not know what he could do.

As each inmate was called into the office for the exam, Wulja and I decided to be among the last ones questioned. When the first applicants came out of the barracks, we learned that each had been given the same problem: how to install wiring for one light controlled from two places. Wulja knew the process, and with a stick he drew a diagram on the frozen ground. He explained the drawing to me, and I tried to memorize it. Eventually, I was called into the examining room, and a miracle from heaven occurred. When I was asked to draw the wiring diagram, I did it as well as an experienced electrician, just as Wulja had shown me. They liked my drawing and my explanation in perfect German. Most of the inmates from Poland did not speak German but conversed with the Germans in Yiddish, which was close enough for everyone to understand.

The Todt management needed only two electricians, and an inmate from Vilna and I were accepted on the crew. My co-worker was an electrician who had been working in his trade at home, so he was very well qualified for the new job. This young man had been one of the first to arrive at the camp from the Vilna Ghetto and was in good physical condition, considering the terrible living conditions; he must have worked indoors on a less strenuous job assignment than mine. I met him after we had completed our exam; he seemed to be a very pleasant person. I was sorry to hear that Wulja, who was a master electrician, had not been accepted to work in his trade. I thanked him for his much-needed help and expressed my sorrow that we would not be working together. I promised that I would somehow try to compensate him for his devotion to me, but a few days later he was transferred with other inmates to Nerete, and a long friendship ended abruptly. I will never forget Wulja's unselfish help, which gave me one more tool for survival.

The following day, we two Jewish electricians were assigned to a group of three gentiles. John was from Poland, Tony from Holland, and the third man, whose name I have forgotten, from Luxembourg. A Todt man was in charge, but the three gentile electricians were sympathetic to our situation and were helpful to us. They had been recruited in their native lands and worked for a German company called Licht und Kraft (Light and Power). They had been sent here under duress to install power lines and wiring for the German SS and Todt men's living quarters, which consisted of numerous barracks. We all worked under the supervision of the Todt organization. From the outset, I had to be cautious not to reveal my limited knowledge of electrical work. I watched the professionals perform their tasks. I had to pretend that the work they were doing was familiar to me; in reality, it was not too complicated for me to comprehend, and I was soon ready to work with my co-workers. In the beginning I helped them, but they later allowed me to work on my own.

John was a rough-spoken individual who was in his late twenties. He was always conscientious about his work and tried to accomplish as much as he could to please his German superiors. Tony and the electrician from Luxembourg were easygoing men in their early thirties. They never argued about their assigned work but did not go to far to try to please the Germans.

I most frequently worked with Tony, and we got along very well. We conversed in German, which brought us closer together. He spoke a great deal about how much he missed his family in Holland and showed me pictures of his wife and two small daughters. He wanted to know about my life in Riga and the destiny of my family. His hatred of the Germans was so great that it often slowed my work on our assigned project, for Tony saw me as his confidant and shared his inner thoughts with me. He revealed that when his vacation came, he planned to go home and not return; instead, he wanted to join the underground resistance in Holland. Our co-worker from Luxembourg expressed similar intentions. John spoke very poor German and felt more comfortable with the other Jewish electrician, who came from Vilna and with whom he could converse in their native Polish.

My new job required a great deal of walking, which I did not mind. I was happy to be able to move about and not be stuck in one place. I felt like a free bird who could fly around the open wasteland to look for nourishing crumbs. In the morning, I had to walk a mile or so to a barracks, where the electricians met with their Todt supervisors. After we had received our assignments, we dispersed—individually, in pairs, or all in one group, depending upon the urgency and size of the job. We worked in the various living quarters and warehouses of the German SS Einsatzkommandos and Todt organization, which were several miles from each other. The German living quarters consisted of barracks, which were very well kept by female Jewish inmates from our labor camp. These women had a fairly comfortable life; they worked indoors, were cleaner and more neatly dressed than other inmates, and received enough food to prevent hunger. They also had the opportunity to listen secretly to the radio and inform other inmates about the situation on the front, which boosted everyone's morale and encouraged us to survive. The news spread quickly until it reached everyone in the camp.

We had to travel on foot to our various job assignments. There were no roads, so we followed man-made tracks through the empty, snow-covered fields. At times, the tracks were obscured by snow, and we had to find our way out through the bushes in the open wasteland. It took me a while to become familiar with the different locations and to know how to find them without getting lost. When I had mastered the complicated orientation, one problem remained: my footwear. My boots had fallen apart as a result of the constant moisture and had been replaced with a pair of wooden Dutch shoes called *klumpes*. I had to master walking in these shoes, and I learned that wooden shoes were very different from leather ones. To wear the klumpes properly, I was not supposed to bend my legs or my toes but, rather, to make slow, sliding movements. My feet had to be wrapped with rags to prevent blisters caused by the harsh wood finish on the inside of the shoes.

The shoes kept my feet warm and dry but prevented me from moving quickly. A solution came about when I was assigned to install porcelain insulators on utility posts for high-tension wires. To reach the top, special climbing hooks were fitted to our shoes, but for me to use them I needed a pair of regular work shoes. Since mine were wooden, I would have been unable to join my co-workers on these assignments, so my supervisor often loaned me a pair of boots for the job. After a while, as a reward for my good work, I was allowed to keep the boots, which made me very happy. The blisters I had suffered from the klumpes healed quickly, but the scars remain to this day. Still, from then on I could walk painlessly and comfortably. My new shoes became the next hiding place for my gold coins and the small picture of my mother.

One day while I was working in a supply warehouse for the SS and Todt, I noticed fluffy bath towels on the shelves. Thinking of my father and Boris, I took two towels from the shelf and wrapped them around my chest. When I returned to the barracks, I gave the towels to Father; he was delighted to have them. The following morning, before he left the barracks, he wrapped the towels around his body to protect it from the freezing weather. The next day, I stole two more towels; I gave these to my cousin Boris. He, too, wrapped the towels around his body and was more comfortable working outdoors. I tried to steal two more towels for myself, but someone was always present when I walked into the warehouse. Eventually, however, I succeeded in getting towels for myself. I knew that if I were caught stealing German property, my life would be in serious jeopardy. To the Germans, the towels meant comfort in their daily lives; to us, they were a necessity for daily survival. They not only kept us warm but served as a shield from the lice that fed on our blood. From then on, the entlausung at the frozen well was changed for the better. Instead of taking off our undershirts, we simply unwrapped the towels from our bodies and shook them against the ice.

I became very well acquainted with my Jewish co-worker. We were two of the most fortunate inmates in our camp, as we were free to explore our surroundings. At times we would leave our work sites and visit

the isolated farms nearby. One of us was always on the lookout for anyone suspicious in the area. The farmers we were able to reach were friendly
and willing to help. They knew who we were, so no explanation was
needed for our presence on their farms. Some gave us bread, others gave
us potatoes; everything was appreciated, and we always thanked them for
their generosity. The food we obtained was divided in half, and I shared
mine with Boris and my father when I returned to the barracks. At times
Tony and the Luxembourger electrician brought me some leftover food
they did not care to eat. Both would say apologetically, "We would like
to help you more, but we do not get much food either." I tried to explain
that I understood their dilemma and was very grateful for everything
they did. They always expected less work from me; both of them would
say, "Just relax, take it easy; do not exhaust yourself."

I was eager to work in the German living quarters, where I found a
window to the outside world. The Jewish women there gave me the latest
political and fighting news, which they learned from listening to the
radio or overhearing private conversations among the German SS or Todt
men. This information gave me the motivation and strength to continue
fighting for my survival and eventual freedom. The women told me that
despite the unfavorable news from the front, the Germans were still acting like fanatical dreamers—like conquerors of Europe. Their forces were
retreating from all fronts, yet they could not see that they would never
obtain the lands they desired.

In time, I became the morale booster for the men in our barracks.
Many inmates would wait for me to return from work to find out whether
I had any new and encouraging information. The report from the front
in the winter of 1943 gave us the boost we needed to deal with the
difficulties of camp life. After more than two years of successive military
victories, the German blitzkrieg efforts had come to a halt. The Soviet
forces had begun a massive attack across the eastern front. These attacks
soon became so damaging to the Nazis that, reluctantly, Hitler's armies
were forced to retreat. General Paulus and his army surrendered, and the
Soviets retook Stalingrad. In 1943, Soviet forces advanced rapidly on all
fronts. One of the fiercest battles took place around the city of Kursk.
Leningrad was still under siege, and the German forces endured heavy
casualties there. At the same time, the Allied forces were preparing for
the Normandy invasion.

Several railroad tracks around our campsite experienced very heavy traffic. Hospital trains constantly made stopovers for maintenance on their way back to Germany with wounded men. When the trains left, our men found potatoes, carrots, and other vegetables on the side of the tracks. The food was safer now because these soldiers were not sick but injured. The freezing temperatures did not let up, and it was very hard for Father and Boris to work outdoors all day. I tried to provide them with additional clothing, but it did not help. The cold killed more inmates than the shortage of food. The mortality rate in the labor camp rose considerably, and our bunks had many empty spaces. When our Riga transport had arrived, there had been too few sleeping places for us all. Now, a few months later, the nares were becoming emptier by the day.

At this point my behavior sank to its lowest level. I lost all sense of decency and, with a few others, participated in gambling on human lives. We would bet on which men would die during the forthcoming night. The tragic individuals were judged by their poor physical condition and unstable mental behavior. I became accustomed to dead bodies, as I saw them on the bunks nearly every morning. Unfortunately, the first to expire were the German Jews from the Riga Ghetto, who could not adapt to the new, difficult surroundings of Vaivare. By this time my heart had become so hardened that the corpses around me did not bring me down. Paradoxically, they had the opposite effect, increasing my determination to outlive other inmates and overcome the hardships in the labor camp. I looked forward to our day of liberation.

One morning my father and Boris were slow to get up. I paid little attention, since I, like everyone else in the barracks, was in a hurry to get dressed, have some coffee and a piece of bread, and be ready for the morning roll. When we were in line on the Appelplatz, I noticed that Father's and Boris's faces were puffed up and bluish in color. I knew these were the first symptoms of deterioration as a result of exposure to cold and of a decline in the body's resistance because of malnutrition. These signs could mean, as we said in the camp, "the beginning of the end" of a person's life. I was very disturbed, for I could not imagine the moment when Father's name appeared on the betting table. It was unthinkable that I would bet on my own father's life for the sake of recreation. I asked him how he felt and whether he noticed any swelling in his face. He acknowledged that he felt swelling there, as well as in his feet. He never complained about himself, and I did not expect him to say anything unpleasant. He always justified his condition by saying it could always be worse.

After roll we went our separate ways, as always. I was bothered all day by Father's and Boris's appearances. I decided that I had to find a way to get some nourishment for them, even if it meant jeopardizing my own life; I was determined to save their lives. My goal was to locate a farmer with whom I could trade my gold coins or some clothing in exchange for food I could steal from the Germans. I was familiar with the landscape in this part of the country: I knew every tundra bush, footprint, and sled track. Fortunately, the German SS and the Todt knew me as the electrical maintenance man who walked freely from one location to another, so it would not be suspicious if I were found walking in some remote place. I began to look for new sled tracks that might lead me to a farmer who had never met me. Near the end of the day, I found fresh tracks that led to a forest in the distance. I followed them, feeling they would eventually lead me to a farmer's house. Soon, I reached the forest and was surrounded by a variety of trees.

Finally, I reached the edge of the forest, but the tracks continued. It was a daring undertaking to walk across an open field, but I had no choice. In the forest I had been camouflaged by bushes and the high trees, but my movement here was completely exposed; I was noticeable from miles away. From a distance I might have looked like a dark speck gliding along the clean, glittering snow. My parents' faces were constantly on my mind: Mother, as my savior in heaven, and Father, for whom I had to be a savior.

At last, in the distance I noticed a farmhouse. As I approached the house, I looked for a watchdog in the snow-covered yard but did not see one. I knocked at the door, and the farmer opened it immediately; he had seen me coming through the open field for some time. He greeted me warmly and let me into his house. He noticed my frozen face and shivering body and allowed me to warm myself at the wood-burning stove. He offered me hot coffee and food; I ate delicious homemade black bread with an assortment of cheeses and sausages. I was a novelty to this Estonian farmer, since none of the inmates would have dared to journey here. He spoke in broken German, but we understood each other very well.

He knew I was Jewish and that we were being mistreated, and I told him I was working for the Germans as an electrician.

I was ready to offer him my gold coins, but before I could speak he called me to the window. He wanted to show me his backyard and the fence that led from the house to the barn. Then he said, "I would like to have electricity in my barn. You see the porcelain insulators on the fence? I installed them but could not finish the job because I lacked wires. Can you provide me with the necessary wires in exchange for produce?" I liked his proposition and thought to myself, If I can strike a deal using wires, I will be able to keep the coins for a future hardship. My reply was to the point: "Can you give me butter, bacon, bread, and other produce in exchange for the wires?" He agreed, and the deal was made. I told him I would be back with the wires within a week. The friendly farmer had known the purpose of my visit from the outset. Without my asking for anything, he filled my pockets with potatoes and pieces of bread. I left the house and made my way back to the camp, happy that my first undertaking with a wealthy farmer was such a success. My promise to deliver wires to him had been made without thought of the consequences that could follow—I had, in fact, put my life on the line.

I walked as fast as I could through the open field and was relieved when I reached the forest. The walk back was much easier, since I knew my destination and the familiar road ahead. I had only one problem: I did not know what time it was. The sun was setting fast, and I had to arrive at camp in time for the nightly roll call. Where the snow was not deep I tried to run, but it soon became very difficult to move at all. In addition to my body weight, I was carrying the additional load of the potatoes and bread. My legs became progressively weaker, I was perspiring from exhaustion, and my breath was condensing to icicles on the scarf that covered my mouth. Finally, I made it out of the forest and found myself surrounded by the familiar low bushes of the tundra. My fear diminished somewhat, but I was still running late. My body was soaking wet, but I kept on until I reached the camp gate.

When I arrived, the inmates were already on the Appelplatz; I could see Father and Boris in the distance waving at me, indicating my place in the lineup. I rushed toward them, knowing I was very late. My father asked me where I had been, but I just smiled and winked at him. He quickly got the message that I had lots of surprises for our evening meal.

We stood at attention for the roll call and then returned to the barracks, where our troika enjoyed the treats I had obtained from my new acquaintance. We had enough supplementary food to last us several days.

A week passed, and the materials I had promised the Estonian farmer were on my mind. When the opportunity came, I stole two boxes of wires from my work site. I had to get rid of them before someone noticed they were missing, so I made my way to the farmhouse the next day with both boxes under my arms. I knew my way down the long road, but I needed good luck so no one would see me in the open spaces. I walked as fast as I could. My eyes were focused forward, and my mind was ahead of my body. I did not stop until I reached the forest, where I allowed myself to rest for a few minutes and made sure nobody was following me. My arms were somewhat numb from carrying the wires, but I did not care how I felt as long as I did not meet with foul play at the hands of the farmer or the Germans. When I finally reached the open field, I stopped again to inhale more of the pure air before I thoroughly surveyed the surrounding area. Nothing was moving, and no sounds were audible; in that part of the country, everything is dormant during the winter months.

I crossed the snow-covered field with renewed vigor and determination. The farmer had seen me coming from a distance and was waiting at the door; he seemed very happy to see both me and the wires. A large bag of produce had already been prepared for me. I was told this was the first installment and that I should come back the following week, when there would be another. I took my payment and thanked him for his generosity. I left the farmer's house holding the bag close to my body, as though it were my most treasured possession. I took a break under a pine tree in the forest and slowly opened the bag: There was butter, sausages, cheese, bread, and potatoes. To my amazement, I also found a pint of homemade whiskey; the only thing missing was the bacon I had requested. I was happy with what I had received as my first payment, but I was faced with the dilemma of how and where to distribute it. Slowly, I filled my pockets and other garments, making sure the bulging areas protruded as little as possible. When this delicate work was finished, I continued the walk back to my quarters.

I was beyond the forest and crossed the tundra as fast as I could. My heart was pounding so hard I could feel every beat through my heavily padded clothes. I knew that if I were caught with this illegal food, my existence would be made miserable in a cruel way. I was disturbed but continued down the unmarked road that led to the camp. My passing through the heavy snow became more difficult with every step. To amuse myself, I began to talk to the bushes: "You bush, you are too tall; you are too bushy, too fat for this place; you have too many branches; you bush, with very few branches, you are worn out and will not survive this winter; ah, you are the best-looking one of all I have seen." This one-sided conversation with the bushes helped me to continue on and to keep my mind focused.

I felt much better when I got closer to the camp and could see the high, red flames from the bonfire. I thanked the invisible force that had protected me and given me the strength to reach home on time. At the gate, the Estonian guard was standing in a wooden booth, protected from the wind; I passed him with a smile and a wave, acknowledging his presence. He smiled back, and I was relieved to have passed through the camp gate. It was after sunset, and the inmates were preparing to line up for the evening roll. Boris winked and Father smiled at me as they noticed my enlarged chest and hips and my protruding pockets. After roll, we entered our barracks excitedly, and every man received his daily ration and hot coffee. Then the three of us crowded on the top bunk Boris occupied and had our meal—the feast of the year. I showed them everything I had obtained; we carefully cut each food item into smaller pieces for convenience and concealed them by carrying them on us at all times. We had not seen such a variety of food in years. As we enjoyed our meal, I told them about my experience and the friendly Estonian farmer. One at a time, we took a sip of the homemade whiskey with a bite of a sausage sandwich. This was a truly memorable evening, different from all other nights; we went to sleep with bellies filled with food. It was also very special for me, knowing I was able to help Father and Boris in their struggle to survive.

The following day life returned to normal. My fears had passed, and I could watch the fruits of my daring mission help my dear ones. The food I brought home lasted quite a while. Father and Boris had a sip of whiskey daily to keep their bodies warm during the unending freezing weather; within a few days, their facial swelling had been reduced and their normal coloring reappeared, which made me very happy. After several days I visited the friendly farmer once again. Just as before, he was extremely generous; another bag of various smoked meats, butter, and bread had been prepared for me. This time, though, he had also included a large piece of bacon. His valuable food prolonged our lives and helped to strengthen us for future challenges. I bow my head in great gratitude to a friend, a nameless rural farmer in Estonia, for his high sense of values and his desire to help another human being in need.

When spring of 1944 was upon us, the melting snow prevented me from going long distances. Although I had an open invitation to visit the farmer, I could not get to him. The open fields were flooded, and the muddy country roads were impassable by foot. Father and Boris still could not leave their workplace, so I became the sole provider of additional food for our trio. We were in good physical shape now, thanks to the help we had received. I was cautious about my unlimited free movement in the countryside, for I did not want to jeopardize the good relationships I had with my Todt superiors and my gentile co-workers. At times I did visit other farmers on the way to or from work. They were accustomed to being visited by hungry inmates of the camp; therefore, their generosity was limited, and they would sometimes give me nothing. At other times I succeeded in begging a few potatoes or a small piece of stale bread the farmer did not want. Even this was enough to partially satisfy our hunger; every little piece of food was a great help. Anything I brought into the camp had to be concealed from the other inmates, so I had to be careful not to arouse the suspicion of anyone in our barracks. As hard as it was, I succeeded in keeping the food a secret. It was hard to see my friends go hungry, which made me much more aware of how fortunate I was.

My spring dreams came true. The sun tenderly began to warm our worn, skinny bodies, and I looked forward to the day when we could shed some of our shabby winter clothes. The rail traffic became heavy; the German hospital trains, filled with sick and wounded soldiers, passed the camp one after another. The soldiers occasionally sang the famous German national anthem, "Deutschland, Deutschland über alles [Germany, Germany over all]." We also heard the moans of those who were bedridden. The men who were mobile stared at us through the windows as though we were wild animals. The increase in rail traffic gave us incentive to continue fighting for our survival. The Soviet military advancement on the front could be felt at Vaivare, as the heavy fighting neared an end in our favor. Despite all of the German casualties on the front, the dismantling of Soviet industrial complexes was proceeding at full speed. Open railcars loaded with steel beams and girders arrived uninterruptedly for Father and the rest of the men to unload. I was dreaming that a glorious end to my tragic story would arrive by summer. The morale in the camp was high, but, unfortunately, lingering hunger diminished hopes.

With the warmer weather, my working conditions changed somewhat as well. Tony was about to leave for a vacation in his native Holland, and the electrician from Luxembourg was also returning home. Both were very happy to be leaving Estonia, and neither had any intention of returning. I was now working only with John and the other Jewish electrician. We were very busy and had to work hard to fill the outstanding work orders with fewer workers. John, the only remaining foreman, became very demanding and followed us to every job site, which prevented my co-worker and me from calling on farmers for food. When John was under the influence of alcohol, he became very violent. He wanted to go back to Poland but was not permitted to do so. His vacation was scheduled for when Tony came back, but I knew that day would never come and that John was here to stay. The Todt organization had drafted an extensive development plan for the region, and several barracks had already been erected and needed to have electrical wiring installed. John was unhappy about these additional assignments and occasionally took his frustration out on me. I tried my best to please him, assuring him that all of the work would be finished to the satisfaction of our superiors. He was very moody and unhappy in Estonia and was jealous of his friends who had left for their homes. My Jewish co-worker knew how to handle him, though, and he always managed to reconcile differences pleasantly.

One day I received a work order to repair defective light fixtures in the living quarters of several high-ranking SS officers. It was one of my most memorable days, which began on a positive note but ended with a very sad occurrence. The SS officers' living quarters were several miles apart, and I could move from one to the other without John following me. I easily completed all of the repair work before the day was over. I also managed to stop at a farmhouse, where I was given a few potatoes. At the end of the day, I strolled through the open fields, whistling a tune.

I had a habit of doing this whenever I was pleased with the day's events. I returned to the camp, thinking that our trio would not be hungry that night; after a long time with no extra food, we would enjoy baking the potatoes on the stove in the barracks. When I entered my quarters, however, I faced the most serious dilemma of my life.

Father was waiting to tell me he and Boris had been selected to be transferred to another labor camp a few hundred miles away. I was stunned by such unexpected news. Within minutes, I had to decide whether I should join them or remain in Vaivare and continue to enjoy my good job and livable food supply. I knew I must not be parted from my father, no matter what might happen to me. He was delighted when I told him, "I am going with you and will not leave you alone." The new camp was located in a small town called Sonda, where we would work in a sawmill. The work unit of two hundred men was already organized and ready for transport the next day. With great effort, I managed to be included in this group. The fact that I was an electrician made it difficult for my transfer to be approved, but luck was with me again. I was glad our troika had survived this treacherous camp and would stay together, for better or worse.

9

Sonda, My Next Home

My last day in the labor camp at Vaivare began like any other, with a
wake-up call before sunrise, early morning cleanup, the meal of black
coffee with leftover bread, and the morning roll call by our lagerführer
and his Jewish subordinate. After roll, the two hundred men selected to
move on were congregated, and my era in Vaivare neared its end. Army
trucks with armed Estonian SS soldiers arrived in the yard to transport
us to our new labor camp in Sonda. We boarded the trucks and were on
our way. My love for life had paid off; my will to survive was stimulated
in Vaivare through inhuman suffering and had developed into an increased capability to fend off hunger and physical abuse. I did not regret
my choice to leave the camp, since I felt strongly that each day presented
another opportunity for self-preservation and that in the end my freedom would be achieved.

After a few hours' ride along a country road, we arrived at our new
campsite, which consisted of only one barrack with a spacious Appelplatz
in front. The entire area was surrounded by a high, barbed-wire fence.
The barrack was newly erected and included the necessary facilities; everything inside was new and clean. As in Vaivare, our beds consisted of
individual two-story bunks with straw bags. The camp lagerführer was a
young, noncommissioned SS officer from the Einsatzkommando unit.
The camp elder and his assistant were young men from Vilna whom I
had never met. By profession, the elder was a butcher, and his assistant
was a barber; both were rough, shrewd individuals. Of all of the inmates,
only our troika and a young man named Henry were from Riga; the rest
were from Poland. It is significant that a majority of the men were butchers

from Vilna; this was a select group of able-bodied men in good health. A boy of bar mitzvah age, accompanied by his father and uncle, were the second troika in our midst. This trio, like ours, stayed close together and shared their meager food.

After a day's rest, we were ready to go to work. I requested an assignment as an electrician in the sawmill but was denied, since the mill employed its own electricians. We soon discovered that our men would not work at the sawmill, as we had been told, but in the forest to provide the mill with necessary timber. Only local Estonians worked inside the mill; we had been deceived by the SS in Vaivare so they would not have problems getting the strong, healthy workers they needed. We were sent to the forest in small groups, each of which had a function to perform: we had become lumberjacks. We cut down trees and loaded the logs onto trucks to be transported to the mill. I worked with my father and Boris, trimming the downed trees by cutting off branches with a handsaw or an axe. All chopping and cutting were done manually, which required a fair amount of strength.

The routine in our new camp was the same as it had been in Vaivare, but the living conditions were much better. The barrack was clean and less crowded, with good facilities for washing. The problem with lice was considerably diminished, and we no longer needed to undergo the daily entlausung. Once a week we were sent to the public bath in town. Everyone was very concerned about keeping the barrack clean and sanitary, as well as about taking care of individual hygiene.

Sonda was located in the heart of the Estonian timberland, which was an ideal location. In addition to the sawmill, the town had a slaughterhouse that secretly provided leftover meat to the camp, thanks to the good relationship between the lagerführer and the Jewish elder. We were excited to frequently find small pieces of meat in our soup, but the Jewish camp elder and his assistant benefited most. I was told they ate steaks and other delicately prepared foods in the company of the lagerführer.

The young SS kommandant had his own quarters in the barrack and felt comfortable enough to mingle among the inmates. I considered him a hunk with a six-foot-tall human body and very little brain tissue—a "cheesehead," as we inmates often called him. This noncommissioned officer probably realized he could have been sent to the front and become another German casualty in the war; instead, he belonged to the elite SS Einsatzkommando unit and was fortunate to be out of the fighting zone. He was "somebody" among the weak and helpless incarcerated Jews. In Sonda he could enjoy the fresh, clean country air and exercise his unlimited power over the camp inmates. He often drove to town to satisfy his sexual urges with local Estonian fräuleins, to whom he falsely depicted himself as a brave German soldier.

The living conditions in our camp were dependent upon the elder and his assistant, who knew how to handle the young, inexperienced lagerführer. The inmates generally benefited from the good relationship between the elder and the lagerführer but still suffered from hunger. We received insufficient nourishment for the hard work we were forced to perform. Our troika had an additional problem in this small, confining camp: We found ourselves among a close-knit group of Vilna men. At times it was difficult to live with our fellow inmates, as we were looked down upon because of our Yiddish dialect, the way we performed our work, or other habits they did not like. These men did not hesitate to make fun of us, and their domination and intolerance of the few Riga inmates became unbearable. They stuck together and expressed bias toward us, not realizing we all faced the same destiny. Their harsh life in the Vilna Ghetto and the labor camps had caused their attitude toward other inmates to toughen in an attempt at their own self-preservation. They judged people not by their mental abilities but by their physical strength.

To overcome our mutual misunderstanding, Father tried to speak to the Vilna men in a friendly and reasonable way, but his well-meaning attempts failed. We thought their unwarranted hatred of us might dissipate over time. I recalled how, as a small boy in Riga, I had often overheard the words *Vilner kacovim* [Vilna butchers], which were used to identify a person who was exceptionally rude or who used abusive and obscene words in daily conversation. I never understood the full meaning of these words until I had to live and work closely with men they described.

Eventually, two factors changed the conduct of the Vilna butchers, as we called them. First, they realized that our troika was as able as the rest of the men in handling the work in the forest. In fact, our accomplishments generally garnered us considerable respect from our co-workers. The second happening was the development of a friendship between my father and the assistant elder. They were both interested in politics, and on their days off they would debate world affairs, as well as the eventual outcome of the war. This relationship caught the attention of the Vilna inmates and led to a friendlier alliance between our factions. We were no longer considered outsiders by the men in our labor camp.

Unfortunately, Henry, the fourth Riga man, faced a different fate. He was a lonely, strong-minded young man, with a history of negative experiences with co-workers in previous camps. Henry was severely undernourished and could not accomplish as much work as the rest of the men in the forest. He sometimes left the work site to look for farmhouses in the area at which he could obtain extra food, so his fellow workers soon labeled him unruly and lazy. One day he left his job to call on a farmer and was given several raw potatoes. When his group returned from work, he was searched by the gate guard, who found the food in his pockets. He was detained and then brought out to stand in front of the men during evening roll call. Our lagerführer accused him of leaving the job site unlawfully and canvassing for food. Henry tried to defend himself, explaining why he was forced to beg, but the SS man was not in the mood to listen and began to beat him with a leather jockey's whip. It was horrible to see his bleeding face.

After a lengthy whipping, Henry was dragged to a bunker that had been built as a lockup facility for prisoners who were being punished. It was like an oversized doghouse covered with earth, and only a hinged door was visible; from the outside it looked like a bomb shelter. Henry was put inside, and the wooden door was locked behind him. He was fully dressed and had a blanket but received no water, food, or additional bedding for two days. When the guards finally opened the door to feed him, Henry lay dead on the sandy ground. This young, mild-mannered man, who had fled from Nazi Germany to Riga with his parents in the late 1930s and then lost them in one of the concentration camps, had met his own gruesome death in the wasteland of Estonia. I asked myself angrily, Did one of the Vilna Jews report him to the authorities, thus indirectly taking his life, solely because he was a German Jew from Riga? Such inhuman treatment was difficult to tolerate; Boris and my father were also very disturbed by this tragic death of a fine young man. We never attempted to discuss the matter with the Vilna inmates, since we feared for our own safety; instead, we closed our minds and shut our mouths. For a few days the incident shook up some of the more socially conscious inmates, and the mood in the barrack became noticeably tense, but this attitude slowly dissipated as if nothing had happened. Our lives returned to a daily routine, but the memory of the young Jew named Henry lingered in my mind.

Our tiring work in the forest continued with little change. Although spring of 1944 was already upon us, it was barely noticeable in the deep wooded areas. The tall pine trees obstructed the warm rays of the sun, which could not reach the frozen, snow-covered ground. I still wore my shabby, worn-out clothes, which gave me little protection from the chilly air. During working hours we made a bonfire and at times moved near it to warm our cold hands and feet; at mealtime all of the men gathered around the fire. A truck would deliver a tall canister of soup, our only warm meal of the day. The soup was watery, but one could find some slivers of meat and crushed potatoes. Thanks to the donations of meat from the local slaughterhouse, this meal was considerably more nourishing than those we had received in Vaivare. Nonetheless, soup and a piece of bread did not fully satisfy our ever-lingering hunger, although deaths from hunger or cold did not occur in this labor camp; I was grateful not to see a large bonfire of inmates' corpses. I had no way to obtain additional food from outside sources; after witnessing Henry's fate, I did not dare to knock at the door of a local farmhouse.

With the passage of time, our hunger became severe. One day my father came to me with a solution to our problem. "I think I can trust the barber," he said, meaning the assistant elder of our camp. "He seems to be the right man with whom I should do business." "What do you mean, Father?" I asked. He replied, "Over the past few weeks I have had several conversations with him, and he told me about his secret dealings with the slaughterhouse in town to improve the food distribution here." After a pause he continued, "Do you think we should give him one of our gold coins in exchange for some leftover meat or bread?" "That is a very good idea. The only thing I fear is that he might double-cross us," I said, thinking again of Henry. After mulling it over, I agreed with Father that we could take a chance with one of the five gold coins I carried in my boots. I thought that if any problems arose, Father could say he had found the coin in Vaivare.

During his next conversation with the barber, my father suggested that he could obtain an old Russian ten-ruble gold coin in exchange for some meat. The barber accepted Father's offer without hesitation, and it was agreed that he would provide several pieces of edible meat in exchange for the coin. Our troika feared the possible outcome of this deal, but we soon began to receive small, concealed packages containing baked meat that could be readily consumed. Much of it was not meat but, rather, pieces of cow organs: liver, lungs, kidneys, and stomach. We did not mind, as long as the food was edible and satisfied our hunger. Father was glad his undertaking with the head of our labor camp had been successful and that our worries had been unjustified. Every few days the barber secretly gave Father the promised packages. Our fight for survival was again strong.

After a few weeks the assistant elder told my father, "This will be the last package you receive from me. The slaughterhouse people will not give me any more for your coin." Father said nothing and took his words in good faith, although we had received fewer than the agreed-upon number of packages. The actual cost of these organs was a small fraction of the value of the Russian czar's ruble, but to us oppressed and hungry men, gold had no value since it was inedible. Until now, we had not been able to use the valuable coins to improve our desperate health condition. Father, Boris, and I could have died of hunger while the valuable coins lay untouched in my boots, so we were happy to still our hunger pangs with the ready-cooked meat—be it lung, kidney, or a piece of stomach. After a long time, Father traded another gold coin; again, we received baked bits and pieces of organs the slaughterhouse would normally have put in the garbage. That "garbage" gave me and my loved ones a new lease on life, improving our mental and physical strength and giving us hope.

Eventually, the sun's rays penetrated the thick branches of the pine trees, and we could finally take off our old, worn-out winter clothing. The snow melted and the grass appeared, with wildflowers in the open expanse of the forest. As nature became rejuvenated by the warmth of the sun, so did our men. They enjoyed the sparkling rays of sun and the fresh aroma of pine; with the change in the weather, a considerable change occurred in our co-workers' attitude toward our troika. All harassment ended, and we helped each other like a close-knit family. We had been so estranged only a few months before but were now bonded in friendship.

Father made more deals with the assistant elder, and I soon had only one gold coin left. Father received the small packages of meat at different times and places so as not to arouse the suspicions of the other inmates. Eventually, the assistant apparently formed the sudden, unfounded notion that my father had stocked away a fortune in gold rubles. We assumed he had decided to find them without harming us, for we often found our bunks ransacked when we returned from work. Only then did we realize that somebody was after our supposed fortune, thinking it was tucked away in our straw bedding. It was not enough that we had given the valuable coins away for much less food than they were worth, but somebody had now become greedy and wanted to obtain them for nothing. We had no proof of who had done the ransacking, but nobody except the barber could have been responsible, since it was done while the other men were at work. It would have been impossible to have searched anybody's bed without the knowledge of the camp elder or his assistant. At any rate, whoever had looked for our coins was probably disappointed.

The seeker of our fortune was so desperate that he searched our clothing in the bathhouse. One Friday when we returned from the shower room, we found our pants and jacket pockets turned inside out and our socks removed from our boots. Our last gold coin had not been found, for I had wrapped it in a piece of cloth and pushed it into the pointed toe of my boots. If the interloper had shaken my boots, it might have fallen out. We had to find a way to outsmart our foe so we would not lose that coin; following this incident, whenever we went to the bathhouse we never all went into the shower room together. Our nest egg was watched at all times by one of us, and our clothing and boots were never again touched. Father continued his friendly discussions with the camp's assistant elder but stopped the food dealings with him, since he feared harm might come to us. He made it clear to the barber that no more gold coins were available.

Our camp elder and his assistant, who worked as a team, were widely admired by the inmates in our labor camp for providing better food and a calmer atmosphere in the camp and at our workplaces than we had experienced in previous labor camps. After Henry's tragic death, no more casualties occurred as a result of "natural causes," meaning deaths caused by hunger and mistreatment. The inmates were peaceful and, for the first time in a long time, were thinking of a better future. I had a vision of becoming a free man again, but our wishful dreams were soon cut short.

At the end of August 1944, rumors spread through the camp that the rapid advancement of the Soviet Army on the front could mean our labor camp would be evacuated. Within days the persistent rumors had become a reality. Early one morning we were ordered to pack our few belongings and leave them on the bunks. After neatly making our beds, we left the barracks for morning roll call. I noticed that our guards around the fence had been joined by several Estonian soldiers. Our lagerführer and the Jewish administrators became nervous and engaged in short conversations among themselves. Finally, the lagerführer announced that he expected the arrival of higher SS officers, who would inspect us.

Soon a private military car and a canvas-covered truck entered the camp, and several high-ranking officers from the Einsatzkommando stepped out. The rear gate of the truck opened, and several German SS soldiers, armed with machine guns, jumped off. We realized that something terrible was going to happen to us, and the memory of the massacre of the Jewish ghetto police in Riga sprang to mind. We were ordered to stand at attention while we were examined. This meant we could not move or converse, so I looked at my father and he looked at me. I exchanged glances with Boris; at times, our gazes crossed, as though we were signaling a last farewell. With the nervousness of our lagerführer, the presence of the newly arrived SS officers, and the heavily armed SS soldiers in the background, I found myself in a very hostile environment. Finally, the highest-ranking officer, accompanied by our lagerführer, began to walk between the rows of inmates, thoroughly and systematically checking each one's appearance. He picked his victims with a raised arm and a pointed finger, saying, "You, out; go to the truck." Both men walked slowly and carefully, selecting their men. I looked straight ahead and could only hear from a distance, "You out, you out; go to the truck."

The loud, deadly words of the SS officer quickly grew near. My body froze, and my heart felt as if it were beating a thousand times a minute. I occupied my mind with one concern: the fate of my father. I thought, What shall I do if Father is called out? Shall I go with him, as I did before, or shall I let him go alone to face certain death? What shall I do? I hoped it would not come to that. At this crucial moment of my life, only my father was on my mind; I could not think about myself, for

I was in a complete state of shock. The officer was slowly moving from my right, intently observing every inmate. The dismissals were repeated several times, and the officer's growling words sank so deep in my mind that I thought I would go insane, idly standing, glued to my spot. The selected inmates left the lineup and walked slowly toward the truck. I wanted to pray to God for our safety, but my experience had shown me that the God of any religion had abandoned me and my people. Some gods seemingly supported or sympathized with the Nazis. To pray for my salvation, I could only rely on my immortal mother in heaven; she was the only goddess upon whom I could call to rescue me at this decisive moment.

Before I could utter a prayer, I heard the SS man's distinctive voice say, "You; go to the truck." He was pointing to the boy from the other troika, who did not move. The officer said, "Come on, come on," but before he could finish the words "go to the truck" the boy's father interrupted the determined officer and said, "He is my son—please leave him here with me." The SS man paid no attention and called on the boy again. "Faster, faster; go to the truck." Suddenly, the loud, crying voice of a child sounded throughout the Appelplatz: "Papa, Papa, Papa!" "I want to go with my son," said the father nobly. "You can go with him," replied the officer, and the pair left our lineup and vanished under the canopy of the military truck, the father holding his son's hand. This loss saddened me greatly. I had often wondered how the boy had been able to survive the severe camp life in Vaivare; he and his father and uncle had arrived there long before our transport from Riga.

The selection continued. The officer passed the boy's uncle and stopped in front of my father. I noticed that Father had puffed his cheeks out to alleviate their sunken appearance and had straightened his posture as much as he could. He was trying to look his best, and his desire to live could be seen on his strained face. Slowly, the SS man moved away from him without lifting his arm. I felt relief. O God, Father is safe, I thought. Then the German officer neared me, and I, too, puffed out my cheeks. I feared him greatly, for he could end my life by pointing his finger. He looked at me for a split second and then passed, continuing toward Boris. I stayed at attention, then I noticed that he had passed my cousin and was slowly moving farther and farther away. My only concern was that Boris and Father were safe.

Down the line, I could hear the SS officer's words again: "You, go to the truck." When he and the lagerführer had reached the other end of the line, twenty men had been confined in the truck. Without delay, both men joined the other officers, and after a short conversation, they departed, giving a brisk "Heil Hitler" salute. The soldiers who stood at the rear of the truck closed its gate. I could see the dust the truck raised as it hurried away; in a few minutes it had completely vanished from sight. The twenty innocent men, who represented 10 percent of our camp's population, were on their way to be massacred. Their mute, mass grave somewhere in the forest of Sonda will never bear a marking or a trace of the people who committed the gruesome crime. This genocide of innocent men was known in Yiddish as the "Zen Percent Akciye," or the "Ten Percent Solution."

Our lagerführer returned and dismissed us, but none of us moved. We stood like wooden soldiers, glued to the ground. The camp elder looked around and then began to shout "Why are you all standing? Move, move; go to the barracks." With expressions of outrage and sorrow, the inmates slowly began to disperse. Everyone was tense and lost in thoughts of what had just happened; it was an unexpected experience that none of us would ever forget. Later, at another evacuation camp, I met inmates from other labor camps who informed me that gestapo headquarters in Berlin had ordered every evacuated Jewish labor camp to reduce its population by 10 percent before transporting everyone to Germany. There were hundreds of Jewish victims before the urgent German retreat from the Baltic countries ended.

Our men left the lineup as though they were leaving the funeral of a devoted friend. I held the boy's grieving uncle without saying a word, for the poor man had just lost his brother and a bar mitzvah–age nephew. I walked into the barrack, where a dead stillness hung in every corner. None of us could yet comprehend what had occurred on the Appelplatz. Everyone was mourning for the unfortunate men whose lives had been snatched away with the point of a finger. We all felt as though we had returned from heaven and been granted new lives. Father sat on his bunk and wiped the cold sweat that appeared on his forehead. "Ohhh, was *that* a roll call. I will never forget this one," he whispered to me. Boris removed his jacket, and his entire body was soaking wet from this tragic experience. With the passing hours our pain slowly subsided, and the men began to converse in whispers, as though we were confined to an area in which our regular voices were not permitted. Our troika was happy to be alive to face the uncertain future together.

My last day in Sonda was far from over. Late in the afternoon, our evacuation began. Each inmate received coffee and a somewhat larger than usual ration of bread. After the meal we were ordered to our second lineup of the day on the Appelplatz. A large corps of heavily armed Estonian SS soldiers appeared and surrounded the camp, I supposed to ensure that nobody escaped. Another roll call took place as the men stood five in a row, ready to leave the camp. The soldiers surrounded us; under the leadership of the lagerführer, we marched through the camp gate and walked toward the small Sonda railroad station. When we arrived, I noticed the familiar boxcars on the tracks, ready for our evacuation. The men were evenly divided among the cars, and our troika wound up in a group of inmates with whom we had worked in the forest. We knew each other well and felt like one large family; I was glad to be with friends. We were ordered to board the boxcars; after everyone had found a place, the Estonian guards put in our toilet bucket and shut the heavy sliding doors, and we were on our way to Germany. The guards accompanied us in their comfortable, private railcar.

I left the God-forsaken country of Estonia without having observed nature in full bloom or hearing a birdsong. I had walked through miles of open prairies and deep forest but had never seen a print of any wild animal. I left behind my perished countrymen in unmarked graves and departed from this land, in which I had encountered the cruelest days of my life. Plagued by cold, illness, and unending hunger, this place brought to life the darkest pages in the history of mankind. It was the setting for a frightful experience that will stay with me to the end of my days.

10

The Road to Germany

The long transport train left the small, urban railroad station of Sonda without delay and moved very quickly, as though we were supposed to arrive in Germany by a certain time. In the eyes of the Nazi leaders, the train carried priceless, indispensable cargo—the Jewish survivors of a labor camp. It seemed to me that no obstacle would slow the train, for the engineer seemed to think the track belonged only to him and blew the steam whistle frequently to gain the right-of-way at every crossing. He may have wanted to warn the people on the ground: "Here I come with my heavy load of Jews."

Since we were traveling south, the weather improved considerably; this was the opposite of our trip north to Estonia, when the extreme cold had plagued us. On this transport everyone easily found room on the straw-covered floor, and although we had no blankets it was warm enough that we were comfortable. After a short time, the exhausted men were ready to fall asleep. We put behind us a day filled with difficult and tragic events that would long linger in our memories. I chose a comfortable corner of the boxcar next to Father and Boris and lay down to rest my tired body. The speeding train and the relentless squeaking of the wheels on the track seemed to echo the hasty retreat of the German Army from the conquered foreign land. More noises came from the frequent clash of the car couplers, but such disturbances did not bother me, and I fell asleep immediately.

In the middle of the night the train stopped. The loud conversation and footsteps of the soldiers, as well as the rattle of their automatic rifles, woke me. I looked up through the window, but it was too high to allow me to see what was going on outside; I saw only the pitch-dark skies. For a moment I was very scared, as the previous day's massacre came unbidden to my mind. Mistrust of our "friendly masters" arose as I thought, Maybe we are not being sent to Germany after all; any acts of foul play can be expected from the SS Einsatzkommando. They call us subhuman creatures; perhaps they will let us off the train in an open field and kill us all right there. This time, however, my fears were caused by paranoia, for the stop had been only for a change of guards for our transport at the border, and then our train left Estonia.

The Estonian soldiers left, and the German SS unit took over the supervision of the train. To make sure they were receiving the proper "merchandise," they opened the doors and checked the contents of every boxcar with flashlights. They announced that they were the new accompanying guards, asked us if everything was in order, and gave water to those who requested it. After a short stop, the train began to travel at its original high speed.

By the early morning hours, we were already on Polish soil; then we stopped unexpectedly again. The big sliding door was pushed wide open once more, and the sudden brightness of the morning light blinded me. By the time I could see, the German soldiers were standing by the door with a bucket of water and a sack filled with small loaves of army bread. The water and a cup were put into the car; the bread was thrown to us. We had to be able to catch well, or the food would land in the dirty straw on the floor. I felt we were fed like cattle and that I was one of the calves, receiving just enough food to hold me over until I reached the slaughterhouse. Every man received a loaf of bread, and I ate mine with a hearty appetite. The sanitary conditions in the car were such that under normal circumstances I would not have been able to even think about food; now I was simply glad I had something to eat.

The quiet, subdued atmosphere in our boxcar slowly changed, and the men felt like talking again. We tried to guess our destination and what kind of treatment we could expect from our new masters. Gone were our sad faces of yesterday, and little was said about the action of the SS Einsatzkommando in Sonda. As the saying goes, "Out of sight, out of mind." We had to prepare our minds and bodies to fight off new, unforeseeable challenges to our survival.

Our stop helped my well-being, as it gave me relief from the constant vibration of the train and a chance to enjoy the fresh country air. The small ventilating window in our car may have been sufficient for cattle but was too small for the many human occupants. With the door open, we could all breathe freely. Unfortunately, our pleasant rest ended quickly when the doors were closed and locked to make sure the precious cargo would not be lost or stolen on its journey. My short-lived, bright summer day slipped back into darkness. Our conversations stopped abruptly, as every man went back to his previous place on the straw. The train began to move, and its monotonous sounds made us drowsy; we lay motionless, not even thinking. At midday, bright rays of sun could be seen through the barbed-wire–covered window above my head and peeked through the split openings of the old wooden walls of the boxcar. A complete quiet reigned; only the friction of the wheels and the puffing sound of the steam engine could be heard.

I could not doze off as the other men did, so I lay on the floor and looked through the small window. My eyes were looking at the blue sky, but my mind was trying to fantasize about life as a liberated young man at age twenty-three. I thought hard but made no headway; it was as though my mind was covered with an invisible web. I could not imagine a free man's life or the end of my present existence. My thoughts were dominated only by the memories of the deaths I had witnessed caused by hunger, cold, and disease. I recalled the burning of the corpses of my countrymen, my life in the inferno of Vaivare, how I had learned to adjust to my hostile surroundings, and the terrible death of that young man in Sonda. Last but not least, I wondered why twenty innocent men had been taken away from us on our last day at Sonda. The loud cries of the child before he was sent to the truck still sounded in my ears: "Papa, Papa, Papa!"

I thought of the five hundred men deported from Kaiserwald. Would I be one of the very few to stay alive? Would I be able to tell the world of our oppression in the wasteland of Estonia? I shook my head, frightened by such horror-filled thoughts. I realized that I had to change my way of thinking. My strong will prevailed, and the flashbacks of past experiences ceased. As a reminder of the Estonian ordeal, I had three visible scars: the one on the back of my neck from my infected boil, the unhealed mark on my toes from wearing wooden shoes, and a partially frozen toe caused by the subzero temperatures. I did not need to add any mental scars to the wounds I already had. Now, at last, I could sense an end to the war and to my suffering. All that remained a question was whether I would survive to see it.

Between thinking and snoozing, another day passed, and we were into the second night of our journey to a secret hideout. During the night the train had stopped again; another piece of bread was given to us with some water, and the smelly bucket of urine and waste was exchanged for a clean one. After a short stopover, the locomotive had renewed its puffing, and the train again rushed toward its destination. Finally, during a beautiful sunrise, the train stopped. I was awakened by heavy foot-steps and heard conversations between our guards and some strangers, who turned out to be newly arrived SS soldiers. This was the second time a change of guards had taken place. When the new guards opened our door, I noticed that the train had reached its destination: the city of Danzig.

I was glad to leave the stinking cattle car in which I had been locked up for almost three days. Our troika and the others lined up to be counted; it was as though the SS believed one of the prisoners had somehow mi-raculously disappeared. After we had been approved, the kolonne was led for a short walk to the river. Under the strict supervision of the guards, everyone boarded a small steamboat moored there. Most of the men, including Father and Boris, found a seat below the deck. They were glad to be able to sit up; during the long train ride we had all been either lying down or standing. I stood with a few others on the upper deck to observe our new environment. Next to me was another inmate about my age. I remembered having seen him in our camp barrack, but he worked in another unit, so I had not had the opportunity to become acquainted with him. I learned that he was from Vilna and that his name was Joseph. We commented on our surroundings as the boat moved slowly down the river, and we were soon conversing freely. I immediately noticed some-thing special and different about this strange young man, something I thought might lead to a close friendship.

I was overwhelmed by his soft-spoken Yiddish words and his kind views about life and nature. I liked his way of thinking; it corresponded with my own. Until now, of all the young people I had met, I had not found anyone like Joseph. Most of the time we looked ahead, as though we were eager to reach a future home that would reclaim us from our grief and misery. We dreamed that this unknown, secret place would eventually lead us to our freedom. In essence, nobody knew where we were headed, but it was pleasant to converse with someone so much like myself. The fine breeze, fresh morning air, and wide blue skies made me feel as though I were on a pleasure cruise as a free man. Several feet away, though, was a relaxed SS guard to remind me that this was not the case.

The river was narrow and calm, and Joseph and I observed the landscape on both banks. Most of the area consisted of cultivated farmland, but in some places the farmers were already tilling their fields for the upcoming crops. I watched with great interest and noticed gestures of sympathy some of the laborers in the field made toward us. As our boat slowly passed, they all stopped working, and every one of them looked at us sadly. I felt they wanted to warn us about the terrible place to which we were headed. They did not resume their work until our boat was out of sight. This moving scene impressed me so much that it remains in my mind to this day. After a few hours of the pleasant boat ride, our transport arrived at the shores of a concentration camp whose sign read "Stutthof."

11

Stutthof Extermination Camp

The inmates slowly embarked from the boat, completely surrounded by the accompanying soldiers. Looking at the heavily armed guards I thought, Is the SS showing off its mighty force for us, the defenseless Jews? They could gain much more for their country if they showed this force to the enemy. I guessed that these young, healthy soldiers would rather stay with the half-starved Jewish inmates than be killed for the sake of their beloved führer and fatherland. Our men, like well-trained soldiers, quickly lined up in rows of five. Father, Boris, and I were in one row; my new friend, Joseph, was behind me. I knew nothing about Stutthof, but I imagined it was a terrible place to be incarcerated. We walked to a tall, ornamental wrought-iron gate; spanning its entire width was the inscription "Arbeit macht frei [Work makes you free]." The guards let the kolonne go through, and I entered the grounds with feelings of despair and horror. We were led like frightened sheep to the slaughter. I saw nothing that could harm me. Suspicion entered my mind, since this terrible place did not look as bad as I had envisioned. The yard in which we found ourselves was clean and well kept, with bushes and trees in the distance.

We were led to the receiving building, where the entire staff of SS officers awaited our arrival. They asked us a few questions and explained the procedure we would have to follow; we were also advised of the camp rules and regulations. It was here that I received my new name, Pflichtling [Prisoner] 95933; my old identification number was taken from me. My few belongings were placed on a long table; I was permitted to keep only the razor, shaving soap, and shaving brush I shared with my father. Our clothes were taken to be disinfected and steam cleaned while we took a shower. When we had finished we were given clean underwear, and our old, worn-out clothes were returned to us, still warm from the steam treatment. We were apprehensive about what would come next.

Nobody was in a mood to converse, which was just as well, as we had little to say. The men just looked at each other and shook their heads with bewilderment. The small changing room was very crowded, and everyone began to push and shove, sometimes rather fiercely. In the chaos I lost my last ten-ruble gold coin, which had been wrapped in a small piece of cloth and kept in my shoe. It slipped away from my watchful eyes as if to say, "You will not need me anymore." I was glad I still had the small, well-hidden picture of my mother, which I cautiously put in my shirt next to my body for safekeeping; it would have been a disaster if I had been separated from this printed image of my mother. I told Father what had happened to the gold coin. We were not disturbed by our loss, as the possession of such a coin in this camp could have brought us more harm than good.

As we marched through the different sections of the camp on the way to our living quarters, I noticed inmates of different nationalities who wore clean, decent clothing and did not look malnourished. My initial impression was that this place was not as bad as everybody had imagined; then we reached the Jewish section of the camp. Our kolonne arrived as morning roll call was ending. Some inmates had already left for work, and those who remained were gathered in the yard. They were dressed fairly well, but their faces showed definite strain, and they were evidently underfed. When our group approached, they were astonished to see us in such a deteriorated condition; they observed us with fear and distaste, as though we were human scarecrows. Their first question to us was, "Where did you just come from?" When they heard we had been in Estonia, their frightened and amazed looks changed to sorrowful and sympathetic ones. They had been informed of the harsh, deplorable living conditions in the Estonian labor camps. They extended a warm and friendly greeting and gave us encouragement to continue our fight for survival by saying, "Our geula [salvation] will soon come; it is just around the corner."

The inmates were all from Riga; some were German Jews who had arrived there after the closing of the large ghetto in 1941. Father, Boris, and I were delighted to be among our countrymen again, for we were the only ones in the Estonian transport who had come from Riga. We were called to enter the barrack to find our assigned sleeping place. I found myself in my new living quarters: a large barrack with individual two-story bunk beds and tables for our meals. As experienced concentration camp inmates, our troika quickly picked the bunks nearest the exit door. In case of any emergency or turmoil, we would be the first to get out. Each bunk had a straw mattress, a pillow, and a blanket. The barrack was very clean, and every bed was neatly made; this indicated to me that strict rules and regulations were enforced.

When our men entered the quarters, we found ourselves face-to-face with several Jewish disciplinarians, the capos. They were considered the rulers of this barrack, and their direct superiors were the SS supervising officers. The capos wore nice clothing and blue berets to signify their promotion, as well as for easy identification. They were better housed and fed than the rest of the inmates. Most carried a short whip hidden in their sleeve, with which they occasionally abused the inmates. I recognized three of these men from Riga: Mischa Glickman, David Kagan, and Harry Kussman.

Mischa Glickman was physically well built, over six feet tall with broad shoulders. I had worked with him for a short while in Riga, transporting furniture from Jewish homes to the quarters of the German occupying forces. He was a powerful man who had an excellent knowledge of German. To show off his physical strength, he would pick up heavy pieces of furniture and carry them down several flights of stairs. When officers were present, he would ridicule and humiliate his co-workers because of their weakness and inability to handle furniture as he could.

David Kagan, who had been my camp elder in the Ilgeciem Cement Factory, was a ruthless abuser of the inmates. He, too, had sought recognition from the SS lagerführer in Ilgeciem for performing well with the prisoners entrusted to him.

Harry Kussman and his wife had lived in the same apartment building as my family. He was the one who had offered to hide me in his home when the abusive German officer was looking for me. Kussman had sheltered me for several days until the officer finally left the neighborhood, and my family was very grateful for his help. Because of our resettlement in the ghetto, we lost track of this generous man. As soon as he saw Father and me enter the barrack, he approached us with friendly words and asked where we had last been. When my father told him, he expressed sympathy for our plight in the Estonian labor camps. He then abruptly interrupted our conversation and said firmly to Father, "Katsel [our last name], listen—this is a very disciplinary camp. Do as I say—no questions asked." He showed us the leather whip hidden in his sleeve, then continued, "If I hit you with this whip, it is because I have to, not because I want to. Do both of you understand what I am telling you?" We quickly replied, "We certainly do; we understand you very well." With these words we concluded our dialogue with Harry Kussman.

Glickman, Kagan, Kussman, and a few less familiar rulers of our barrack had been recruited by the SS camp leadership to discipline their fellow Jews, for which they were handsomely rewarded. They received better food and living quarters and also established a good name for themselves. They received acknowledgment for their work from the SS officers, which allowed them to climb the concentration camp "corporate ladder" for future assignments. Back in Kaiserwald, the SS Einsatzkommando leaders had used convicted German criminals to carry out their cruel disciplinary orders; in Stutthof, they utilized Jewish inmates who had promoted themselves by "properly" handling their fellow prisoners in previous camps. Later, the same capos selfishly increased their intimidation and physical abuses, for their brutal behavior in Stutthof eventually paid off.

After a short stay in the new barrack, we were sent to join the rest of the men in the yard; they had arrived in Stutthof from Riga only a few days before. I was very eager to find out how things were at home, and they wanted to learn about our life in the Estonian camps. My countrymen listened to our stories of tragedies and suffering with great anxiety, emotion, and sorrow. Fortunately, most of these men were from various kasernierung around the city and had been subjected to very little abuse or harassment by their German masters. They had not suffered from hunger and exposure to the cold, so it was no wonder that they had been so surprised by our appearances. Our fragile-looking men, who walked like puppets on strings, must have looked like aliens from another planet. I was told that many Jews remained in the kasernierung, although the Germans had accelerated the removal of all Jews from Riga. Kaiserwald

Concentration Camp had been closed, and the inmates had been brought to Stutthof. Witnesses reported that some men remained there, but their fates were unknown; it was assumed they were the 10 percent to be annihilated. Among them had been my Uncle Ljova.

The longer I spoke to my countrymen, the more we had to talk about. I learned the fates of many of my friends who had been victims of the brutal SS, others who had died of natural causes, and still others who had been brave enough to escape and go into hiding. Among the several hundred men from home, I was happy to find a man and his son who were named Kalika; I knew the boy from high school. He had been an importer and distributor of bananas in Riga, and I jokingly asked the father, "How is the banana business these days?" He replied with a smile, "It is good, but it could be better if only I were a free man again." My friend and I talked about our carefree school days and our activities. Father was glad to find in the elder Kalika a man with whom he could discuss past business experiences.

Among the inmates were people who had been incarcerated in Kaiserwald; after their departure it had closed down. These men had very grim news about the last days of the camp. After I had left for Estonia, the living conditions had gone from bad to worse. Intimidation and physical abuse reigned in every barrack, and many people died from illness and malnutrition. The situation worsened with the advancement of the Soviet armies on the eastern front. The SS command feared the enemy might discover the murderous atrocities it had committed against the Jewish population in Latvia, so the leaders increased the workforce for the Stutzpunkt. The doomed inmates wore black patches on their outerwear for identification. Every few days, several men were selected from this marked group and transported to the mass graveyards around Riga to eliminate all traces of the massacred German and Latvian Jews.

Our troika was so enthusiastic about meeting these long-lost countrymen on German soil that we could not leave them alone. To our surprise, we discovered that the Riga men were well-informed about the military situation on the fronts, whereas our lives in Estonia had been completely isolated from the rest of the world. As a result of our hasty evacuation from Estonia, we knew about the crumbling of the German Wehrmacht on the eastern front. Now we learned that General Paulus's Sixth Army had been defeated at Stalingrad and had retreated despite

Hitler's call to "fight to the last round of ammunition." For the first time we heard that Field Marshal Rommel's armored units had completely pulled out of North Africa. We were surprised to hear of the successful landing of the Allied forces on the beaches of Normandy and of their rapid advancement into France and Italy. At this time, Rome had been freed by the U.S. armed forces. I finally understood why we had abandoned Sonda so rapidly; the siege of Leningrad had been lifted, and the Soviet troops had deeply penetrated Estonia and Latvia. The Nazi radio announcers called this rapid Wehrmacht retreat from the eastern occupied countries a "tactical retreat." This encouraging news from the front meant our dreadful days were slowly coming to an end and that the probability for ultimate peace was on the horizon. I was mentally uplifted by this information about the state of world affairs. My discussions with the men from Riga brought me happiness and an inner fulfillment I had not experienced for a long time.

My first enjoyable afternoon in Stutthof passed by quickly, and the day soon ended. A bell rang for the lineup of the evening roll in the Jewish section of the camp. The barracks elder, with some SS Death's-Head officers, went through the lines for a thorough count. The number was confirmed by our SS officer, but we could not leave. Only when all headcounts from each barrack were correct were we dismissed. That first roll was the longest I had experienced during my incarceration in the camps. I wondered about the need for the interminable headcounts. Was this our daily harassment or some kind of punishment, or was it a way to kill the free time the SS had on their hands? I was never interested in learning the answers to my questions, since time became meaningless. In this camp, time stood still.

When roll call was over, the inmates hurried to their barracks to receive the daily food ration; the evening meal was a bowl of soup and bread with margarine, about as much as we had received in previous camps. We had experienced as much excitement as our bodies could absorb in one day; it had been very emotional for everyone. Before falling asleep, I chatted with Joseph, and we arranged to stay together at the morning roll call.

The following morning, before sunrise, the men in my barrack were awakened by the orderlies. An announcer called out, "Today nobody will go to work. All inmates must witness an execution at the Appelplatz." I had barely had a night's rest, yet I had to get up and witness the destruction of a human being. Our troika left the barrack with Joseph and lined up on the Appelplatz. I could see a newly erected wooden gallows meant for two people. Following the order, every inmate remained in his place after roll to witness the public execution of two inmates. I reminded myself of Kussman's command to do as we were told, so I waited for a seemingly endless amount of time with the rest of the men until I noticed an entourage of well-groomed, high-ranking SS officers at the gallows.

A short while later a car drove up, and two young men stepped out with two armed guards. The men's hands were strapped behind their backs, and the guards led them to the raised platform. One of the officers announced to the attending inmates, "These two Russian prisoners tried to escape from this camp. For such an unlawful undertaking, they will be punished with death by hanging." He warned all those present that they would face the same punishment if they attempted to escape. Each prisoner was then ordered to turn his head toward the gallows. The two guards blindfolded the Russians and guided them to the place where the nooses were hanging from a heavy wooden beam. The soldiers put the ropes over the prisoners' heads and tightened them at the necks. The bodies of the Russians suddenly dropped straight down with no other motion, as the two trapdoors simultaneously opened below their feet. The SS officers walked away, and the cruel execution of the two young men was over.

Before we were dismissed, every inmate had to pass the victims. Their bodies were left hanging, unattended, for the rest of the day. This inhuman display served as a warning to the Jewish inmates of the camp. I was told this was the first public execution in Stutthof. I had to look up at the elevated platform to see the two dangling bodies. It was very unusual to observe the hanging of two human beings. For a young man, the gruesome scene was difficult to take. I had to control my emotions for the sake of self-preservation. My hardened feelings soon brushed away the tragedy, as they had on many other occasions on my long road of persecution.

The Jewish section of Stutthof consisted of several large barracks in one row with space between them. In front was the Appelplatz, which also served as the outdoor gathering place for the inmates. We could walk freely from one end to the other. The entire Jewish section was surrounded by a high, barbed-wire fence with a wide opening that was the entrance to the gentile sections of the camp. The barrack I occupied was at the very end of the Appelplatz. It had a dividing wall on the inside and two entrances from the outside; mine was next to a narrow gravel road that wound around a large, windowless, red-brick building. On the other side of the road, I could see only the side and rear of this long brick building, at the very end of which was a high smokestack that climbed toward the sky. I later found out that the gravel road started at the women's quarters and ended at the gas chamber and crematorium—the building with the smokestack. I was as close to the "death factory" as I could be without being on the inside.

A few days after my arrival in Stutthof, I noticed people on the visible stretch of the narrow road. Every day I observed small groups of women walking slowly to the place of annihilation—the gas chamber—under the supervision of female SS guards. Those who were able often pushed a four-wheeled open wagon that carried the physically handicapped. These women were partially naked; their bodies were covered with gray camp blankets, but some of their limbs protruded. The Germans did not even have the human decency to provide clothing for these doomed women. Most of them quietly moaned and sobbed, knowing well where the road led; the walk or ride they were taking would be their last. It was difficult for me to stand helplessly and see these women suffering only because they were of the Jewish faith. I thought, Not so long ago these helpless women were our grandmothers, mothers, and daughters, who lived happily, surrounded by their beloved families. Now they have been abandoned by God and man.

I could hear mumbled Hungarian words, so I assumed they were Hungarian Jews or, as the inmates called them, majaros. I thought about my own mother and how she must have felt when she walked the last steps to her death on a bitter winter day in 1941. With time, my eyes and mind became numb to these unpleasant scenes. When one of the wagons appeared, one of the inmates would call the others to come to the fence: "Hey, here comes the parade—the majaros are on their way to heaven." This unwarranted behavior can be explained psychologically: Because of the inhuman lifestyle we led, we had lost all human feeling and become nothing more than two-legged animals. To keep our minds stable, we had to create humor from every situation. I became one of the spectators to this tragic show; by this time my eyes had no tears. I did not dare to pity anyone, including myself. It was a gratifying feeling to stand on the side of the fence where life still existed, whereas on the other side only death was present.

My father, Boris, and I were very disturbed over the public executions and the daily parade of women being led to the gas chamber. The unending smoke from the crematorium chimney was a frightful reminder that we could be next. It reminded me of the open bonfire in Vaivare, where our lives had been spared; whether we would die in Stutthof remained to be seen. By now I knew I was witnessing the greatest crimes against humanity the world had ever seen. Some days I observed the heavy black smoke rising from the high smokestack. I wanted to cry out, "O God, why did You create Adolf Hitler, a human monster to the humble Jewish people?"

It was a foregone conclusion that Nazi Germany was desperately waging a losing war. What boggled my mind was how many more innocent people the regime would take with it in the fading days of its existence. The unscrupulous Nazi leaders were still living in a dream world; they would not admit that they were slowly but surely being defeated by the Allied military forces. As the war neared an end, nothing could deter the Death's-Head officers from their insane goal—the unrestricted dominance of the concentration camps and the continuation of endless atrocities against the Jewish people. The SS leaders were ensuring their rapid destruction through their own deeds. The traditional method of mass murder by shooting proved too inefficient for them and too psychologically stressful for the executioners. Instead, the newly built gas chambers and crematoriums could more efficiently exterminate victims on a large scale. It seemed to me the Third Reich had sealed its doom long ago by using a large part of its military resources and energies to annihilate the Jews in Europe.

I found myself immersed in the morals and discipline of Stutthof; I followed every rule and regulation. It became normal to drop everything, stand at attention, and quickly remove my cap when a German in uniform passed me. This was another humiliation to which I had to adjust. In this camp, our troika was completely dependent on the food ration, which was too meager to nourish us but too substantial to allow us to starve to death. Hunger was not only felt in our stomachs but was part of our conversations. Somehow, we felt relieved when we talked about food we had enjoyed before the war or about the meager food rations we had received in previous camps.

Although the standing order was that every inmate had to stay within our compound, I began to survey the gentile campsites in an effort to obtain or find a source of extra food for our trio. I did not dare to venture too far from my barrack, since I had to watch for anyone in a military uniform who could prevent me from fulfilling my goal. I noticed that the inmates of each gentile section wore different colored triangular patches on their outerwear: The Polish inmates wore red triangles, priests and other religious figures wore white, political prisoners of any nationality wore purple, and the Jewish inmates were supposed to wear yellow. We had never received our patches, however, because of the sudden heavy influx of Jewish inmates, so we wore only our prisoner numbers.

When I walked into the section in which the inmates wore purple triangles, I was taken by surprise. This was the political section where only adversaries of the Nazi regime were incarcerated. Most of the men were Latvians, so I could understand them. Without telling him who I was or where I was from, I initiated a conversation with one of the men in German. He told me they had been brought here from Riga as political prisoners. I dared not reveal my identity, since I still harbored a deep fear of Latvians. From a distance, I saw some familiar faces. Among the well-known politicians was the son of Latvia's first president; there were also several socialist leaders, such as Bruno Kalnins. Their headquarters had been across from the building in which I had lived in Riga, and I remembered the men from my childhood years. I spoke to a few of the Latvians but did not converse with them in their own tongue; nor did I reveal my true identity. I still feared they could harm me if they discovered I was Jewish and a Latvian; they knew Jewish inmates were forbidden to enter their section of the camp.

My fear subsided somewhat when I heard some unkind words about Nazi oppression. One Latvian told me he regretted having lost his freedom simply because he was a member of the Socialist Party. He missed his family and did not know their whereabouts. During our conversation he lit a cigarette, and I asked him where he had obtained it. He replied,

"From the Red Cross—we regularly receive packages from them that contain food, tobacco, toiletries, and other useful items we do not get here." He paused, then asked, "You are receiving packages too, aren't you?" Wishing it were true, I answered, "I arrived here recently and have not yet had a chance to receive a Red Cross package." The Latvian told me he was sharing the barrack with Norwegians. I did not ask for, nor did he offer me, cigarettes or anything else. I slowly made my way closer to his barrack to see if I could find something useful or some leftover food. The inmates were relaxing at the window; some smoked pipes, others smoked cigarettes, and small packages of food were stored on the windowsill to keep them cool.

I hoped one of the men would offer me some food or tobacco, since they could see I was not as well nourished as they were. Most likely, they did not see fit to give me a handout, for the satiated do not understand the hungry. I did not ask for anything because, in my mind, the Latvians remained untrustworthy people. Even if they were incarcerated in the same extermination camp as I, they could still have an anti-Semitic bias. I decided I would rather remain hungry than trust my life to the Latvian inmates, so I left the yard empty-handed.

I had seen that not all inmates in the camp were treated equally. Here, too, the Jews were the lowest of any group. In spite of the severe penalty if I had been caught, I continued to visit the barracks of the gentiles for the sake of seeing people of different nationalities, as well as for the possibility of receiving something edible. I asked myself, Why am I excluded from receiving Red Cross life-support packages? Why do they have more and I so little? My chances for survival are dwindling every day; why are theirs secured? Every time I visited the gentile section of the camp, I returned to my barracks without a crumb of bread or even one cigarette; this filled me with anger and rage.

The humanitarian Red Cross and the entire world had abandoned the Jews and placed our destiny in the hands of the Nazi tyrants. We were left to fade away within the grim walls of the concentration camps. Even the mighty air forces of the Allies ignored our pain and suffering when they flew over Germany. Numerous industrial and residential complexes all over Germany were turned to ruins by Allied air raids, yet not a single camp barrack or crematorium smokestack was scratched. Bridges and rail crossings were destroyed, but not one track leading to the gas chambers was touched. The decent leaders of democratic countries on both sides of the Atlantic fought hard to achieve liberty and justice for all but the Jewish people, whom they had forgotten. Nobody spoke out against the attempted destruction of an ancient people and their culture; it was the Jews who had provided early civilization with the first commandments of law and order. It has been said that all evil needs to succeed is for good men to do nothing. With the exception of a few righteous Christians who had the courage to defy society by resourcefully saving Jewish lives, the world stood in silence, willing to witness the elimination of European Jewry.

Some inmates in our barrack knew the dates of the Jewish holidays, according to our calendar, from memory. They told us that Rosh Hashanah, the start of the Jewish New Year, would begin the following evening. The high holiday arrived, but I felt no different. For me, it started like any other day, with a cup of black coffee and a few bites of bread. Still, memories soon flooded my mind. Father was not a pious Jew, but on this holy day he had always attended the neighborhood synagogue, where he had held a permanent seat for many years. He would put on the suit he wore only on special occasions. The rest of the family was always beautifully dressed in its best clothes as well: my mother wore a new dress, and the four children wore outfits she had carefully selected. A holiday spirit infused the streets of Riga: the traffic was somewhat diminished, and every Jewish business establishment was closed. The gentiles could feel the Jewish New Year celebration in the air.

Our synagogue was a small prayer house that seated approximately a hundred people. It had been established many years ago by a landlord who had converted the first floor of his apartment building into a house of worship that carried his name. The prayer services were conducted by the cantor, who was hired especially for the holidays, and all services were conducted under the guidance of our rabbi. Sometimes during the services my father would express his love for me by covering me with his prayer shawl. When I had my bar mitzvah and received my own prayer shawl, he then gently pointed in the Mahzor (holiday prayer book) at what the cantor was chanting. During these prayers I would look eagerly through the curtain that divided the men's and women's sections to see my mother and sisters all dressed up. I waved at them lovingly and received Mother's gentle smile in acknowledgment. The small synagogue was always filled for the high holidays, and the congregates looked forward to hearing our old rabbi's droshe (sermon). He recited passages from the Torah and then skillfully compared them to the current complex political situation.

I vividly remember how this scholarly spiritual leader called me to the bima (pulpit) at my bar mitzvah. When I had completed chanting a portion of the Torah, the rabbi gently patted me on the back and praised me for my excellent performance. My mother and father and my grandfather Schleime also congratulated me for my exceptional chanting of the prayers. I was proud of myself; this was the high point of my young life. The following day we had a great celebration in our house. Both close and distant relatives and friends came to the party; our house was filled to capacity. I heard congratulatory speeches accompanied by happy Jewish songs. We toasted throughout the evening for a happy and healthy life for everyone in attendance. All the kind, memorable words made my mother and father very happy—they were very proud of their eldest son. This event was, and remains, the happiest moment in my life.

The day of Rosh Hashanah was upon us; it was the Jewish calendar year 5704. Several inmates in our barrack still knew some prayers from memory and gathered for a short service before leaving for the morning roll. I did not participate but stood close and listened. Eventually, every inmate came to the Appelplatz to participate in some way in the short religious prayer.

I noticed a crowd of men gathered at the adjoining barrack. On previous days there had only been a few of them. They appeared fairly well dressed, with no marks of mistreatment or malnutrition. After roll call I asked Father to help me find out who these Jews were and where they had come from. We approached the men and found, to our surprise, that my distant cousin Urik Joffe was among them. He noticed us, and we greeted each other with outstretched arms. With a bewildered expression he said to Father, "Imagine, Abrasha, of all places I have to meet you in this rotten one—and on the day of Rosh Hashanah." "I am very happy to see you alive—you look marvelous," replied Father. We had not seen each other for a long time and had been unaware of each other's fates after the German occupation of Riga.

Father and I had endless questions for Urik. He revealed that his group of several hundred people was the last remnant of our Jewish community in Riga; the city had become Judenrein. They had left Riga by boat in a great hurry, since the Soviet troops had advanced to the outskirts of the city. After the liquidation of the large ghetto, some of the workers became kaserniert in Lenta—and he was one of them—not for the sake of their protection but to secure free services for the officers of the gestapo. These jobs ranged from washing and sweeping floors to cleaning garages and repairing cars, tailoring, shoemaking, and repairing watches. The Jewish craftsmen were pleased to live under the protection of the powerful gestapo institution, and they received sufficient nourishment and comfortable housing. The entire Jewish workforce consisted of several hundred men and women who worked together but did not share the same living quarters.

Urik spoke a great deal about the advantageous work conditions in the gestapo shops and about the close relationship the workers had enjoyed with the privileged officers of the organization. When he left, Riga was steeped in chaos: The Germans were fleeing the rapidly approaching Soviet forces, and the Latvians were in disarray, not knowing what to expect from the Soviets since they had considered the Germans their liberators. It was tragic that the Latvians did not know they were being manipulated for the good of Hitler's Third Reich and that they had become victims of a cleverly designed racial policy. The Latvian Nazi sympathizers and collaborators became so desperate that they fled the country by any possible means. Multitudes of cars and horse-driven buggies jammed the streets of Riga and the highways throughout Latvia. The citizens knew their day of reckoning was upon them and that they would have to answer for their deeds against the Jews. We were also told the tragic news of what the remaining Jewish population had experienced. Here, too, the 10 percent rule had been put into effect before any group of Jews was evacuated to Germany. Such a liquidation procedure was now all too familiar.

After a lengthy conversation with Urik and other countrymen, we went to join the people from our own barrack. By that time everyone knew about the new Jews from Riga, but I was among those who could understand their grief to the fullest. I felt sorry for the recently arrived men, since they would have to undergo a tremendous adjustment to this camp. They had never been subjected to the living conditions of a concentration camp, in which the greatest crimes in history against a human race were committed. To these men, this incarceration would become a daily battle for a very minimal existence. Stutthof was, in many ways, different from other camps, where prisoners would slowly fade away from lack of nourishment. Here, these inmates would not have a chance to expire on their bunks while they were asleep; instead, they would meet with a much more gruesome death. Inmates who did not look healthy or who were incapable of performing some kind of work were destroyed like diseased animals. They were put to sleep in the gas chamber and burned in the oven of the crematorium. My life was spared only because I was still able to work, and my skills could be used in the service of the Third Reich.

Rosh Hashanah came and went, as did the ten days of Awe, which ended with the day of atonement, Yom Kippur. This was a day of fasting and praying for the forgiveness of the sins one had committed during the past year. It was also a time to pray for a healthy, prosperous, and happy new year, for which the inmates in Stutthof had long been yearning. I hoped the coming year would be one of salvation from Nazi bondage for me and for every Jew living under their regime. Under normal circumstances the full day's fast would be a strenuous undertaking, but in the year 5704 it was a natural event, because we frequently ate little for many days at a time.

My new acquaintance, Joseph, became my closest friend in the camp. We spent our days together in the yard and looked for opportunities to find some food to supplement our meager daily rations. Across from our barrack stood a small structure that served as the food distribution kitchen for various barracks in our section. Nobody was allowed to come near it, but we spent many hours observing the building from a distance, looking for a way to enter the premises. Eventually, our persistence paid off. One morning, the kitchen had a shortage of workers during mealtime. The man in charge noticed us and called us over, asking whether we would be willing to deliver a kettle of coffee to our barrack. We accepted his offer and were happy he had seen us, for this could be our best opportunity to get into the kitchen. Our aim had been to distribute something more edible, but we did not mind starting with coffee.

After only a few days on this job assignment, a terrible accident occurred. By that time, we were well acquainted with how to handle the tall aluminum container filled with hot coffee; it was heavy, but two side handles made carrying it considerably easier. One day, Joseph's foot slipped off one of the steps that led from the kitchen. I was holding the container handle with all my strength and managed to keep it straight, but some of the coffee spilled out onto Joseph. With great difficulty we managed to deliver what remained. Joseph's left foot was badly burned; he received medical attention but was in severe pain and unable to walk. I felt very bad about this unfortunate occurrence and could not sleep for several nights, plagued by the thought that it might have been my fault.

Since nobody could stay in the barrack during the day, my friend sat on the steps all day except during roll call, when I would pick him up and help him walk to his place in line. The rest of the day I sat next to him to keep him company and spoke with kind, soothing words, since I could not help to ease his pain in any other way. After a week he felt better but was still unable to move easily. One afternoon, I went for a long walk; when I returned, Joseph was missing from his usual spot. I desperately searched for him, but in vain. Later I was told he had been taken away by the camp orderly. I never saw him again; my dear friend died before I had a chance to say good-bye to him, and our short-lived friendship came abruptly to a tragic end. I was very disturbed by this incident and did not know how to relieve my grief, but I realized that no physical or mental anguish, as painful as it might be, could interfere with my fight for survival.

I did not go back to my kitchen job; instead, I responded to a call for work for which I was to receive an extra bowl of soup. I became part of a twenty-man volunteer group. After morning roll we were led to an open field in which there were boulders of different sizes, shapes, and colors. The SS guard assigned us to clear the field; every inmate was given a wheelbarrow with which to transport the boulders several hundred feet, where they were then placed in a pile. I assumed I was working for a good cause, since this field could be used for the benefit of the camp population. On the first day, we were not rushed, although we worked constantly. At midday we were dismissed and were rewarded for our efforts with a bowl of soup. Eventually, the work became increasingly difficult, but the soup sustained me; it was the only remedy for my hunger. After several days we were told to stop clearing the boulders from the field; instead, we were to take them off of the pile and return them to the open field. This backward assignment angered me; I concluded that the SS people at the camp had no intention of clearing the field and putting it to good use. They merely wanted to wear us out; it was an example of more evil intent that threatened our lives. I decided not to let them weaken my body and make me ripe for the gas chamber. The following day I joined Father, Boris, and the other hungry men without work in the spacious yard of the camp.

The days in Stutthof passed quickly; they were filled with night-mares, deception, hunger, grief, and pain. I felt as though I were on an island of insanity as the end of 1944 approached. The Jewish section of the camp was bursting with people; with every German retreat from conquered lands in Eastern Europe, a transport of enslaved Jews arrived. The gestapo made sure that when it retreated its treasures would not be left behind. Stutthof became the transfer camp for all evacuated Jews; our Appelplatz, once barely occupied, soon became very crowded.

The cold weather came sooner than we had anticipated, and the change took a toll on the inmates. I noticed that more men were unable to walk around the camp; they were the unfortunate prisoners who were called muselmen. Their bones protruded, and their glassy eyes sank deep in their sockets. Some days the weather was so cold that all of the inmates stood tightly against each other on the Appelplatz, creating a circle. The body heat kept the entire group warm and protected us from the wind. While we were exposed to the cold, our daily roll call became much longer; the men in the lineup were counted and recounted numer-ous times. The camp population had expanded to such a degree that the SS officers had a difficult time taking an accurate count of the inmates. The lightly clothed, undernourished prisoners had to stay in line until the kommandant approved the final count; only then was everyone dis-missed.

The atmosphere in the camp became very tense, as none of us knew what would come next. I was concerned about our destiny, and we expe-rienced feelings of hopelessness and despair every day. There was no way to tame the Nazi monsters—who were destroying innocent human lives under the cruelest circumstances—while they faced humiliating and pain-ful military defeats throughout Europe. At the end of the war, they would be forced to give a detailed account of their atrocities; any decent man in the ranks of the SS leadership would have decreased the genocidal activ-ity in our camp, but the reality was just the opposite: The gas chamber

and crematorium were never closed. I suppose the intent was to annihilate all European Jews before the war ended, thus avoiding full account-
ability for these people's disappearance. The Germans were more concerned with getting rid of the Jews than with seeking victory on the
battlefield.

To my sorrow, I noted a great increase in the traffic on the narrow
road that led to the gas chamber. Group after group of heavily guarded
women passed us, and fumes and smoke rose constantly toward the sky.
In our crowded yard, one saw inmates congregated in tight circles; they
looked like chickens in coops, ready for shipment to the market. I was
living an existence in which death was the sole focus. The concealed gas
chamber and crematorium provided an easy method for removing us
from the face of the earth, leaving no trace that we had ever been here.
Every inmate felt as though we were confined in a bubble that could
burst at any time. Hundreds of Jews were brought into the overcrowded
camp, and nobody knew what would happen next, although only two
routes remained for the massive number of inmates to take: the road to
freedom or the road to heaven. Having fought such a fierce battle to
reach my final day of incarceration, I did not want to experience physical
destruction just before my liberation.

Finally, the long-awaited day arrived: The bubble surrounding us
was burst wide open, for which every inmate was very happy. The camp
administrators began to create individual work groups for shipment
throughout Germany to boost the shrinking workforce in the fading
days of Nazi power. Every few days, such units were organized and sent
out. In every instance the jobs were announced ahead of time: how many
men were needed, where they would be sent, and what kind of work they
would have to perform. This sounded encouraging, but with few excep-
tions it was not so. The SS officers in charge portrayed the new job sites
as very favorable to avoid discouraging the inmates from volunteering.
Our trio was very careful in selecting an assignment; from our many
experiences, we knew not to take the optimistic words of the officers at
face value. We paid attention to how the announcements were made, how
the men were selected for the job, and whether they were screened for any
special qualifications. It would be hard for someone who had not been
incarcerated in several life-threatening camps, as we had been, to understand how we judged every recruitment. We had developed the intuition

that guided us in choosing which work group we should join.

Every time volunteers were called upon to join a new unit, Boris would ask my father whether we should consider registering. Every time, Father would reply, "I am suspicious about the job site information they have given." He did not like either the place or the kind of work the men would have to do. Since there were plenty of volunteers, nobody was forced to join any of the new groups. Father's negative attitude toward every position irritated Boris, but there was always a reason not to register. Since nobody knew the actual conditions of the new workplaces, I left it up to Father to decide which work group we should join.

Several days passed, and Father still insisted he did not feel right being sent to an unknown work camp. "My heart tells me we should not go there. There is something about these new places," he would tell Boris and me. I fully accepted his intuition, but my cousin was reluctant to agree. He was eager to leave this extermination camp, for the inhuman surroundings affected him greatly; he was fearful of not being able to survive if he had to stay much longer. He became envious of every group of men that left the camp. One day it was announced that a group of two hundred men, predominantly chemical engineers and technicians, would be organized for shipment to a chemical factory in Czechoslovakia. Boris was delighted, for he was a chemical engineer and saw a chance to work in his profession in a country in which he had attended the university and spoke the language. Happily, he approached Father, proposing that this place would be suitable for all three of us. He described the advantages that could be gained from working at the chemical plant. Father had to decide quickly whether we should register for this work group.

After thinking it over for several minutes, he determined that we should not go and strongly discouraged Boris from doing so. "My dear Boris, something tells me not to sign up for this new assignment. I will wait for another one that is more to my liking. We will not stay in this camp forever." Boris exclaimed furiously, "Abrasha, I always listen to you, but you now must listen to me. I cannot let such an excellent opportunity pass me by." Father replied tenderly, "I beg you, do not go; do not leave us. Let us all stay together." A strongly rebuke followed: "Abrasha, I do not want to wait for something better. This job is fine; it is what I want. I am sorry, but I am going to register for this transport."

I, too, felt this was not a good idea, particularly when I realized that in addition to the professional chemists, they were accepting inmates who had no experience in the field merely to fill the work order for two hundred men. I thought, The posted announcement called for chemists, but they are taking anyone. Something is not right—could this be another clever ploy by the cruel Nazis? I thought about my cousin, who had become like my adopted brother. We had begun our plight together as one family and hoped to be freed in the same way; I thought we could never be split apart. We had learned how to live together, as well as how to love and help each other, for the sake of our mutual survival. Like best friends, we had talked about common interests and concerns and made plans for our future.

As hard as he tried, Boris could not convince his Uncle Abrasha to join him in the transport. A few days later he left us and this frightful place, satisfied and fulfilled. He looked forward to being in a country where he had spent many wonderful years, for he loved Czechoslovakia and its people. Upon his departure, he thought we would meet again when we were all free men. We remained in the camp, heartbroken over the unexpected tragedy that had split our troika apart. I imagine Boris became disillusioned when he arrived at his destination; he saw neither the country nor the people for whom he had yearned so greatly, and it was too late to correct the misjudgment that would cost him his life. After the liberation, I searched for him at every information center, but he had vanished without a trace. I found out eventually that he and the rest of the transport had been the victims of German deception. They had not been sent to Czechoslovakia to work in a chemical plant; rather, they were sent to work in the coal mines of Natzweiler, where most of the inmates—including Boris—perished.

My father and I remained strongly convinced that we, too, would soon leave this concentration camp. God had given us a precious commodity: hope. Since logic could not help us, we had to live with the hope of a better day—and that long-awaited day was soon upon us. A week after Boris left, an announcement was posted that five hundred inmates would be selected for factory work in the city of Magdeburg. We liked the selection process and felt safe joining this group. On the day the new workforce was to be selected, well-dressed German men came to our campsite. They seemed to be representatives of the plant to which we were to be sent. Father liked what he saw, and his intuition told him to register for this transport.

The men were very particular in selecting the workers; every inmate had to run in front of them, then return and raise his hands and feet as the Germans intently observed every move he made. I felt as though I was on display at a slave market with the buyers trying to outbid each other for ownership. It reminded me of the play *Uncle Tom's Cabin,* which I had seen in Riga many years ago. At that time it had been on the stage, but now it was real. Just as in the play, I had to show them my body to prove I had the physical ability to fulfill the required work. In addition to running and raising my hands and feet, I was also examined for blemishes. After the physical checkup, every man was interviewed by the factory representatives. I had to tell them my trade and how long I had worked at it and also had to answer many other personal and general questions. Finally, I was told I had been accepted, and I could see they were pleased with the choice. Father was also selected, and both our names were put on the approval list. The selection of all five hundred men took three days, since many inmates were rejected.

Before our transport departed, we were sent to the camp bathhouse, and new winter clothing was distributed to every man. I was glad to finally get rid of my old, worn-out clothing. After a bath, the kolonne of five hundred men was herded into waiting boxcars for the trip to Magdeburg. To my amazement, around a hundred female Jewish inmates were added to our group. Father and I left this extermination camp with no regrets, although we did not know what the future would bring on our next assignment. We had escaped this gruesome, ghostly place without a scratch or a painful mark on our bodies and were the sole survivors of a five-hundred-man work group that had left Kaiserwald for another strange place called Vaivare. Once again, we were the masters of our own destinies.

12

Buchenwald's Labor Camp Number One

A glimmer of hope for my survival came when I left Stutthof. Under heavy guard, our kolonne arrived at the railroad tracks and was quickly loaded into the boxcars that would bring us to the city of Magdeburg. The interior of the car was familiar, since it was like the previous cars I had occupied, but the circumstances were different. On past occasions I had been railed to a camp located in a country that had been conquered by Germany; this time I was riding on German soil on my way to a German manufacturing plant to help their war effort. I felt as though I were in solitary confinement. I feared what might be in store for me in the country that hated Jews the most. I thought about my cousin, who had left us recently. Until then, we had all been faithful to each other and had not wanted any harm to come to a member of our troika. I had many worries about Boris: Was he having difficulty adjusting to his new environment? Was he really working as a chemist, the profession he loved so much? Most of all, I was concerned that he might not be dressed warmly and may not be well fed in the approaching cold winter months. At times I would peek through the small ventilating window to see the German landscape. The wintry sun tried to penetrate our boxcar, but the window was too small for any rays to reach the occupants.

After a two-day ride, the train stopped on a private track near the factory. The inmates were rushed to disembark and were guided toward the main entrance. Our kolonne was so heavily guarded that I was reminded again of the ancient slave market; the only thing missing were shackles on our wrists and ankles. From a distance, Father and I noticed a white sign with large black letters that read "Buchenwald"; underneath that it said "Arbeitslager I." The name *Buchenwald* immediately caught my father's attention. He looked at me sadly, then said quietly, "Af tsores." He was telling me in Yiddish that we were in trouble. To me, the name was gruesome. I was very disturbed and wondered, Had the SS become so smart that they had behaved themselves well in Stutthof at the time of our selection to fool us so they could bring us to Buchenwald Concentration Camp without difficulty? Had they outsmarted all five hundred of us? My anger and disappointment soon subsided when an unexpected, magical moment arrived. I found out that we were not going to Buchenwald but to the Polta Werke (Plant), a labor camp in Magdeburg; I was happy I had not been deceived.

The men were led to a small campground, and the women were guided to separate quarters. The men's camp consisted of two large barracks with a fairly large yard surrounded by a high, wire-mesh fence with one large sliding gate. The entire campsite was heavily guarded; when we entered, all men had to face the barracks. The Jewish leaders of the camp had already been appointed by the SS officers; I suppose they were being rewarded for their efficiency at Stutthof. David Kagan was the camp elder, and Harry Kussman and Max Finkelstein were the barracks elders. The five hundred inmates were evenly divided between the two barracks, which were new; the interiors were spotlessly clean and neatly arranged. Each building had a sleeping and eating area, but our camp had no kitchen facilities, so the food was cooked and prepared in a kitchen elsewhere in the plant. The washrooms in the barracks had hot and cold running water. The sleeping area consisted of two-tiered bunk beds with a straw mattress and pillow for each bunk. The eating area had several tables with benches large enough to comfortably seat every inmate. Most of the men were Latvian Jews, but some were from Germany, Poland, and Lithuania and had been transported to Riga before Stutthof.

Before the war, the Polta Werke had manufactured aluminum household goods; however, because of the change to a military economy in Nazi Germany, it became a manufacturer of various types of shell casings, ranging from ordinary military rifle ammunition to heavy artillery shells. It seemed the factory desperately needed workers, so the plant administration wasted no time. The following day, department heads of different branches of the plant arrived at our camp to interview every man and find out what his skills were and the extent of his knowledge of the profession. To secure a good job, every inmate became an expert in a given trade. After the interview, each man was assigned to work in a particular department in the plant.

Each barrack worked a twelve-hour shift, and the shifts changed from day to night hours every week. I was selected to work as an electrician, and Father became an experienced mechanic who was assigned to operate a machine. Although the work schedules were unusual, everyone was happy with his situation. This was the first time in our internment that every man was treated as a human being. We looked forward to going to work the following day, but our pleasant expectations were short-lived, as bad news reached the Polta Werke. After our transport had left Stutthof, many of the inmates had become ill with the infectious disease typhus, so our entire transport was put under a strict quarantine to see whether anyone would become sick.

The time of the quarantine was the longest ten days I had ever experienced. I feared becoming a casualty of that dreadful disease; I had never been ill during my entire Nazi internment. A restlessness could be seen on every inmate's face; none of us could find activities to occupy our minds, so we just sat, waiting for something to happen. We looked at each other, searching for a pale face or listening for a cough or a complaint of body pain. In the end, fortunately, our concerns were unfounded: nobody was infected. We were finally allowed to enter the plant and begin our assigned jobs. In the meantime, we had enjoyed a lengthy rest, so it could be said that the unpleasant experience had done us a lot of good; as the saying goes, "All's well that ends well."

Everyone was eager to start work. Our two hundred and fifty men began with the first shift, at eight o'clock in the morning. Under the guidance of SS guards, we left the campsite and soon found ourselves on the second floor of one of the many buildings in the plant. The guards remained outside the building. The German plant supervisors greeted us and showed every man his workstation. I was met by the electrical maintenance supervisor, who explained what my job would be: I was to make necessary electrical repairs and make sure all motors and lights were in working order. He gave me a portable toolbox with the necessary tools. My work area consisted only of the second floor, where I could move around freely. My father became a mechanic in charge of a large machine that cased artillery shells. Most of the men became operators of various machines, but a few had to settle for janitorial and machine-oiling jobs.

One section on the floor was called the Bonderei, and working there required extraordinary endurance and strength on the part of the workers. The work consisted of heat-treating metal parts to temper them and then cleaning off the oily residue. Both processes subjected the workers to a great deal of heat and hot steam. The jobs were performed in an extremely hot room over a pool of chemical tanks in which the parts were treated and cleaned. The room was so hot that the men worked without shirts, and their bodies were protected by long black rubber aprons. The job was extremely difficult for gentle, undernourished inmates, who received no extra soup or bread as a reward for their strenuous efforts. The few men who worked in the Bonderei were able to perform the hard work only because their spirits were kept high by the belief that freedom was near.

My father liked his job. Round pieces of brass were delivered to his machine in a wooden crate, and he inserted one piece into a large press. He pressed certain buttons, and a ready-made artillery shell casing came out. He cooled the casing and then washed it in hot water. He wore white cotton gloves at all times so he would not scratch the smooth, soft brass shell surface. In the beginning, many defective shell casings had to be put aside as unusable—he had to obey strict quality control standards. In time, and with the instructive help of his supervisor, he mastered his trade. His quality record improved so much that he was praised by his German superior. Father was proud of his accomplishment. He would sometimes pick up a two-foot shell casing and show it to his co-workers, saying, "Take a look; how do you like my perfect doll?" At his place of work, he had no worries about personal hygiene problems, as he had plenty of hot water and rags at his disposal. I admired his soft, clean hands, which had never been so nice. Not only could he keep his body clean, but he would also wash our underwear right at his machine. The only thing that did not please him about his job was that he could not leave at his discretion. When he had to use the washroom, he had to notify his supervisor that the large production machine would be stopped for a short time.

After receiving instructions from my German supervisor and getting oriented to my new workplace, I was ready to tackle the electrical repairs on the second floor. The first floor held the factory offices, and another manufacturing department was above us in which our inmates did not work and were not allowed to enter. My assignments were fairly easy. At first, I was busy with delayed electrical wiring repairs and cleaning up electrical equipment, but within a few days all of the neglected maintenance work was finished, and I was left with little to do. I moved around the plant, ready to tackle any emergency repair work that might be needed. I made sure my supervisor could always find me in case he had some unexpected work. At times, the twelve-hour shift seemed to go on forever.

My supervisor treated me fairly well, although he often used abrasive language. I thought he was one of very few who understood my predicament and was sympathetic to my living conditions. He never spoke to me about my problems, but I liked his approach at work and the way he handled himself as a boss. He frequently removed the garment he wore to work—which bore a Nazi Party membership badge—to lend me a helping hand. He taught me complicated wiring diagrams for the large manufacturing machines without hesitation. Sometimes when I had nothing to do, he would make sure I was occupied by having me dust electrical motors or perform some similar menial job.

Although I could move around at ease, many of the men worked very hard under constant duress from their supervisors. Some were even threatened with physical and verbal abuse for not having produced enough. Every time I looked at those supervisors I thought, Oh, you Nazi slave drivers. The time will come when you will have to account for your words and deeds. It was no secret that the German supervising staff in the plant had little feeling for the Jews; they were interested only in getting the most from the helpless men to promote their own accomplishments to their superiors and prove their devotion to the führer. Was it possible that the Nazis for whom we worked still wanted to save their beloved homeland when the end was already in sight?

I thought back to the time of our ancient Hebrew forebears' slavery in the land of Egypt and how they built the pharaoh's pyramids with their bare hands. After around two hundred years, the Hebrews were free and left the pharaoh's land, only to be pursued by his legionnaires in their chariots. The Hebrews traveled by foot through the hot desert until they reached the shores of the Red Sea, which stopped them from going further. The legend tells us that "to prevent them from being massacred or taken into slavery again by the pharaoh's legionnaires, a miracle had to happen, and so it did—the Red Sea parted in front of the Hebrews and made a passage, enabling them to cross." A miracle had saved my ancient ancestors, and I wondered whether I would live long enough to see a modern miracle that would save those of us at Polta. I felt the Nazis would no longer be able to pursue the Jews on this soil, just as the ancient pharaoh's legionnaires had tried and failed. I visualized the fall of the sturdy, powerful German Nazi regime; my hope was that their homes would be converted to ruins and that their spirit and hopes would vanish.

During the winter days of 1944 and 1945, I enjoyed living in a warm, clean barrack and working indoors, where no freezing winds could penetrate my body and no rain or snow could affect my well-being. There were no worries about entlausung or rushing to the daily roll and no more beatings or abuse by gentile or Jewish capos. I was happy to have reached this place. Still, hunger prevailed for me and the other men in the work camp. As always, food was the main topic of conversation, both in our barrack and at our places of work. The long hours, insufficient food, and continuously suppressive environment made us all fatigued and physically weak. Everyone sought opportunities to obtain additional nourishment.

Our ingenuity and creativity caused us all to become entrepreneurs, although in a somewhat limited way. Since none of the inmates received utensils for everyday needs, a demand was created for knives, spoons, and other useful household items. Our men knew how to make these items from pieces of scrap metal with the help of the tools available in the plant. The men in our barrack bartered these homemade utensils with other inmates for bread, margarine, a slice of sausage, or any other food item in our daily rations.

My father developed a prosperous business as well. He was one of the few who had soft, clean rags at his disposal, and in his spare time he would unravel the cotton rags and wind the threads on a piece of cardboard. They could be used for sewing, so he began to barter individual pieces of cardboard for food. To make the thread more useful, one man created sewing needles from small scrap wire by sharpening and hardening one end and drilling a tiny hole at the other. A long-standing problem was solved, and we were now able to sew on lost buttons and repair torn clothes. On Sunday, our day off, everybody was busy in the bar-racks. Some men fixed torn pants or shirts, some sewed on buttons, and others congregated in small groups around a table to exchange usable items. Like chips in a gambling casino, pieces of food, thread, needles, and other items were spread all over the table. We created our own flea market, which was more entertaining than lucrative.

One evening when I was working the night shift, I heard unusual noises coming from a corner of the plant; it sounded like pots and pans were being struck against each other. I rushed to the nearest window to see where the sound was coming from. It was very dark outside, but I could see a large yard with dimly lit lampposts every few hundred yards. In the yard I saw a man unloading several tall aluminum containers, which I recognized. They held the soup that was delivered to us daily, and I thought they might contain some leftovers, so I sneaked out into the yard. Before I could proceed I had to overcome some obstacles, such as deciding on the shortest and quickest route, so I would not be caught committing such a crime.

I knew the main entrance could not be used, since the SS guard was watching the door downstairs, and the emergency exit doors were too far away from the yard. I had only one option: to use the stairway that led to the first-floor office. The door that led to this stairway was continually monitored by a watchman who made rounds throughout the plant. At certain intervals he would check this door and then punch a time clock to indicate the time and day he had checked for any irregularities. I went to this door to see whether it was locked and, if not, whether I could open it from the other side to enable me to get back on the floor. I waited for the watchman to appear; when he left, my obstacles were cleared. I told Father of my intentions. He asked me which exit door I would use, wished me luck, and I was on my way. The operation was risky, as I was not supposed to leave my work site.

As I was about to open the exit door, I looked around to see whether any German supervisors were there to see me leave. I left carefully and walked down the two flights of stairs. I found myself in a vestibule with two doors: one leading to the office and the other to the yard. I opened the outer door and rushed to the aluminum container in the distance. When I reached it my eyes popped wide open; I knew I had found a real catch, or a maline, as we inmates called it, since the large pots still contained plenty of soup. I scooped up the soup with my hand. If it had not been liquid, I would have filled my pockets. I ate as much as I could, then left the area. When I got back to the second floor, I told Father about my great discovery. He was happy and relieved that I had returned without incident. I expressed sorrow that I could not bring some of the delicious soup back for him.

I knew this was the kitchen for the foreign workers in Polta. After their meal, the large pots were brought here to be washed. Most of these laborers were Ukrainians brought to Magdeburg to be employed by the Polta Werke. They lived in a separate campsite on the premises of the plant and could move about the grounds freely. They received better treatment and nourishment than the Jewish inmates.

When I saw all the soup that was being wasted, I knew I needed to acquire a small, portable container for my next journey to the kitchen. My father asked a co-worker to make us a pot with a swivel handle and a cover, and within days we had one in our possession, traded for a piece of bread. Father and I could now enjoy the soup as a supplement to our meager food ration. The additional food I acquired at night gave us enough sustenance to quell our hunger during the coming week of day shifts.

After a few weeks, my great discovery was no longer a secret; other inmates had made the same realization and went after the leftover soup as well. Only a few men were able to undertake the challenge. For some, the risk was too great, in light of the fact that the war was slowly coming to an end. For others, it was impossible to leave their work sites. On some nights I was unable to go to the yard because of my heavy workload. Sometimes the watchman would lock the exit door, and there was no way for me to get out; other times, I would find the containers completely empty. My co-workers would frequently get there before I could, taking the little soup that was left.

The soup containers were returned from the Ukrainian living quarters and work sites at different times. I had to watch the storage enclosure, which was time-consuming. I also had to find a time to leave that would not arouse my supervisor's suspicions. I saw the soup business as a private enterprise, in which I had to watch for competition. My greatest competitor in obtaining the soup was my friend Chonke, as we inmates called him. At times we would both return empty-handed, angry at each other for having scooped up the last drop of soup and left the other with nothing. Still, I considered him my friend in misfortune; we felt we had something in common. We talked about getting the soup out of the deep containers, which were often very soiled; nevertheless, that did not discourage us from filling our cans.

Once, I had a profound misunderstanding with my father, which left a deep scar on our future relationship. A week had passed, and I had not been able to get to the containers. Our hunger made us irritable; years of experience taught me that hunger can convert people to beasts. I could not go out because the watchman had locked my exit door. I knew the door could be opened from the outside; the problem was how to get to the other side. I looked for any openings, much as a hungry rat looks for a hole in a tightly guarded enclosure. I was driven to despair; when nobody was around I opened the window and crawled out, barely holding on to the window ledge. I gripped the drainpipe located near the window and slid to the ground. I quickly dipped into the containers and filled my own container with soup, then ran back to the building. As I had guessed, the doors on the main and second floors did open from the outside. In no time I was safe on my floor.

I rushed to Father to leave the soup can for safekeeping, since I was in a hurry to get back to my post. I told him we would have the soup during our rest period. He set the can in a safe place under his machine. During the rest period I came to Father to eat the soup with him, but the can was empty. Father looked bewildered and could not explain how the soup had disappeared. I became furious, and said loudly, "You ate all the soup! I risked my life—I could have been killed. You did not leave even a spoonful for me! You know I am just as hungry as you!" I was so excited that I began to shout profanities at my father. He kept saying he had not eaten the soup and did not know what had happened to it. I accused him of lying, but he insisted he would never take food from his own son.

The argument continued, on and off, all night. Throughout the years we had never had an argument; it was a shame that as we neared the end of our suffering, such an unpleasant episode had to occur. If my cousin Boris had been with us, such a fight would never have taken place. When we were together as a troika, there was always a third person to smooth out misunderstandings between the other two. When we returned to the barrack, our argument continued. Finally, we went to sleep, barely talking to each other. The next day my father continued to tell me he was innocent; he was also deeply hurt, not so much by my unwarranted accusations as by the fact that I did not believe him. He was bothered by the fact that our argument had been overheard by inmates in the barrack and at the plant. A few days later, I came to my senses; I was very sorry about my behavior toward my father, but it was too late to retract the words. I suppose the pressure of the camps had finally taken its toll on me. Nonetheless, the incident did not stop me from returning to the kitchen for the soup we shared.

Around twenty years later, when he visited me in Chicago, my father finally told me how much I had pained him. He said, "Remember that incident at Polta? I never took the soup in that can of ours." After all those years he still harbored bitter feelings. I thought all night of how much I had hurt his feelings; so many years later, he was still trying to justify his innocence. After a sleepless night I asked him, "What can I do to show you my sorrow and regret over my behavior?" "Forget it; I brought it up only because we spoke about our sufferings at Polta. You have done enough already; I am now your guest in America," said my father. From that moment I realized the extent of my father's warm heart and his devoted concern for me: He did not want me to carry the heavy burden of guilt. He is no longer around, but I can sincerely say, "Rest in peace, my dear Papa. I miss you and love you very much."

My twelve-hour work shifts left little time for socializing with the inmates from the other barrack. Both buildings were on the same campsite, only about a hundred feet apart, but I had little chance to get to know the other two hundred and fifty men. When I was working, the other group was sleeping, and so it went, day after day. I saw the others at the plant during the shift change, which lasted only a few minutes; I had just enough time to exchange a few words with the man who replaced me on the next shift.

The camp elder, Kagan, appointed several men to make up the Innerdienst, a group of barracks orderlies. They saw to it that the daily food rationing and soup distribution proceeded in an orderly manner and made sure all of the strict rules and regulations of the barracks were observed. The orderlies did not work at the plant but were occupied with keeping our barracks clean and well maintained. They enjoyed an easy life; for their work, they were rewarded with extra food and a separate sleeping area. With the help of these men, the camp elder could closely monitor and supervise the inmates in both barracks. The Innerdienst men behaved roughly and acted like strongmen in fulfilling their duties in the barracks; they were similar to the capos in the concentration camps. The self-styled leader of this small group was named Nachke. The men in the barracks, myself included, were frightened of these men and did not dare to undertake anything that would not be to Nachke's liking. Before the war, I had seen him daily at his job in a kosher butcher shop around the corner from my father's business in Riga. I never imagined this well-mannered teenager would become a brutal, domineering person whom every man despised.

At times, even our barrack elder, Max Finkelstein, went out of his way to please this tough group of men. Max was a tall, slim, mild-mannered man with a soft voice; how such a man had obtained the rugged job of barrack elder was beyond me. He always acted with restraint and discretion toward his fellow inmates. When he lost his temper, he would raise his voice threateningly and say, "You'd better listen to me, or I will punch you in the nose. I will poke your brains out—do you hear me?" I never saw him put these threats into action; he tended to use words instead of his fists. As the barrack elder, Max was responsible for distributing our daily ration of soup. The tall aluminum containers were delivered from the kitchen to our barrack, and the inmates would form a long line to receive the soup.

Max's long-handled ladle served him well. He would use it to mix the watery soup so the few slices of potato and slivers of meat in the pot were evenly distributed; if possible, he would include a piece of meat and a potato in every inmate's serving. My father always asked, "Max, mix up the soup one more time—maybe you will be able to fish out a potato." Max would say, with a smile, "Fine, I will try." When he poured the soup into my father's dish, he would ask, "Are you pleased now?" Father always replied, "Very much so. Thank you." After a while, when one of us reached the front of the line, Max would jump in before my father could open his mouth. "Can you see? I am mixing the soup twice, just for the sake of you and your son." As many weeks passed, we developed a cordial friendship without saying much to each other.

Father and I ate our meals at an assigned table. Each table had its own Innerdienst man who saw that the area was left clean after the meals and that everything proceeded in an orderly fashion. His biggest task was supervising the slicing of the rationed loaf of bread, for a careful and lengthy procedure had to be followed to make these portions as even as possible. Before the process began, each loaf was measured several times with a homemade ruler. In spite of the careful cutting, some pieces were always a bit smaller or larger than the others, since every loaf was unevenly shaped. After all of the bread had been cut into individual rations, one inmate would be turned away from the table, and the orderly would point to one of the pieces. The inmate would call out the name of one of the men, who would be given that piece of bread. The procedure lasted until everyone had received his portion.

Sunday was my most enjoyable day, for we could sleep late and rejuvenate our tired bodies. This was the day on which we could pay attention to personal grooming and cleaning, repair our clothing, and still have time left to discuss the war and our tragic situation. Father and I often conversed about what we would do and where we would go if, one day, we were free men again. We agreed we would never return to our homeland, especially not to the evil city of Riga, for the Latvian soil was too deeply soaked with Jewish blood. We could not live with the Latvian people, as most of them had participated in some way in the destruction of the Jewish communities throughout the country.

We had given up hope of finding our family alive or even of finding their burial place. "Yes," we said, "our love for the land where we lived most of our lives is gone forever." The only place to go was to the ancient land of our people, Palestine, in which Jerusalem was located. What was now a wasteland had been rich with milk and honey until the Romans had driven our people out; since that time, the Jewish people have moved from one country to another. They have always treated their hosts with dignity and honesty; they have fought and died to protect every country they have lived in, but little acknowledgment had been granted them. Despite all of their efforts and work, the Jews were persecuted. We were ready to begin a new life in a Jewish homeland; we were ready to build and, if necessary, to fight and die for an independent Jewish state that would absorb and protect its people from future persecution, wherever it might take place. Although we had family in the United States, my father had no desire to settle down there.

During the winter months of 1945, things went fairly smoothly. I was accustomed to my daily routine in the barrack and to my work in the plant. I considered my co-workers to be my friends and knew that in a time of need I could depend on their help. The hardest part of the job was working the night shift and trying to sleep during the day. My body was used to sleeping at night, and any rest I got during the day was never enough. As much as I tried to adjust, I always felt tired. The greatest advantage of night work was the possibility of pilfering soup. At times, this soup was sour, but it still tasted delicious to me. I was pleased to be in this labor camp that served the Polta Werke. We had no snow, rain, or windy days, and sticks and whips were never used. There were no muselmen with expressionless faces in our midst, and no men drifted into oblivion. I could tolerate this place until the day of my salvation.

One beautiful, clear day, on which I was working the day shift, felt somehow different from any other. The Jewish women, who were in a separate department, did not appear for work, which seemed strange. No one could discover why, and our worry turned to panic when we had not seen them by the day's end. I thought something had surely happened to the women. I wondered whether they had been harmed and hoped I would not share a similar surprise later that evening. When we returned to the barrack, however, everything seemed to be in order. Later we found out why the women had not shown up for work, and although they were not harmed, the reason was extremely cruel: The SS guards in their camp had made them witness the hanging of a young Ukrainian woman accused of sabotage at her workplace. This horrible proceeding had lasted most of the day and kept them from their jobs.

When spring 1945 arrived, the working conditions at the plant slowly began to deteriorate. Allied aircraft appeared over Magdeburg; every time the planes flew over the city, the civil defense sirens went off. Production had to be stopped, and everyone, including the Jewish workers, had to go down to the air-raid shelter. At first, this happened only occasionally, but as the days passed the sirens went off frequently. Every time I went to the shelter, I felt I was closer to my liberation. Some days our men had to stop their machines several times; every time this happened it affected production in the entire plant. At times, Father could not operate his machine for several hours a day, because the delivery of new materials needed for production had been delayed as British and U.S. planes dropped bombs over Magdeburg day and night. In the early morning I saw heavy black clouds that looked like a shining sunrise, and the wafting, smoldering smoke in the distance seemed a colorful rainbow. How wonderful it was to witness the gradual destruction of Nazi Germany. This Allied bombardment greatly affected the morale of the German population, as both property and lives were lost. Our supervisors could not sleep at night and came to work exhausted, and their negative attitude was felt strongly throughout the plant. The inmates, on the other hand, enjoyed the night's rest and smiled to themselves every time they heard a loud, devastating bomb blast.

The bombardment of Magdeburg did not slow—rather, it increased—but no matter how strenuous the bombardment was during the night, we still had to work the following day. Some of the supervisors were not able to come at all, and others showed up late with smudged faces and soiled clothing. During the night, they had been busy helping firemen put out blazing fires in their neighborhoods. The Germans were outraged to see the destruction of many homes and buildings by the U.S. and British air forces. The inmates would look at each other with smiles and the common thought that the Germans were getting what was coming to them. The Allied planes were in Germany's air space frequently and at all hours. We had a unique Yiddish expression for the Allied air raids—"Ot kumen di feigalech mit di kneidlech"—which meant, "Here come the birdies with the matzo balls." Our work was now interrupted every few hours, and several of us stopped going down to the shelter. I wanted to witness the destruction of this plant, regardless of any danger to my own life, but not one bomb was dropped on the Polta Werke. At times I looked at the sky, searching for the friendly planes, and said, "Where are you? I am waiting for your visit. You are my rescuers—how much longer do I have to wait for you to free me from my Nazi shackles?" I often saw heavy black smoke wafting toward the blue skies over Germany. I had watched rising smoke many times before, but this smoke was different: It came from German homes and factories burning in their own land. The other smoke I had seen had come either from Jewish flesh and bones on an open bonfire or from a crematorium chimney.

In March 1945, the Allied air force bombardment over Magdeburg became considerably heavier; the planes dropped bombs almost uninterruptedly. The production of artillery shells at Polta was limited to a few days a week. Our German supervisors, dusty and exhausted, showed the strain of sleepless nights. Mine would occasionally complain about how hard he had worked the previous night, cleaning up and removing debris from his and neighbors' houses in complete darkness. I watched everything that was happening around me with enormous delight. As March passed, the scars of the perpetual Allied blasts became more visible throughout the city, and black smoke was seen constantly over the city's skies. Production at the plant finally ended because our supervisors could not come to work; they were busy taking care of personal problems at home and were called to duty to the civil defense. About thirty of us still went to the plant daily to do cleanup work. My father and the remaining inmates were sent to the city to dig trenches for the civil defense, mostly along the Elbe River.

It looked as though the German authorities were preparing for a staunch defense of Magdeburg to stop the quickly approaching U.S. Army. The civilian population was notified that when the U.S. armed forces reached the outskirts of the city, a fifteen-minute air-raid alarm would go off. At that time the defense of Magdeburg would start in full force, with all those in the civil defense participating. As I was working in the plant, I constantly heard air-raid sirens going on and off. The workers were warned that they needed to be sheltered in a safe place during the air raids, but we soon ignored the alarms and did not go down to the designated shelter. The loud, roaring sirens were a symphony to the inmates' ears.

Finally, on April 9, 1945, at about ten o'clock in the morning, I was at the plant listening to one of the many air-raid sounds, but it seemed to last longer than usual this time. I turned to a co-worker and said, "Do you hear the siren? It is going for a long time; could this be the long-awaited fifteen-minute warning for the civil defense to take up arms? Could it be that the Americans are approaching Magdeburg?" We ran to the clock at the end of the hall. We watched the movement of its hands; the minutes ticked by quickly, and the shriek of the warning siren kept on as never before. We had to be certain this was the real thing, since our next step might lead us into the hands of our captors. Exactly on the fifteen-minute mark the blast stopped, which frightened us, as we did not know what to do next.

We were very excited and could not speak or act; only our smiling faces revealed our happiness, for our dreams had become a reality. I thought the Americans were on the outskirts of the city and that I was only hours or, at most, a day away from freedom. I looked around but saw nobody on the floor. The German supervisory staff had disappeared unnoticed, and the several other German workers who had been cleaning up with us were scrambling toward the exits. My friend and I were left standing alone. "Let's go hide," I spontaneously called to him, and we quickly ran to look for a safe hiding place.

Chicago, immediately after author's arrival, 1947. *From left:* Boris, Herman, Betty, Shirley, and Ralph.

Tamara and Boris during courtship, Gary, Indiana, 1947.

Tamara and Boris's wedding photo, Chicago, 1948.

Boris's reunion with his father, Chicago, 1965.

Boris and Tamara Kacel with Israeli Prime Minister Menachem Begin at his house reception, 1981.

Community leaders of Peterson Park's B'nai Brith Lodge #2050, 1969. *Standing, from left:* Herman Gershberg, Irving Cairo, Julius Wagman, Max Sakol; *sitting, from left:* Erick Salm, Boris Kacel, Sam Fox.

Abram, at grandson's wedding, 1988, in Chicago.

13

My Escape to Freedom

With a prayer on my lips, I lived through the fifteen-minute warning sirens in Magdeburg. I will always remember the sound of April 9, 1945: the beautiful sound of my freedom. In a spontaneous reaction to the many years of frustration, anger, and mental fatigue, I ran, without a thought of what would happen to Father or me. I knew he would look for me, concerned about my safety; I did not mean to abandon him, but the excitement had overwhelmed me. I thought only of the freedom and liberty that were so close at hand, thanks to the approaching Americans. I was sure there would be a great celebration among the men and that I would be reunited with Father, when in truth the first few minutes of my imagined liberation could have been the last minutes of my life.

My co-worker and I could not find a suitable hiding place inside the plant, so we ran out into the yard where not a soul could be seen. I was drawn to the smokestack from the boiler room; I imagined we could find a good hiding place there. What we found was a secluded pile of coal in the back of the boiler room, and we scooped out the shiny black pieces with our bare hands to form a cavelike opening, somewhat like an igloo, that served as a hiding place. After sitting there for several hours, we became curious about what had happened to the rest of the men who had been in the plant. My friend decided to go explore the situation, so he went into the building where we had worked to see whether anyone was there. A few hours passed, and my friend had not returned; I became somewhat panicked. I thought, Did he willfully abandon me? Was he apprehended by the guards dressed in civilian clothes? I sat well into the middle of the very still night but heard no voices. Eventually, I was forced from my hiding place to look for food; the kitchen seemed the logical place to look.

As I made my way out of the hiding place, two armed plainclothes guards came out of the kitchen and immediately took me into custody, because they knew who I was. I tried to defend my presence in the unauthorized area, but they did not want to hear my explanation. "You are a runaway from your camp," they said. "Come with us," one of them added, brandishing his gun; I did not resist or contradict him. They brought me to an abandoned campsite on the plant property where there were several barracks, all vacant. We walked into one, and the guards left me there, warning me not to leave; every half hour they would check on me. When I asked how long I would have to stay there, I was told, "At sunrise you will be disposed of." They left without giving me a chance to ask for clarification of their statement, although I knew what it meant. I would be executed in the early morning hours—the Germans customarily performed executions at sunrise. I realized I was in trouble. I have to escape from this place; I have nothing to lose; I will not let them kill me, I thought. The guards left me in a state of agony, fear, and despair. I had learned long ago that I had to take my destiny into my own hands whenever possible; here, too, I would have to find a way to get out of this dilemma before the night was over.

My insatiable hunger kept me from thinking rationally. I went out into the empty yard to look for food and to find a way to escape. The entire campsite was surrounded by a solid wooden fence about ten feet high. Dim lights were mounted on every post, their beams aimed at the fence. This area of the plant was unfamiliar to me. I walked into a few of the empty barracks to find some clue as to who had occupied them. I guessed foreign laborers must have lived there, since they had individual frame beds, and the foreigners generally had more privileges than the Jews. Raw vegetables were scattered across the floor. I picked up some carrots, potatoes, and sugar beets and returned to the barrack where the guards had left me. The vegetables were the first thing I had eaten all day. After my small meal, I lay down on one of the beds for a short rest before attempting my escape.

The guards came back to check on me a few times. The second time they brought two other inmates they had caught in the plant—brothers from Kaunas, Lithuania. I did not know them well, since they had lived in the second barrack and worked the shift opposite mine. They were also told not to leave. Once the guards had departed, I told them of my plan to escape, to which they readily agreed. We had to determine the approximate time between the guards' visits without a clock, but after they had checked in a few times we knew about how much time we would have. We began by looking for weak spots in the wooden fence but found none. All of the boards were solid and fastened tightly to the crossbars; it would have been impossible to loosen them with our bare hands. Jumping over the fence was not an option because of its height. We became discouraged, as the night was coming to an end. On our last try, I found one board that consisted of two pieces, and after several attempts we were able to loosen the lower part.

The brothers had a German army rucksack, a knapsack. They had thrown it on the floor in anger, considering it to be unlucky—it was this large green knapsack, sticking out from their hiding place in the plant, that had attracted the attention of the guards. Before we could proceed with our escape, we had to prepare some food, so we went to the other barrack to gather more of the vegetables. I picked up their discarded bag and decided that for me it would be a lucky charm. I put my beets, carrots, and potatoes inside, and the brothers put their food into their pockets. After one more visit from the guards, we were ready for our escape, which we knew had to be completed within the next half hour. We rushed to the fence where the loose board was located, slowly removed it, and crept through the opening. When we reached the other side of the fence, however, we encountered another problem: a barbed-wire fence. We were fortunate to find that the bottom part of the fence was loose. One of us lifted the wires, creating enough space to crawl underneath, but the space was so narrow that I had to crawl flat on my stomach to get through. With each other's help, though, we managed to overcome the final obstacle to our escape.

The night was pitch black, and we could not see anything in front of us, so we walked very close to each other so we would not get lost and kept very quiet to make sure no one would hear us. After a short while, several German policemen with flashlights sprang out of nowhere and confronted us. They called out, "Halt, halt; stop, stop," shining their flashlights at us while we scrambled to all sides. I knew we were in trouble again.

I found myself standing next to a wooden fence that had a tall swinging gate. The policemen went after the brothers, and when I heard that they had been caught I had an extra minute or so to open the gate and hide behind it. The policemen must have seen my shadow moving past the gate and assumed I had run into the yard to hide. A few armed men checked the yard with their bright flashlights; they soon left, disappointed, without closing the gate behind them. Some invisible, friendly force—perhaps God Himself—had protected my life again: If the police had shut the gate, they would have found me standing there. To my sorrow, the brothers from Kaunas were taken away, so my acquaintance with them was short-lived. I tried to look them up later, but they had disappeared without a trace.

I stayed where I was for a long time; I wanted to make sure all of the Germans were gone for good. Eventually, I shut the gate and went to survey the area for a safer hiding place. The night was so dark I had to hold on to the buildings to keep from walking off the sidewalk. I came to a small wooden structure; in the dark, it seemed to be a row of sheds. I approached the yard and found I was correct. They were individual wooden storage sheds under one roof, each with its own door. All of the doors were padlocked but one; I opened it and walked into the shed, closing the door behind me. I decided to hide here, hoping it would be the last time I would have to do so.

I was exhausted from the incredibly busy night, but before I settled down for a good night's rest I took a board and leaned it against the unlocked door. The sound it would make dropping would warn me if any intruder tried to enter the shed. I fell asleep faster than I can ever remember having done and slept as though I were in the world's most comfortable bed.

Sounds of children playing in the yard woke me. The bright rays of the sun were pouring through the slits of the wooden walls of the shed. I had to remain very quiet and limit my movement; any little squeaking sound or shadow might catch the attention of the children or adults in the yard. I was very hungry and treated myself to some carrots and beets. When I had finished my breakfast, I made a scratch on the wall so I would not lose track of time in this isolated hideout. I wanted to investigate my strange new surroundings and the people in the yard, so I found several peepholes along the outer walls. I could see little, since the houses in front of the shed obstructed my view, but I was encouraged to see much of Polta's main entrance gate. The second-floor executive offices were also visible. This gate had once been a very busy section of the plant, but everything was still now. Although it had seemed that I had walked a long distance from Polta, I had wound up practically across the street. In the darkness I had not been aware that I was walking in a circle and, by pure luck, had found this shed.

After surveying the area on one side, I turned to the door on the opposite side to find out what was happening in the backyard. The boards of the door were far apart because of their old age, and I could see the entire yard clearly. The building I saw was a two-story structure with several rear steps that led to the backyard. It seemed to be a row of townhouses, probably occupied by young couples with children. I could see several mothers caring for infants in baby buggies on this beautiful June day. The younger children played with their toys and dolls; a few rode tricycles in the yard. A small group of older children played hopscotch, and others kicked a ball, pretending to play soccer. I enjoyed observing their activities; I had always liked children, and I watched the way these innocent little human beings enjoyed the outdoors under their mothers' supervision. They were laughing and smiling, unaware of the difficult time in which they lived. I noticed that one boy wore the uniform of the Hitler Youth; his presence reminded me to be constantly on guard. No men, young or old, were visible in the yard; I suppose they had all been called to duty to defend, protect, and preserve the Third Reich. The men were sent to fight, and often to die, for a lost cause. Others had been recruited for a very successful and, to them, noble cause: the persecution, abuse, and murder of innocent civilians—Jews and other nationalities.

Despite these thoughts, it was wonderful to watch happy families spend leisure time together in their own backyards. They were unconcerned with what went on with other, non-Aryan families in Germany or in the countries their führer had conquered. I thought of the shattered lives of the Jews and the few Germans who opposed the Nazi teachings. Sitting in this quiet, self-confined enclosure, I could vividly remember how the German Jews had arrived in the Riga Ghetto. They were only a small number of the evacuees; the majority had not lived to see the ghetto. I thought, too, of how they had died in various camps because they were not properly dressed and fed. Then I looked at these beautiful children at play and thought of my own sisters and brother. What had they done to be annihilated—they had been born to Jewish parents. To me, gentile and Jewish children were the same. They came into this glorious world to live; they were meant to enjoy everything it had to offer and everything parents and educators could teach them. Only outside, evil forces reshaped innocent children's minds to hate and to kill. I felt the twentieth century had turned into one of tyrannies.

Thoughts of my siblings stayed with me. I recalled the Yiddish words "Shtetl Riga vu ich hob myne kindershe yorn farbracht," which meant "My little town, Riga, where I spent my childhood years." We had spent many entertaining hours together in our house, in our backyard, at public parks, and on the shores of the Baltic Sea in the summer. We might have enjoyed each other's company even more in our maturity, but my family was swept away with massive gunfire. I will never forget the cold winter night in 1941 when my dear yiddishe mame and her three youngest children marched to their destruction and incineration. The weary mothers, fathers, children, and elderly were driven on foot in one long procession. Some mothers held their babies close to their breasts as they followed one another down a street filled with sparkling white snowflakes. They likely had a prayer on their lips: "O Almighty God, help me and my child." The loud cries of "Mama, Mama, Mama" must have been heard the world over, yet the world stood still; nobody answered the mothers' prayers or the children's cries. I am sure my mother tried to protect her children from harm, but the strenuous and fearful one-way march ended tragically in the forest of Rumbuli.

My thoughts turned again to these happy German children at play, and I hoped that when they reached adulthood they would have no bigotry and hatred in their souls. It would make a world of difference if these children denounced the crimes committed by their elders. Only they could see to it that the gruesome black chapter in German history did not repeat itself.

The sun was about to slip under the horizon, ending my first day in hiding. The large yard that had been filled with children and their mothers was now empty. No gunfire was heard, and not a single aircraft could be spotted in the sky. Everything was still and quiet, and I was impatient to see and hear some military action. Was this the calm before the storm,

I asked myself. This day had been the most strenuous of all for this heartbroken young man. I was alone, fighting for my survival and thinking of Father; I wondered where he was at this late hour. How awful he must feel, having spent this past night and day without me. Was he thinking about where I was? He did not even know whether I was alive. Did he think I had meant to abandon him at the most crucial crossroads of our lives? Grim scenarios occupied my mind, but even feeling such deep sorrow I managed to fall asleep.

Most of my time in the shed was spent observing the children and their mothers in the backyard. At night, I looked at the sky and asked the stars above to watch over me. The vegetables I had stored were enough to sustain me. The raw potatoes could not have been tastier, even if they had been baked or fried; they were a delight to my growling, empty stomach. I had no water, although a faucet was attached to the front building. I did not dare appear in the yard; I could be seen during the day and heard at night. Any desire I might have had for drinking water was squelched by my tremendous fear of being apprehended. I had made two scratches on the wall, yet freedom was nowhere in sight. I wondered, What has happened to my brave American liberators? They were supposed to be at the outskirts of Magdeburg two days ago. What has prevented them from entering the city? Was I deceived by the very people I thought were my friends? I had stopped hearing sounds of flying planes and crushing homes and saw no more black smoke rising from burning buildings. I could only go to sleep and wait for a better day to come.

Before the daylight had completely faded, I heard gunshots and artillery barrages. Gradually, in the darkness of the night, the sporadic shooting became a constant bombardment; automatic machine guns could be heard uninterruptedly. The Allied air force was taking its toll; I could hear buildings falling to the ground. Shells zoomed loudly above my head on the way to their targets; my small shed was apparently in the path of a major artillery duel. The bombs fell so close to my hiding place that at times I could hear and feel the trembling of the earth shake my shed. I hoped this was the final assault on the city by the U.S. armed forces.

In the middle of the night, when the shooting had stopped for a time, I went to my peepholes to see whether the buildings within my sight had been damaged. These fully occupied buildings stood untouched by the destructive shells. The sky looked as though it was filled with shining stars, but the lights were actually the explosions of antiaircraft shells. As I watched the firefight outdoors, I was startled by a loud, crushing noise in the shed just a few feet away from me. I looked up and saw a large, round opening in the roof where a bomb had penetrated. Luckily, it had landed on newspapers on the floor of the shed—precisely on the spot where I had been lying only a few minutes before—which had prevented it from exploding. I considered this another miracle; I had left my sleeping place not a moment too soon. If the bomb had landed on me, I would have been torn into pieces. Somebody in heaven was definitely watching over me.

I did not know whether to remain in the shed or go look for another hiding place. Suddenly, I felt very lonesome and abandoned. I wanted to speak, just to hear a voice, or to touch any human being who could understand my predicament. I longed to go outside and tell somebody what had happened in the shed, but I quickly realized I had no friends with whom I could share my terrifying experience. I had to remain alone in the small wooden enclosure. I looked at the hole in the roof that had been created by the bomb and felt like thanking God for His watchful eye and for preserving my future. Looking through the opening to the sky, it seemed the early morning sun was descending from heaven, creating a bright halo around the hole in the roof.

Since I knew no suitable prayers from memory, I composed my own. "My God Almighty in heaven, how can I thank You for saving my life in time for my freedom? Please spare my life and let me be one of the survivors who can tell the free world about my sufferings and the horrors committed by the evil German empire. O God, spare the life of my father, wherever he might be, and give me the strength to survive. Then I shall help to rebuild Jerusalem and will pray at the Western Wall of our ancient temple on behalf of my perished brethren." By the time I completed my prayer, my cheeks were dripping with tears; all of my buried grief and frustrations spilled out. I tried to compose myself, but it was too difficult. I did not return to my previous sleeping space, since any vibration of my body might set off the bomb in the stack of newspapers. I made my new bed in front of the shed's door, aware that my presence would be immediately revealed if the loose door should swing open.

Terrified, I tucked myself in and finally fell asleep, undisturbed by the renewed bombardment. In the late afternoon, I woke up and made a third notch on the wooden wall, hoping the heavy shelling was the final prelude to my freedom. I took out my rucksack filled with vegetables and noticed that I had only enough for one more meal. What I thought would be my day of liberation was soon over, and I had to face another night, during which the bombing subsided somewhat.

By morning, everything had become suspiciously quiet. I scratched another mark on the wall—this was my fourth day in the shed. I looked into the yard; no children were at play, no mothers with baby buggies, no toys scattered. An unusual stillness surrounded the abandoned backyard. I turned to the opposite wall that faced the Polta Werke and looked through the peepholes. There, too, everything seemed strangely quiet. I thought, If the battle for Magdeburg had ended, I would see troops marching, tanks and other vehicles roaring down the streets, and a festive celebration by the victorious Americans. None of these events was occurring anywhere nearby. Once in a while I noticed gatherings of small groups of unfamiliar soldiers who wore extremely large helmets, which I thought I recognized. I wondered who they were, then recalled seeing pictures of Norwegian soldiers who fought with the German Wehrmacht wearing the same type of helmets. I assumed these men had arrived from Norway to bolster the local forces in defending the city.

The following night passed with no disturbances; I heard almost no shelling or Allied aircraft. In the morning, I made my fifth scratch mark on the wall and finished the remaining food. I checked the peepholes to see what was happening outside, but it looked like just another beautiful, sunny day. A few children appeared in the yard; otherwise, the streets were as deserted as before. I was busy thinking about my next move. I was also very aware of the bomb that had not detonated that was embedded in the pile of old newspapers near me. My movements were curtailed considerably because I stayed away from that dangerous area. I decided that under cover of darkness I would have to leave the shelter that had served me so well. My stash of life-sustaining vegetables had been depleted, and I would have to find some food to survive until liberation. To my knowledge, the only place I could find any food was the Polta kitchen. At nightfall, I put my empty rucksack on my back and quietly left the shed, and my time in a wooden crypt came to an end.

It was a fairly bright night, and I could see my way to Polta's main gate, which I walked through undisturbed; no guards were in sight. The kitchen was only a few hundred feet away; as I approached, I was happy to see the empty soup containers in the distance. When I reached them, I quickly poured some of the leftover soup into my mouth; it was sour, but I swallowed it without thinking of the consequences. As I reached for a second helping, two strange soldiers with machine guns ran out from the kitchen straight toward me. They shouted in English, "Hands up, hands up!" I was very scared and confused, yet was able to answer, "I am a Jew, I am a Jew" as I followed their order. "What were you doing here at night?" one asked me. "I am hungry and came here to get some soup," I answered. They searched me for weapons, then a jeep drove up, and I stepped in. We drove to a dark street elsewhere in the city; the soldiers did not tell me where I was going. It seemed I might not have convinced them that I was a Jew, and I was very fearful of these Norwegian soldiers who spoke to me in English. As we rode I came to my senses; I realized these unusual-looking soldiers with the oversized helmets were Americans, not Norwegians. I thought, "Now I am in a mess—how shall I prove I am Jewish?"

After a short ride, they brought me to a place where I was locked up; I do not know whether it was a police station or a small jail. I was guided to a spacious basement; along the walls were several separate cells with steel bars and doors. The room was dimly lit and very smoky and was filled with German war prisoners, most of whom were officers from the Wehrmacht. Some were clean and neatly dressed, but others were dusty, with torn uniforms, and looked exhausted. I noticed that the rank insignias of several of the men had been torn off. I noted my unusual predicament: I had become a German war prisoner. I thought, Look where I wound up—among Nazi officers. How will I get out of here, and how will I be able to convince the Americans that I am not a Nazi but an inmate from Buchenwald's labor camp at the Polta Werke? I felt that only time would solve my newest problem. All of the cell doors were open, but every cell was full; the basement was so crowded I had to squeeze through the men to find a space on the floor. I sat next to a lieutenant from the Wehrmacht, who tried to strike up a conversation, asking which unit I had belonged to and where I had been taken prisoner. I still wore my shabby civilian clothes and did not know how he would react if I told him I was a Jew and the circumstances under which

I was caught. I decided to counter his friendly approach by saying I was too tired to talk.

As terrible as it felt to be locked up with my enemies, as I looked at them I could only think that I had beaten the Nazis; the daily horrors were over, and I had survived. I was happier than I had ever been, for I had lived to see the Nazi Army defeated and the fall of Hitler's evil Third Reich. After a long and strenuous night, U.S. soldiers appeared to let us into the yard. We were lined up and counted, which reminded me of morning roll call in the concentration camps. Under armed guard we were led from the yard to the street, and the long lines of several hundred German war prisoners—myself among them—were led on a long march through the streets of Magdeburg. We reached the outskirts of the city, where a camp for prisoners of war was located. As we awaited instructions, I saw my friend Jacobson, who had lived in my barrack at the Polta Werke. I called his name; he came over, asking what I was doing among German war prisoners. I told him how I had wound up with them and asked how he had come here. He said the U.S. Army had freed the Polta camp three days ago, and he had become acquainted with some of the friendlier officers. He was helping one of them, who happened to be Jewish and was in charge of this camp.

When I heard this pleasant news, I asked Jacobson to help me get out. He replied, "I will go immediately to explain to the Jewish American officer who you are; I am sure he will free you without delay." My friend left and reappeared within minutes with the commanding officer, a colonel, who looked at me and realized I was in the wrong place. "Get out of the lineup—you are a free man," he said loudly. I was so excited that I left hastily, thanking the colonel and Jacobson for their aid. I was on my way out when I realized I had no place to go; I was a free man without a home. I turned around and ran back toward Jacobson. I asked him how I could find Polta, and he gave me directions. "Take this street and go straight ahead—it will lead you to Polta. You will see our boys at the main gate, so you cannot miss it." I asked him whether he had seen my father, who he knew very well. He answered, "No, he was not among the people liberated at Polta." I thanked him for the information and left the yard. That was the last time I saw Jacobson; later, when he was released from his job, he became homesick and returned to Riga.

With a smiling face and a happy feeling, I left the camp and began walking toward the plant, as Jacobson had directed. This walk was very different from previous ones, for I was no longer surrounded by armed guards, and nobody directed me to move faster or in any particular direction. The cobblestones became soft and comfortable beneath my feet; I felt as though I were walking on clouds. My fear and the uncertainty of my life were erased from my mind. I felt like crying out to the free world, "At last, at last I am free, I am a free man and so much more. I witnessed the humiliating defeat of the evil German forces that had sought to destroy me."

For several years I had been forced to walk only on the pavement, so I was not used to being on the sidewalk. After trying for a short time what had been forbidden for so long, my natural instinct sent me back to the pavement. I walked with confidence, slowly but steadily, and looked around my new world. It was wonderful to walk again as a free man without being disturbed by anybody.

Not a soul was in sight, and everything around me had been devastated and looked uninhabitable. Completely destroyed and partially damaged buildings stood unoccupied, and I passed areas where an entire block of homes had been reduced to rubble by the bombs of the Allied air force planes. Proceeding down the wide street, I passed an empty prairie in which many kinds of spring wildflowers were in full bloom. They looked very beautiful, since I had not seen such beauty for some time. The field looked like a rainbow sprung from paradise, but I saw ugly scenes as well, with fallen trees and broken branches all over the streets. There was no need to clear them away, since nobody was out walking or riding.

My calm walk in the clear, warm morning reminded me of my long overdue need for nourishment. No food was available in this wasted part of the city, so I tried to satisfy my smoking habit instead. I picked up some cigarette butts that had been discarded by the U.S. soldiers and put them in my pocket; I could not smoke them right away because I had no matches. As a liberated man, I was completely on my own; there was nobody to hand me a meager daily food ration. I could no longer get supplementary soup from the Polta kitchen, and no more handouts of any kind could be expected. I would have to provide all of the necessities for survival.

My long, exhausting walk ended when I saw the red brick of Polta's administration building. A small crowd stood at the main gate like a welcoming committee, ready to receive me. I walked as fast as I could to reach my old friends. I shook hands with them, exchanged greetings, and happily embraced those I knew from my barrack. The men looked at my disheveled appearance, which reminded me of the time I had arrived at Stutthof from Estonia; then, too, the inmates had looked at my shabby clothes and dirty face and hands. Still, my friends were as happy to see me as I was to see them.

They asked where I had been, so I told them about my escape from the plant, my time in hiding, and the way I had been liberated with Jacobson's help. I was told they had been set free by the U.S. Army three days ago. I asked whether they knew of my father's whereabouts; to my sorrow, I received another negative answer. I was so happy, however, that I was ready to start celebrating this day of liberation with my friends. To my disappointment, they had already had their own festivities a few days ago. I felt out of place, for these men had already found apartments and had plenty of food. None wore his old camp clothes, and they all looked neat and clean. I, on the other hand, had no place to sleep or food to eat. My first happy gathering with the other camp survivors ended painfully.

Nachke and his men stood near us next to a covered truck. I was told he had found a warehouse cooler filled with meats and dairy foods and had supposedly hidden some of the goods in the truck. I asked him, "Can you give me some food? I just left my hiding place—I became a free man this morning." He asked abruptly, "What do you have for me?" I told him I had nothing to give him. "Go there," he said, pointing to a cluster of undamaged buildings. "Over there you will find everything." He was looking for valuables and meant to suggest that I should loot the apartments. He was trying to start a black market, right in front of Polta. Knowing his brutal character, I said nothing and left him. I was so heartbroken that I decided to go to my old barrack and occupy my old, familiar bunk.

I walked to the building but found nobody there. I went to Father's and my bunks, as though I might find some clue regarding his where-abouts; nothing helped, and every bunk was in disarray. I was filled with grief and frustration and did not feel like staying there by myself, so I went to visit the other barrack. Two men about my age were sitting at the table. They had chosen to remain in the environment most familiar to them, as they were not over the initial shock of having lost their slave status overnight. Their adaptation to a new world order as free men would have to come gradually. At the end of the barrack, a few men were lying in their bunks and moaning from stomach pain. I asked the men at the table what was wrong with the others. They replied, "They are ill because they stuffed themselves with too much food during the celebration."

I told them about the ordeal of my liberation and that I had not eaten for the last day and a half. They felt sorry for me and offered me freshly baked bread and a variety of foods in cans and jars. Seeing the agony of the men in the back, I limited my food intake to the delicious bread and some coffee. I knew my stomach would have to adjust slowly to a free man's nourishment. The young men were very kind, and I was impressed with their behavior. I knew we all had a common understanding of each other. They gave me food and satisfied my immediate needs; I may have forgotten their names, but I have never forgotten their friendship.

Everyone had different reactions to liberation; for some, deeply ingrained attitudes that were no longer appropriate took time to fade. I had problems adjusting as well, but my prime obligation was to find my father and renew the lost bond of his companionship. I was very sad about not having found him; in this hour of freedom, I wanted to share my happiness with someone who was special to me. We had shared the darkest days of our lives, and now we could not enjoy the day of our freedom together. This would have been the perfect time to have told my father how much he had meant to me through all those years.

14

In Search of Father in Magdeburg

I had returned to Magdeburg, the only home I knew in this foreign country. Although I was somewhat confused and bewildered, I felt comfortable amid familiar surroundings, although our three R's—rules, regulations, and regimentation—were gone and had been replaced with more immediate concerns. My life in the camp had been guided and controlled by my superiors, which left me no option but to do what I was told and worry about keeping up my strength. Things were different now, and I had to be concerned about my personal needs.

The two young men I had met in the barracks were very helpful. We laughed a little and cried a little but did not want to reminisce about the pain of the past, except my friends told me what had occurred in the labor camp during my absence. We recognized our good fortune in having survived the inhuman conditions of the concentration camps; we now had to face new challenges one day at a time. We decided to live together; we would look for an apartment the following day. After the plans had been made, we went to sleep. I felt I had given the two men the inspiration needed for a renewed life.

It was a restful night; my old bunk suited me fine, but my father was constantly on my mind. I wanted to help him, but I had no idea where he was. Unconsciously, I had a sense of guilt, feeling I had let him down. I tried to convince myself that this was not the time to deal with my feelings; my priorities were to find a place to live, obtain enough food, and find decent clothing. Only then could I undertake the difficult task of finding my father.

The next morning the three of us rose quickly, and I put on my lucky rucksack—my sole possession. Our first stop was at the daily gathering place of our friends at the Polta gate, where we heard the latest news about the rest of the world and updates on our now-scattered friends from the camp. For me, this place was ideal, for only from a gathering of our people would I learn my father's fate. Although the war continued, guns had been laid to rest in our part of Magdeburg.

On the other side of the Elbe River, the Americans had encountered ferocious resistance by a small SS unit, and sniper fire could be heard. Mingling among the freed inmates, I soon gathered the first clues regarding my father's whereabouts. On the last day in the camp, about a hundred inmates had been sent to the other side of the Elbe to dig trenches for the civil defense. The bridge was knocked out by Allied aircraft, and the men had been forced to remain there. I hoped Father was one of the men stranded on the other side and that as soon as the resistance of the SS unit ended, one of us would be able to cross the river so we could be reunited.

The general mood of the men was very upbeat. Most of the survivors intended to leave Magdeburg as soon as possible. With the help of the well-organized Bricha (an underground Zionist organization), many intended to leave for Palestine through secret routes that avoided the stringent British blockade of the Palestinian shores. Under pressure from Arab leaders in the Middle East, in 1936 the British government had adopted a declaration known as the *White Papers.* Jewish emigration to Palestine was considerably curtailed, and the blockade was strictly enforced to prevent the excessive flow of new arrivals. With the full participation of the Royal Navy at sea, the army on the ground, and the air force in the skies, the British accomplished their task. Some of the men wanted to join the underground fight in Palestine to free the land from the British Mandate handed down by the League of Nations after World War I and establish an independent Jewish state. I was unable to make any plans for the future without my father at my side, so my companions and I left to search for a new home.

We needed to find an abandoned apartment in an undamaged building. Many Germans had left their homes to escape the war zone for a safer place or had gone into hiding in the country because they were involved in Nazi activities. Some distance from the camp, among some damaged buildings, stood a two-story building that had been untouched by the bombs. We looked through the window of the first-floor apartment to observe the conditions inside. All of the furniture and knick-knacks were still in place; everything looked fine. Our persistent knocking at the door drew no answer, so we decided to take over the apartment. As we were about to break the lock, two young German women came through the gate of the yard. We told them, "We want to get into this apartment." In a frightened voice, one of them replied that the apartment was occupied; the owner was out of town and was expected to return shortly, so they could not let us in.

We let them know that we would not be deterred; we wanted to occupy the apartment. This pleased the women, who had thought we had come to loot the place. After liberation, our camp survivors had become well-known to the citizens of Magdeburg for their aggressive behavior. Looting for food and clothing had become common, but no molestation ever took place. Reluctantly, the women, who lived on the second floor, let us into the apartment. Everything was clean and neatly arranged, and there were enough beds for the three of us, as well as furniture in the living room and kitchen. We were reminded that we could not stay long, since the owner would arrive from the country in a few days. This did not bother us, since we knew nobody would dare evict us. I was pleased that we had been able to secure a home so easily.

Our next step was to find clothing and food. In the few grocery stores that remained, we could get food without paying or producing a ration card; we merely asked or pointed a finger and were given anything we desired. The tragedy was that very little food could be found on the shelves, so we were forced to scavenge in collapsed or abandoned buildings. We knew the Germans had stored their food in cellars during the war to better preserve it, but clothing would be found only in apartments whose occupants had fled. Much of what was left had already been ransacked by our friends, so we had to go to a neighborhood the other survivors had not yet visited. We eventually found cellars that were untouched, and we found a variety of canned fruits and vegetables, preserves, and other edible items. It took a few days to bring everything we had found to our apartment. We also had freshly baked bread each day from the neighborhood bakery; early in the morning, when the long line from the store extended to the sidewalk, I would simply walk in and receive a loaf or two. The Germans in the line could only look at me with sad, frightened faces.

In the abandoned apartments we found closets filled with clothes and coats and drawers packed with underwear and shirts, but we took only items we liked and that fit. My friends and I roamed freely from one building to the next, even when the Germans were present. The German population was, understandably, very unhappy about the outcome of the war and about our presence in the city. The several hundred Jews freed from the Polta Werke had essentially taken over Magdeburg, and the local residents were very uncomfortable. They graciously tolerated every move we made, as they understood our feelings and the fact that they had become the most hated people in the world.

Within a few days, my roommates and I were well established in our first home since the long, traumatic Nazi ordeal had begun. It was hard to get used to a normal, human way of life; it is easy to take the slaves out of slavery but much harder to do the reverse. I had to use extra effort to remember to walk on the sidewalk. I developed a dislike for food I had liked before, and my body began to reject food it had once accepted. My body chemistry needed time to make a complete readjustment, both physically and mentally. I had to overcome some fears and insecurities on the inside, and I was filled with hatred and revenge on the outside.

One day I decided to say a final, symbolic farewell to my old, evil home. Undisturbed, I entered the Polta plant and walked into our labor campsite, reminiscing about morning roll call and the other outdoor activities. I went to my old bunk and looked around: There were no loud conversations among the inmates, and stillness and sadness dominated. The bunks were no longer neatly made and covered with blankets; only torn straw sacks and old blankets were visible. The empty tables that had once been shiny were covered with a layer of dust, and the once clean floor was soiled and cluttered with debris. I became very sad and sentimental; being here brought back many traumatic memories. I looked at Father's bunk and even imagined which bunk Boris would have occupied had he been here with us. As I walked through the barrack, heavy tears streamed down my cheeks, different from any tears I had shed before. I used to cry because of my suffering and pain; I now cried with happiness because I had survived so many hardships and abuses. I wept for my perished mother and siblings and, most of all, for my father. Gone were all of my school and neighborhood friends and my uncles, aunts, and cousins from Riga; from a large family tree, only one little branch had survived—me. I was left alone in the land of my persecutors.

As I took my last look at the barrack, I knew I was witnessing the end of a terrible era in my life and in the lives of many other Jewish men and women. Later, I would be asked how I had managed to survive the genocide of the Third Reich; even with the passage of time, I would not know what to say. In school we wrote complicated math formulas and words that were difficult to spell, but we never dealt with techniques for surviving the unthinkable barbarity of Nazi Germany. As a young man in Riga, my life had been completely supervised by my mother; during the days of incarceration, my guide had been my father. Now I had become an orphan. I was unprepared to solve this complicated puzzle; I had to utilize all of my strength and knowledge to overcome my problems alone. With thoughts of the loss of my loved ones, my emotions became so powerful that I feared I might not survive to enjoy my precious freedom.

In the short time I spent revisiting my barrack, I became emotionally exhausted, yet I walked to the other barrack to see how my sick friends were doing. When I reached their bunks, nobody was there. I noticed some clothes hanging from a bunk, an outfit usually worn by inmates of a concentration camp that consisted of a jacket and pants in gray and blue stripes. This prisoner's outfit belonged to one of the two men who had come from Buchenwald as work replacements for our sick inmates. After the liberation, the inmates had abandoned these garments for civilian clothing. I had never worn such an outfit, but the uniform impressed me so much that I grabbed the two pieces and clutched them close to my chest. I was sorry I could not find the cap that went with the outfit. I decided this striped jacket and pants would be my silent witness to the many years of captivity filled with degradation and hunger, to the years filled with bitter tears and sweat constantly dripping from work and fright. I left the barrack never to return, holding the clothes tightly under my arm as a symbolic shield of a mission accomplished. I returned to my apartment a calm and satisfied young man who had left his muddy and unscrupulous past behind. I was ready to undertake the tasks needed for self-preservation as a free and dignified man.

My living conditions were excellent, and I was pleased with the way everything had worked out. My roommates and I respected and cared for each other as devoted friends, had enough necessities to satisfy our needs, and were on our way to a normal life. At times, we spent days apart, but I accepted this as a usual occurrence between close friends. I became better acquainted with the city of Magdeburg, although most of the streets were impassable because of the heavily scattered debris from the crumbling and destroyed buildings. Wherever I went I met sad, subdued Germans who usually greeted me with false smiles; I replied in the same manner to please them. In the grocery stores and bakeries, I was very well accommodated, even though I never paid the shopkeepers for their merchandise.

After the lengthy, celebratory euphoria of liberation, the former kacetniks (a Yiddish nickname for a concentration camp inmate) settled down throughout the city, and the majority managed to live comfortably. Although there was a shortage of food, we always found a way to obtain something for our consumption. The presence of the kacetniks made the Germans very uncomfortable and frightened, although we never harmed them. We, along with the foreign gentile laborers, dominated the streets, so the German population did not go out unless there was an urgent need for them to do so. The daily meetings of our men at the gate at the Polta Werke slowly ceased as we became occupied elsewhere. Some of the men befriended the U.S. soldiers, especially those of the Jewish faith. A few even found employment with occupational military installations. One of our youngest men proudly wore the uniform of the U.S. Army and was adopted by one of the units stationed locally.

After a few weeks, the sniper shooting stopped in the tiny enclave across the Elbe, and the SS unit surrendered to the U.S. armed forces. The bridge over the river was still impassable, but a few of the liberated men managed to cross to our side. I spoke to them and heard about their ordeal in that small, isolated part of the city, but nobody could tell me of my father's fate, although they did verify his presence. I was told that after the liberation they had been prevented from crossing the river, so many men had headed east toward the Soviet-occupied territory. This encouraging information made me happy, but it was followed with devastating news. During the final U.S. assault on the city, the SS guards had kept all of the inmates locked up in a fenced-in tennis court. The Allies, flying over Magdeburg, assumed the men on the court were German soldiers and bombed them, which resulted in some casualties. After hearing this tragic report, I decided to cross the Elbe immediately to find my father, whether dead or alive. Even if I had to go all the way to Berlin, which was occupied by Soviet forces that were known to be hostile to the Eastern Europeans in Germany, I was determined to find him at any cost.

I quickly undertook the dangerous journey to Berlin. I knew I would likely face a grim future in the Soviet Union if I were apprehended by Soviet authorities. I prepared some sandwiches, then neatly folded the striped prisoner's outfit into my rucksack; this would serve as evidence that I was an inmate of a concentration camp. I left my house early the next morning, crossed the Elbe on a ferryboat, and walked for several miles. I explored every avenue but found no trace of my father or any other kacetniks. I reached a station where I could catch a train that would take me to Berlin, and I boarded with great fear. I soon found myself in enemy territory, the Soviet-occupied section of Germany. The train made several stops, each of which I thought would mean the end of my short-lived freedom. Soviet Army patrols were present at the stations but did not bother the passengers, and I reached Berlin without being harassed. This was fortunate, as I was traveling without identification papers; the only proof of my lawful stay in the city was the outfit in my knapsack. I got off the train at a large railroad station and had no idea where to go. I noticed a few Soviet soldiers patrolling the station, but there were very few, and I was able to avoid them.

I left the station and wound up on the street in completely unfamiliar surroundings. I wondered where I should go now that I was in Berlin; then I thought of the pretty Jewish girl with whom I had worked at the railroad repair shop in Riga. I remembered our pleasant conversations and recalled my last words to her: "I will meet you on Kurfürstendamm Boulevard after the liberation." I decided to go to there, as it was the only street name I knew in the city. Walking from the well-populated area that surrounded the train station to the empty side streets, I noticed that the streets of Berlin looked like those of Magdeburg—they were filled with fallen debris and crumbling buildings. Finally, I found Kurfürstendamm Boulevard and wondered whether I would find my friend. If so, would I recognize her distinctive walk? It would have been nice to have met her on the street of which she had spoken so much. To my sorrow, I never saw her and never learned the fate of the young Berliner girl I had liked so much.

I continued down the devastated street and was disappointed not to see the scenes my friend had so eloquently described. The beautiful trees in the middle of the boulevard were gone, and the uncultivated ground stood bare. The buildings were supposed to be attractive, but they were now dilapidated and abandoned; some were even boarded up. After walking for several blocks, I decided to sit down on the steps of one of the buildings to relax and have a sandwich from my rucksack. I had a good view of my surroundings. The city was empty; not a living soul, not even a dog or a cat, was in sight. I just sat and looked at ghostly Kurfürstendamm Boulevard.

Two young men suddenly appeared from nowhere. I walked over to them to get information about Jews who were living in Berlin, hoping to be led to my father. When I came closer, I recognized them as two brothers from Riga. I knew Petka, the elder, and had seen the younger one, although we had never spoken. I was surprised to see them in Berlin, as the last time I had seen Petka was in the Little Ghetto in 1942. I had assumed he had belonged to the Jewish ghetto police and been massacred with the rest of the group before the liquidation of the ghetto. I approached them happily and tried to strike up a conversation, but they did not recognize me and continued walking. I did not want to reveal my identity or that I knew them from Riga, as I was frightened by their strange behavior and did not know what they were doing in this deserted area. My sudden appearance probably made them wonder who I was and how I had gotten here; each of us may have feared that the other was a Soviet informer. I managed to ask whether they had seen any Jewish people, my father in particular, and received a quick answer that they had met no Jews in Berlin. With this disappointing response, I departed; the brothers' reply served notice that I had nothing more to do in Berlin but should return to Magdeburg.

I walked back to the train station, where the schedule showed my train would leave in an hour. I occupied an inconspicuous seat so as not to be too exposed to the constant Soviet Army patrols. Across from me, I noticed something that looked like a telephone booth. I got closer and saw it was an automatic picture-taking machine. I decided to take a picture of myself dressed in the striped prisoner's jacket, since the picture could be taken only from the waist up. I put several coins in the slot, sat down, and looked into the lens. A moment later I heard a click, and a photo slid out of the machine. It was not the best quality, but I was happy to have a picture of me dressed in the camp outfit, for it was the only such photo I had ever possessed.

The hour I spent waiting in the station passed quickly. I soon left the Soviet-occupied territory behind; I was glad to return to the American side unharmed. After walking several miles, I crossed the Elbe by ferry and was soon back in my apartment. My roommates were surprised by my quick return and eager to hear about my daring journey, but I was sad and disappointed. My short stay in Berlin had been so emotionally draining that I could not spend much time with my friends; I needed a well-deserved rest.

About twenty years later, I was amazed to learn that my father had worked as a cook for a Soviet Army unit that customarily patrolled the area where my Berlin-bound train had made a stop. If those soldiers had apprehended me, I would surely have met up with Father, and he would have come to my rescue, as my friend Jacobson had done in the German war prisoners' camp.

Following my failed mission, I had to determine my next move. The entire Jewish community in Magdeburg was prepared to leave Germany for Palestine, breaking the British immigration restrictions. A date was set for all volunteers to board a train for Italy; from there, they would proceed by boat. My roommates were going with the others in the illegal emigration to build a Jewish nation and asked me to join them, although they knew how determined I was to find my father. Had he been at my side, I would have been ready to help with this monumental task; around two thousand years had passed since the rulers of the Roman Empire had expelled our ancestors from their homeland and renamed it Palestine. The time had come to reestablish a state for and by the Jewish people that would be a home to every persecuted Jew, no matter what his or her origin.

I finally decided to look for a job or to volunteer for the U.S. Army. I went to the American military administration building in Magdeburg for information; I found myself in a long hallway with several doors on both sides, each bearing the name of the occupying officer. I looked for a Jewish-sounding name and found the office of a Lieutenant Jacobson; under his name it said "Labor Relations." I did not know what *relations* meant, but I knew the word *labor* very well. I knocked at the door and entered the office, where a young lieutenant sat at his desk. In my poor English, I tried to explain that I was looking for work, but he could not understand me, so I asked whether he spoke any Yiddish. He did not, but he had discerned that I was a camp survivor looking for work. He told me he had nothing for me, but he led me to the window and pointed to the army field kitchen across the street. I was to go there and see a soldier named Sam, who spoke Yiddish. Before I left, Jacobson took a handful of cigars from the humidor on his desk and gave them to me. I thanked him and then went to see Sam.

When I found him, Sam was already expecting me, as Jacobson had phoned him before I arrived. Sam was a sergeant from Brooklyn who spoke excellent Yiddish; he was in charge of the field kitchen for the unit. He seemed to be a warm and concerned person, for he wanted to know what had happened to my family and told me about his family in the United States. We became instant friends; he offered me soup and treated me to chewing gum, chocolate bars, and cigarettes. He invited me to come each day for a meal. When I left the compound, I felt rejuvenated and mentally uplifted because I had finally found someone in the U.S. Army whom I could trust. I visited daily and received a generous meal, followed by friendly conversation.

One day I asked Sam whether he could do me a favor and find out the address of my aunt who lived in the United States. He was more than willing to help, so I told him the only two things I knew about my aunt: Her name was Betty Delson, and she was a physician in Chicago. I was assured that within a few weeks the American Red Cross would locate my aunt and give him the information.

After a week, Sam informed me that his unit was to be evacuated from Magdeburg, along with the rest of the U.S. occupying forces. According to the agreement of the Potsdam Conference—the last major Allied conference of the war—Germany would be divided into four occupied zones: U.S., British, Soviet, and French. The city of Berlin, which had been freed by the Soviet armed forces, would also be divided into four separate zones. As compensation, the Soviets would receive additional German territory freed by the U.S. forces, including the city of Magdeburg. Sam could not give me a definite date for their departure, but the information made me very sad, since I was about to lose my only

American friend.

The day arrived when my roommates were to leave for Palestine. After a hearty good-bye, they departed, ending our short-lived friendship. At the railroad station, no boxcars awaited them; this time it was regular passenger cars that were quickly occupied by the several hundred free men and women. The long train was filled to capacity with happy people bound for the promised land. In a single weekend, Magdeburg had become free of nearly all of the inmates of Buchenwald's Labor Camp I at the Polta Werke. Only a handful of kacetniks remained, myself included. The city no longer looked the same. Gone were the hundreds of familiar faces on the street and at various gathering places; gone were the vital young people who had been freed from slavery. I was heartbroken because I could not join my friends on their journey. I found myself in a completely different environment—I was no longer surrounded by people who had shared my experiences. The two young German women who lived above me tried to comfort me and take care of me. They cleaned my apartment, and I was often invited to their house for dinner. Still, despite their best intentions, I felt uncomfortable in the company of German women with whom I had little in common.

I continued my daily visits to my dear American friend, Sergeant Sam, as long as possible. One morning, I arrived at the yard where the field kitchen had stood; nobody was there, and the yard was filled with debris. I was told the army unit had received orders to evacuate Magdeburg immediately. I was sorry I never said good-bye to Sam. I had lost my one remaining friend and would never learn my Aunt Betty's address.

As soon as I heard of Sam's departure, I decided to follow the Americans. I packed my rucksack and joined the many others on the highway. I walked many miles before I was picked up by one of the evacuating U.S. Army units heading to Munich. When I arrived there, I sought food and shelter at a United Nations Refugee Relief Agency (UNRRA) camp, where I registered as a displaced person (DP). My first night was completely sleepless, as I was obsessed with thoughts of my father. I had escaped from the Polta Werke under the assumption that the U.S. forces would free Magdeburg within hours and I would be reunited with my father, but nothing had happened as I had expected. I wondered all night at the UNRRA camp if I had done the right thing, moving even farther from where I had last seen my father. Eventually, I decided that since nobody had seen him dead, he must still be alive. I made up my mind to turn around the next day and go back. I hitchhiked, going against the flow of those leaving the Soviet zone; I was one of very few returning. When I finally reached Magdeburg I felt a sense of relief, as though this was where I belonged.

I assumed I would occupy my old apartment, if possible. When the two German women saw me, they greeted me with hugs and kisses. My presence excited them so much that they cried with happiness; they seemed delighted to see me again. I thought, I was gone only a few days, yet their attitude has changed so much for the better. At first I could not understand their newfound admiration, but as our conversation progressed, I began to understand the situation. When the Soviet military had entered Magdeburg, a vacuum was left by the departing U.S. administration. The Soviet soldiers went on a rampage of looting and stealing from the German civilians, often molesting and raping the women. The population in Magdeburg had become hysterical; such things had not happened during the U.S. occupation. My reappearance guaranteed their safety, which explained their emotional welcome.

When I awoke the next day, I went outside to see what was going on. I saw something I did not expect: The streets were void of civilians. Very few Germans ventured outdoors, since they felt more secure inside, but many Soviet soldiers and officers could be seen. I went out cautiously, always aware that I might be stopped by Soviet patrols and questioned about my identity. I made my way through the side streets and soon entered the main thoroughfare, Halberstadterstrasse. As I walked down the street, watching the heavy military traffic, I noticed a small, private car approaching. The faces of the two occupants seemed familiar, even at a distance; as they got closer, I recognized the men as fellow kacetniks Saschka Falkon and Mischka Kukla. When they saw me, they pulled over. After a hearty greeting, I asked them where they had obtained the car, and they told me they had found it abandoned in a garage. In our short conversation, I learned that several of our men had remained in Magdeburg and often met at Max Finkelstein's apartment. As soon as they gave me the address, I was on my way. Max had been my barrack elder at the labor camp, and I thought of him as a decent, sympathetic fellow inmate. He had always had a kind word for Father and me, and he never forgot to stir the soup to find an extra potato for us.

I had no problem finding Max's apartment. I hesitated, not knowing how he would react to my unexpected appearance. I soon went in, and Max and his girlfriend, Bella, greeted me in a friendly way. I told him how I had heard about him and his new home; he asked how I was doing and what had happened to my father. He and Bella listened intently and expressed sorrow over my father's disappearance, but they had no information beyond what I already knew. Max had his own concerns about his elder brother, who was also at Polta; like Father, he had vanished without a trace. All Max knew was that his brother had also been sent to the other side of the river to dig defense trenches. I asked about our kacetniks in Magdeburg, and Max told me the few survivors who remained were working as translators or office workers for the Soviet kommandant and other military institutions. I asked him to find out whether the Soviets needed additional help, since I was available and would gladly work in any capacity. He promised to look into it, although he did not think any jobs were available.

During the course of our conversation, I found out that Max and Bella considered themselves to be married. Bella had lived in Vilna and had been sent with the other women from Stutthof to the labor camp at the Polta Werke. This was the first time I had met her, and she made a profound impression on me. Her slim figure, dark brown hair with a part in the middle, cherrylike brown eyes, little nose, and beautiful white teeth with a smiling face brought extra charm to her pleasant personality. I felt so comfortable in their company that I stayed several hours on my first visit. I still remember that Bella would not let me leave until I had joined them for a cup of tea. I could not refuse my new friends; after enjoying tea and a cookie, I finally left their house, intending to return soon. I was confident that my return to Magdeburg would not be in vain.

On the way back to my apartment, I decided to take a detour through the section of the city most severely damaged by the Allied air force's constant bombardment. I carried huge emotional bruises from my years of incarceration and was soothed by walking in the devastated area where only sections of buildings and the debris of fallen structures stood. Very few people walked through these streets. A leisurely walk through this area helped me to overcome my traumatic memories. In these empty, dilapidated German living quarters, I saw the reflection of my own broken home and the destruction of my loved ones. Under the tons of rubble many innocent Germans lay buried, just as an uncountable number of innocent Jews lay buried in unmarked graves throughout the German-occupied land.

Civil order was slowly taking hold in the city, and it became increasingly difficult for me to get free food. The storekeepers were willing to sell to me without my having a ration card or waiting in line, but they insisted on being paid. Although they would occasionally accept partial payment, I was not working and, therefore, had no money, so I faced an economic struggle for my daily survival.

I eventually solved this problem, but in a way I did not like. The two women who took care of me gave me money, and I would buy food for all three of us. The advantage for them was that I got everything we needed without having to produce a ration card or stand in lines, which they would have had to do. I wondered where they got the money, since neither of them held a job and they were not considered to be wealthy spinsters. They were initially reluctant to reveal their financial source, but I persisted, and they gave in. The owner of the building we occupied sent them monthly payments for guarding and taking care of his property while he was in hiding in the country. They refused to reveal the owner's name or whereabouts, and I accepted that; I no longer cared what anyone did as long as I could get my way and live in comfort.

It became a habit to start my day by visiting neighborhoods that had been destroyed. It gave me mental nourishment to see the once flourishing part of the city now in ruins. I visited Max and Bella daily, and we soon became close friends. Max tried hard to find employment for me but to no avail; all of the jobs with the Soviet authorities had been taken by other Riga kacetniks, who spoke both German and Russian and thus were good servants to the Soviets.

The Soviet administration appointed a burghermeister (mayor) in every town and village, and Magdeburg soon had its own German administration. Appointed head of the Jewish Gemeinde (a community organization) was one of only a few native Jews in the city; the rest were camp survivors who had remained in Magdeburg but were officially considered foreigners. The president had some political power within the new administration and was always ready to help us if we were in need. He was in constant contact with us, and I saw him on several occasions at his house; each time, he was very helpful to me in some legal matter.

The native Jewish community came out of hiding, with some people admitting they were Jews in mixed marriages. Slowly, a somewhat normal way of life began to take shape in the city of Magdeburg.

I was looking forward to the weekend when I would meet most of the remaining survivors at Max and Bella's house. When I arrived, Mischka and Saschka were already there. One by one, our friends arrived. I knew most of them, but even if one did not know the others, it took only an instant for a friendship to be formed. Very quickly, the cozy living room filled with people. Among them were my friends Zamka and Basja, who lived together and, like Max and Bella, considered themselves to be a married couple. Also present was Morris Fonarov, who I knew by his nickname, Fedka. Conversation was constant and energetic; it seemed voices were coming from every corner of the room. Some of the stories were tragic, but most were humorous anecdotes from everyday life at the new workplaces. Many considered their jobs to be rewarding, but others seemed to be wasting time in the Soviet administration offices. A lengthy discussion took place about how dumb some of the superiors were, and I learned that many of my friends were doing very well as a result.

Such was the case with Abraschka, who was called Ben-Ame; he had started as a translator, but his superior, a colonel, depended so heavily on his advice that he had been promoted to a policymaking position. He had his own office and was an influential adviser to the Soviet kommandant's office in Magdeburg. Another friend, Choke, who had been my main competitor in obtaining soup from the Polta plant kitchen, was the coordinator of food and supplies for the Berlin army garrison. He was constantly on the road between Magdeburg and Berlin in the company of high-ranking Soviet officers; we considered such a job a "fat" occupation. We also discussed who was buying and selling on the black market. Our conversations were conducted in Yiddish, our mame loschen (mother tongue). I enjoyed being in the company of my friends, although I mostly listened rather than participating.

Max and Bella should have had a revolving front door, for our friends were constantly coming and going. One day a young Jewish lady came in with a hysterical expression, as though something terrible had happened to her. She had come to see Bella, and the two went into the adjoining room to discuss some intimate matters. After a short while they reappeared in the front room, and the young woman was crying hard. I had never seen her before and wondered who she was, so I asked Bella. She replied, "This girl is Frieda Zevin, my friend from Vilna who worked with me at Polta. She has some personal problems." Bella did not wish to reveal Frieda's problems in front of our friends, but I was sympathetic nonetheless.

When Frieda was ready to leave, I asked if I could accompany her, and she accepted. We said little as we walked, but I soon felt compelled to ask what had upset her so greatly. She was reluctant to tell me her troubles but finally did, saying, "I was going steady with a very good-looking lieutenant in the Soviet Army; we were together almost every day. I fell in love and intended to marry him, but when I saw him today he told me he is being called to Moscow and will not be able to see me anymore." I naively asked whether he was a Jewish officer. She replied hesitatingly, "No, he was not; he was Russian." I challenged her: "If he is not Jewish, why should you care that you lost him?" Frieda tearfully replied, "You do not understand—I was very much in love." Our conversation stopped there, since we had reached her house. I realized I was talking to a foolish young girl, so I said good-bye and left. The next day, I met Frieda again at Max's; there were no more tears, and she was able to speak more easily. Since she had recuperated from her ordeal, we could talk freely about any subject. This was the beginning of our friendship, which grew so strong that we saw each other almost daily, not as lovers but as buddies.

My morning walk through the ruins of Magdeburg now brought more sadness than satisfaction, for every day I saw a number of tragedies that had been experienced by the German population. Children of all ages played on the unsafe streets amid debris and broken glass, and buildings adjoining formerly well-groomed playgrounds looked ready to collapse at any time. Homeless people found shelter in the basements of collapsed buildings where I had once searched for food. I could tell a basement was occupied when the narrow passage off of the street had been cleared to lead to these makeshift living quarters. During the day, the inhabitants sat outdoors on collapsed walls or benches fashioned from materials they had found. At night, they were limited to artificial or no light, as all communication and power lines were out of service.

The fallen trees, broken branches, and crumbling buildings stood as a symbol of the Jewish communities destroyed wherever the Nazis had set foot. The brightly colored wildflowers were now surrounded by over-grown weeds and stood lonely and unattended above the ruins of homes where people had once lived happy lives. God knows how many children, mothers, and fathers lay undiscovered beneath the rubble; I was reminded of the countless Jewish graves that would never be known to the world. The daily exploration of these ruined neighborhoods was a learning experience I will never forget. A few years earlier, I had been forcibly separated from my loved ones; since then, I had sought consolation for their sake. In these quiet, destroyed streets of Magdeburg, I found such solace, which brought me closer to reality. After the end of this vicious war, I saw the sufferings of my enemy for the first time. I witnessed the Germans creating their own unraveling tragedy; in them, I saw the reflection of my unfortunate life.

One morning, I wound up on a small, isolated street, without a soul in sight. It looked as though no one had been here since the Allied forces had bombed the area. My curiosity led me to explore, and as I moved around on the crumbling bricks, I noticed a canvas-covered object leaning against a garage wall. The top was under a layer of dust, and the bottom was covered with debris. I blew off some dust and removed the canvas. To my surprise, I found an undamaged motorcycle; the wide, extending eaves of the garage must have protected it from falling bricks. I cleared away all of the obstacles and pushed the bike out to the street. It seemed to be in good shape: the key was still in the ignition, the tires were inflated, and the tank had some gasoline. It was a beautiful, mid-sized motorcycle. The only problem was that I did not know how to start or operate such a machine. I had ridden my own bike but never a motorized one.

I was determined enough to push the bike all the way to my house, where I thought I might find someone to teach me how to run it. Half-way down the main road, I noticed a group of men. I asked whether any of them had any knowledge of motorcycles; I told them I had been riding this bike when it suddenly stopped running. One of the men was willing to help, so he checked out the motorcycle, and I watched every move he made very closely. He started the motor easily, then I asked him the functions of every knob on the steering handle. After receiving the necessary information, I let him ride the bike to make sure it was in good running order. Just from watching, I learned the basic skills of starting and steering the motorcycle. I thanked him for his help and proceeded home, riding my new possession. When I got to my apartment, everybody was amazed to see me on this beautiful bike; I told them I had received it as a gift from someone who had considered it useless. When I drove to Max's the following day, my motorcycle was the main topic of conversation.

One of my morning walks led to a change in my life in Magdeburg. Among the ruined buildings I saw one of the abusive supervisors from the Polta plant. He had always proudly worn the Nazi Party emblem on his lapel and acted menacingly toward the helpless Jewish workers. I had often observed him and thought he would someday be called to account for abusing my fellow inmates. After the liberation, he knew I was after him, but he had managed to get away every time. I had found him once before, during the U.S. occupation of Magdeburg; at the time, the military police had refused to interfere and arrest him, as they had no standing order to incarcerate German citizens. When the plant supervisor saw me this time, he ran into a building to hide; he probably assumed I had not seen him. Without delay, I turned around and rushed toward the street to find a Soviet Army patrol that would be willing to take him into custody. Unfortunately, the soldiers refused my request, just as the Americans had; they had received new orders not to arrest suspected Nazis but to leave it up to the newly created German police to do so.

I was frustrated and angry that I was unable to do something about this man who had caused so much pain and hardship to others. First the Americans and now the Soviets refused to do anything about him; this was beyond my comprehension. Was I supposed to forget about this Nazi supervisor and remove him from my wanted list? I became so furious that I was ready to take him on myself. I walked into the building where he was hiding and asked about his whereabouts. I was told he lived there but was not at home. I did not know what I would have done to him had I met him face-to-face; he was too powerful a man for me to fight, so I could only have called him dirty names.

The following day, I decided to pursue the matter on behalf of my friends, so I went to the German police headquarters on Halberstadterstrasse. Examining the first-floor signs, I noticed one that said "Kriminal Polizei Politische Abterlung [Criminal Police Political Section]"; this was the department I needed. I knocked at the door, walked in, and saw a tall, slim, middle-aged man sitting behind a desk. I explained my purpose in coming to see him; he listened closely and was very interested in my background. He said he was the chief of this newly organized police department and spoke at considerable length about his political activities. He had been an active member of the German Social Democratic Party before 1933 and, during the Nazi reign, had been in and out of jail constantly. When he became free, he had to accept any manual work he could get to sustain his family; before the National Socialist German Workers Party had come to power, he had been in charge of a police unit in this building. The chief liked me so much that he offered me a job in his department; they had three men but needed a fourth. He did not mind that I had no previous police experience or any knowledge of preparing typewritten reports. I gratefully accepted his offer and within days began my first job.

I was delighted with my new career as part of the Magdeburg Police Department. Our officers did not wear uniforms or carry arms; their only identification was a metal badge in a leather case. I was still plagued by having found no clues about my father's disappearance, but my daily work had to continue. I proudly rode my motorcycle to work and received free gasoline and safe parking in the garage at the headquarters. I became well acquainted with the three other officers in our department, all of whom were former members of Germany's Socialist Party. For several years, they had been harassed by the gestapo and at times had been locked up in various jails. From day one I felt a close camaraderie with them, since we had all suffered somehow at the hands of the harsh Nazi regime. My co-workers were very helpful. They were familiar with police procedures and regulations, and I learned a great deal by watching what they were doing or being coached by them. Within days, I knew all of the legal formalities and had mastered typing with two fingers.

Every morning, we received our daily assignments; we were usually paired up, but for simple investigations each of us was on his own. Our department handled only political problems, such as past harassments and unlawful, brutal behavior by Nazi Party members against other German citizens. The chief explained every pending case, described how it should be followed up, and made sure we handled each complaint within the limits of the law. After investigating someone, we would make an arrest if warranted—this was the part of the job I liked most. I was always delighted to see the surprised face of a Nazi offender when he was taken into custody, as well as the sad faces of his family members. It made me as happy as a child in a candy store, for I was witnessing in reverse what had been done to my countrymen during the war. In my wildest dreams, I had never imagined I would become the arresting officer of a Nazi activist; I loved what I was doing and was paid well for it. All of the men in the office were natives of Magdeburg; I was the only foreigner and Jew, yet I felt comfortable because I was surrounded by people whose lives were in some way similar to mine.

Slowly, I made headway with my work. The short written reports were prepared solely by me, but my co-workers were always willing to help me do the longer ones; our department budget did not provide for a secretary or a typist, so we had to do all of our own paperwork. My strenuous efforts in my high school German classes paid off, as I was able to use my German to satisfy the demands of my new occupation.

One day, I received a telephone call from the president of the Jewish Gemeinde in Magdeburg. He asked me to come to his house, where I was introduced to a Jewish lady in her thirties named Lizel. A native Magdeburger, she was the daughter of a mixed marriage in which the father was Jewish and the mother was German; only after the war did she admit she was part Jewish. She invited me to Sabbath dinner to discuss a problem she was having regarding her house. Lizel lived with her mother in a large home on the outskirts of the city; when I arrived, the dining room table was beautifully set, and the Sabbath candles were lit. After a dinner prepared by Lizel's mother, we went into the parlor.

Several years before, Lizel told me, a Nazi neighbor in their old neighborhood had become the gauleiter (county president) of the district, and he and his family had moved into this spacious house, which had allegedly belonged to Jewish people. Lizel remembered that her father was able to keep his job while other Jews lost theirs, for her mother tried to protect him as much as possible during the Nazi era. When the war broke out, her father was taken away and never heard from again. Her mother, a Gentile, made every possible inquiry but could not discover his whereabouts. Lizel was still in school, and her mother was forced to take a job to support the family. After the war, when the Nazi gauleiter abandoned the house and disappeared, documents were found to prove he had ordered the arrest of Lizel's father. Lizel and her mother had moved into the gauleiter's house and were now seeking to take possession as reparation for his actions and for all the suffering they had both endured for so many years.

The Americans, although the occupying force in Magdeburg, could grant the two women permission to occupy the house but could not give them legal possession. When the Soviets took over the city administration, the procedure to receive legal ownership was started yet again, which is why they needed my help: I knew Russian and would be able to expedite Lizel's claim quickly. At first, the Soviet authorities had been receptive, and it had looked as though Lizel and her mother would win their appeal, but the situation changed when a German administration was appointed. The new burghermeister demanded that the property ownership be decided by the court, so the new authorities had no power to make reparations for all the evil that had been inflicted on Lizel's family by the gauleiter. The situation became even more complicated when close relatives of the gauleiter also put a claim on the house. Lizel had tried to do everything possible to keep her claim from reaching the court, and I, as an officer of a sensitive political branch of the city government, tried to influence the "movers and shakers" in the new administration. I wanted to please Lizel and her mother, since I fully understood their suffering during the Nazi era.

My relationship with these women continued, and they asked me to move into their home. I felt I had outgrown my apartment and was ready to live in a more affluent neighborhood, so I gratefully accepted their offer and moved in. I occupied a spacious bedroom and was well taken care of. After so many years alone, they were happy to have a man around the house. Lizel's mother had converted to Judaism in memory of her husband, and I was comfortable living among Jews again. Both ladies treated me royally and appreciated everything I tried to do for them.

Soon after I moved in, another man appeared in the household. Toward the end of the war, the Italian Army was under German supervision; many Italian officers objected to that arrangement and refused to obey orders. They were then sent to detention camps, one of which was in Magdeburg. Lizel used to stand at the camp's wire fence to observe the good-looking men and bring them cookies her mother had baked. When the war ended and the officers were released, Lizel befriended one of them. They had an affair and she became pregnant, but they were married before the baby was born. The lieutenant moved into the house, and I was no longer the preferred man. Lizel began to take me for granted, no matter what I did for her, and our relationship slowly deteriorated.

A long period of time had elapsed, and I still enjoyed my work as much as I had when I started. The once impassable streets had been cleared of debris; the fallen bricks and glass had been shoved into empty lots where buildings had once stood. My department received many complaints and inquiries about the Nazis' past unlawful activities against the citizens of Magdeburg. The investigations often had to be conducted in the devastated areas of the city, and my co-workers had difficulty finding some of the addresses. I had an easier time, since I was familiar with the neighborhoods where street signs or numbers on the buildings might be missing; still, at times I went to serve an arrest warrant and found the address in ruins. My early wish became a reality, however, when I was sent to pick up the Polta supervisor whom I had pursued for so long; he was to come in for questioning at police headquarters. When my partner and I arrived at his building, we were told he and his family had moved but were given no location. In a way, I was glad I did not have to see him again and was pleased that my last confrontation with him had forced him from his comfortable apartment and into hiding.

I thought police work was an honorable occupation and a very educational experience. I considered myself a lucky man, having survived so many hardships during my incarceration in various camps. My enemy had sought to destroy me; instead, I had lived to see a complete physical and ideological rejection of Nazism by the newly created German society. The once popular Nazi salutes of "Sieg Heil" and "Heil Hitler" had almost been erased from people's minds; the time had come when I could contribute in my small way to undoing the evil teachings of the Nazis and justly prosecute those who had supported the Third Reich's "final solution." My mother, who remained the spiritual guide in my life, would have been proud of the work I was doing on my family's behalf.

My job afforded me a certain degree of monetary fulfillment, and I could obtain anything I needed with my earnings. I was introduced to an elderly German businessman who had been a textile wholesaler; he was now out of business but had hidden large quantities of textiles. To support himself and his wife, he sold various bolts of fabric for suits, dresses, and coats. He would see his buyers, the kacetniks, in his house and show two or three pieces at a time. Like the rest of my friends, I could now participate in these transactions. I bought several yards of fabric in various shades and designs for suits; my best purchase was a large piece of heavy wool for a winter coat, with beaver fur for the lining. The gentleman referred me to a tailor to make the coat, which was greatly admired by my friends when it was done. I quickly acquired a beautiful wardrobe and saved some fabric for Father, should I ever find him.

His absence was the only unhappy part of my life, although I enjoyed the company of my friends, the kacetniks, particularly my buddy Frieda, who became my trusted adviser and companion. A highlight of our friendship came when she surprised me for my birthday with a beautiful silver ring; my initials in Russian were on the face, and my concentration camp number, 95933, and her name were engraved on the inside. For her birthday, I gave her something she wanted very much but could not afford: custom-made leather boots with a side zipper, which were very fashionable at the time. We wore our respective gifts proudly.

Since the police headquarters was just around the corner from their home, Max and Bella became my closest friends. I saw them almost every day and heard the latest gossip about our friends. On weekends, we often had picnics in the outlying woods, but Frieda and I missed one because of an accident. I came to get her on my motorcycle, and we rushed to get to the designated picnic spot on time. We were halfway down the road when one of the tires blew out; because of our high speed, the motorcycle hit the curb. We both ended up on the sidewalk; Frieda had bruised her foot and I my right shoulder. We walked to her house to wash up and take care of our injuries; we then spread a blanket in her backyard, opened the basket of food she had prepared, and enjoyed our own private picnic. To this day, I still cherish Frieda's ring and nurse my injured shoulder.

Everything was going my way until an unexpected call changed my life. It is true that all good things must come to an end, and so it was with my enjoyable work in the Magdeburg Police Department. The problems began when the chief called me into his private office and warned me to watch out for our newest employee; he had been sent by our superiors and had started to behave as though he were in charge. I assured him that I would be very cautious. Nobody in our office knew this middle-aged German man who had become our new office manager. He gave us orders without consulting the chief. Through our conversations I learned he was a longtime member of the German Communist Party. For many years, he had been incarcerated in jails and concentration camps and was liberated from Dachau when the war ended. On the advice of my good friend the chief, I was very careful about what I said in the office.

After a few days, I was notified that I had been singled out to appear at our department headquarters in Halle, fifty miles from Magdeburg. That same day, a man about my age who I did not know approached me in the hallway at work; he introduced himself as a detective whose office was on the second floor. He told me he had heard I was supposed to report to our superiors in Halle and said he had been called to appear the same day. The man asked me whether we could travel together, so I agreed to take the train with him, although it was a puzzle to me how someone who worked on a different floor could know so much about me. He told me he had obtained that information from one of his co-workers. He spoke German with a foreign accent, so I asked him where he was from. He said he came from Lithuania, had been arrested by the gestapo as a member of the Socialist Party, and had spent several years in Buchenwald before joining the police department a few months prior to our meeting. On the appointed date, I met him at the station, and we boarded the train for Halle.

When I entered the spacious building in which my meeting was to take place, I recognized it as the headquarters of the NKVD, the Soviet secret police. I was led into an office where a husky colonel was sitting at his desk, waiting for me. I was asked several questions; he spoke in short sentences and went straight to the point without blinking an eye or cracking a smile. He asked me to evaluate the behavior and work habits of the other men in my department, both in and out of the office. I answered that I had not noticed any irregularities, and it seemed everyone in the office was fulfilling his duties diligently. The colonel emphasized my chief, but I could make no negative observations about this very competent friend. I was ordered to watch more closely and to return in a month with a more detailed report. My new acquaintance was interviewed separately, with the same result; he had to return with a more explicit report about his office as well. We were confused as to why the NKVD had chosen us to spy on our colleagues and wondered why we had to give a critical character description of the conscientious men in our offices. We returned home in great despair.

The next day, my chief asked how my interview in Halle had gone. I could not reveal to him the true nature of my conversation with the colonel; I could not even tell him I had to return later. My answer was short and completely false: "The Soviet authorities wanted to know more about my personal life, since I am from Riga, and what my plans are for the future in Germany." It took me a while to realize what the NKVD was up to: A purge was underway. The new man in the office had been sent by the Soviet authorities; he was a trusted Communist, unlike the chief, who was a Social Democrat. The NKVD was looking for a fabricated excuse to remove my friend from his job and turn the Magdeburg Police Department into a Soviet-run agency. I was horrified at the thought of being a part of such a conspiracy and decided to distance myself as much as possible. I knew what the Soviet secret police represented; they were unscrupulous and evil, with no consideration of individual human rights. As much as I liked my rewarding job, I felt I had to give it up; I knew nothing could be gained by becoming involved in this dangerous, messy plot against the innocent men in my office. Realizing the seriousness of my next meeting with the NKVD officer, I began to think of a way to leave my police job honorably. This undertaking was by far the most worrisome since my liberation and could not be discussed with any of my friends, so I had to make all of my decisions on my own.

The month had passed, and I still could not find a way out of my job, so I had to keep my appointment with the NKVD. The same rough-looking Russian officer immediately asked, with a smile, whether I had any favorable news for him this time. Knowing what he meant, I began to tremble with fear, yet I managed to maintain my composure. I answered politely, "I am sorry to say that the people in my office are performing their assignments more than adequately. I did not notice any extraordinary activities that would harm our department in any way. In my opinion, they are all trustworthy employees of the Magdeburg Police Department. In fact, with the help of the new man in the office, we have become even more efficient." I stopped there, for my intention was merely to inject a favorable opinion of the man who had been planted in our department. Seeing the unsatisfied expression on my interviewer's face, I concluded that he did not like my answers; he had probably expected to hear a completely different, and deceptive, story. To collaborate with the

NKVD officer, I would have had to invent false accusations against my chief and co-workers, and I would never unjustly accuse people I considered to be my friends. Our short conversation ended abruptly, and I was told I was free to go.

I left the office disappointed about the way I had been treated, but I also very much feared for my own safety. The Lithuanian detective who had come with me to Halle had had the same experience, spending only a few minutes with the officer who interviewed him. Deep in thought, we went to the station and boarded the train home, not speaking a single word, since each of us feared the other. When we arrived in Magdeburg we said good-bye, and I never saw him again. The next day, I was back on the job, and no questions were asked by anyone in the office, as no one had known about my second trip to Halle. I was desperate to leave the police force but could not find an appropriate and safe excuse. I thought about leaving Soviet-occupied Magdeburg and seeking shelter in the U.S. or English zones; however, I was convinced I could only find my father while I was still in Magdeburg. Since I could not end my search until I found him, I decided to remain, for better or worse.

On one of my frequent visits to the president of the Jewish Gemeinde, I was introduced to a tall, slim Jewish man in his mid-fifties named Abraham Glanz. He asked me, "Govorish po russky?" I answered, "Da, ja govoru." He had asked whether I spoke Russian, and I had replied that I did. I then asked him where he had learned the language, and he began to tell me fascinating stories about his life. He puffed on a cigar as he talked, relieving unpleasant thoughts of past years; he was probably relieved to be able to vent his accumulated mental anguish to a fellow Jew. He had been born in Russia; after finishing the cheider, the religious primary school, he enlisted in the czar's army for forty years so that as an adult he would not be subjected to the Pale of Settlement imposed on the Jewish population. He became, as they were known, a "Nikolajevskij soldat"; when World War I broke out, his unit was sent to fight against the German Army of Kaiser Wilhelm II.

After a short skirmish, he was taken prisoner and sent to Germany; following the armistice agreement he was released, but he liked the country and decided to remain. Consequently, he lost contact with his entire family in Russia and never did learn what had happened to them. He married a German girl and settled down in her hometown of Egeln, where they opened a tailoring and cleaning shop. As a newcomer, he was not well-known to the townspeople, so nobody knew he was Jewish, which enabled him to feel very comfortable in his new environment. During the Nazi regime, he was not bothered by anyone; his German-sounding name helped to protect him, as everyone assumed he was one of their own. Still, he was very cautious and mostly stayed indoors, so his wife became the spokesperson for the family. They had two children, a daughter and a son, both raised as Germans.

After the end of the war, Glanz openly admitted he was Jewish and was surprised that his neighbors were not bothered to have a Jew in their Judenrein society. He was accepted as the most honorable citizen in town by everyone, especially the burghermeister; he could have had any government job he wanted, but he had no desire to get involved in politics. He wanted to remain a humble Jew and was happy to be left alone in his tailor shop. Glanz told me he was called several times a day to the Soviet kommandant's office in Egeln to act as a translator for the burghermeister or other German officials. I found it incredible that, even after so many years, he still remembered Yiddish and Russian.

He said he had to spend a great deal of time at the office with no compensation, but the job appealed to me nonetheless. I asked whether he might help me by finding out whether the Egeln kommandant could use a full-time translator; he said he would inquire on my behalf through a Jewish army major who worked with the kommandant and with whom he was well acquainted. After a lengthy conversation in German, Russian, and some Yiddish, he invited me to his house to meet his family. I accepted his offer and told him I would visit the following weekend. This unexpected acquaintance with Abraham Glanz began a new, exciting era in my life.

15

The Town of Egeln and the Discovery of Father

It was spring 1946 when I met Abraham Glanz, who everyone knew as Abe, and I kept my promise to visit him at his home in Egeln. The following Saturday I was on my way, eager to see how a Jewish man had fit into a totally gentile society in a small German town. I also hoped to land a job with the forces of the Soviet occupation, which would give me a reason to leave police work. Egeln was about twenty-five miles from Magdeburg, and it took two hours to reach it on my motorcycle. The Glanz family graciously received me into their spacious home, which was connected to Abe's store. Mrs. Glanz and their daughter and son welcomed me and made my visit very pleasant.

Since I had arrived well before dinner, Abe decided to show me the town, and we visited the town square in the center of Egeln. He walked proudly, as though he were the king of Egeln and a Jew liberated after many years in seclusion. Abe pointed out significant buildings, including the Soviet kommandanture where he was trying to find me a job. Everyone who passed greeted him, as well as me; I, too, became an important person and had to keep saying "Guten Tag; Guten Tag."

Abe seemed to be admired by every person we passed; he was like the town celebrity. The people looked on him as one of their own; many stopped just to find out how his family was. Some people may have viewed Glanz as a rare piece, a Jewish antique worthy of admiration who had survived a reign of abuse. During our short walk, he introduced me as his friend to dozens of people who all called him Abe. He also introduced me to several Soviet officers he knew who were stationed in Egeln and spoke to them in Russian. He pointed out the former homes of the local Nazi leaders, all of whom he had known by name. Proudly, Abe emphasized that none remained in Egeln. He called them a bunch of perverts and cowards who had no thoughts of their own and merely followed others blindly.

At dinnertime, we joined the rest of the Glanz family in their dining room, where a multicourse meal was served in my honor. After dinner our conversation inadvertently turned to the problems the Jews had faced during the Nazi era. Mrs. Glanz, a mild-mannered lady with a soft voice, explained the difficult and frightful life she had led during this time, beginning with Kristallnacht in Magdeburg and other cities. Nobody but she had known Abe was Jewish, and she stressed the fact that he had not associated with anyone to avoid exposing himself. The entire family had suffered as a result, especially the children, since their father did not participate in any school or outdoor activities. They told me they had initially harbored some suspicion about their father but did not know what to think. Only after the war did they discover the truth, and they felt sorry for him, forced as he was to hide his Jewish identity for such a large part of his life. As young adults, they were happy they were part Jewish and wanted to learn about the Jewish culture and traditions to which they had never been exposed. I heard of many dreadful hardships and sleepless nights Abe and his wife had been forced to endure during Hitler's reign. They were glad the experience was behind them so they could finally have a normal family life.

The next day after breakfast, Abe and I went to look up the army major to whom he wanted to speak about my employment. We approached the major, and I was introduced to him as Glanz's new friend from Magdeburg. The Jewish officer was very happy to meet another Jew. I introduced myself as being from Riga, and he told me about his family; he came from Moscow and was married but had no children. By profession, he was a chemical engineer and had been sent to Germany as part of a team that conducted research at the chemical plant in the village of Westeregeln, which was within walking distance of Egeln. I asked whether the kommandant or anybody in his unit needed a full-time translator; he was delighted to hear that I was willing to work in Egeln, but he warned that the kommandant there was a Russian colonel who had little tolerance for Jews. He thought it best that he approach the colonel when the latter was in a receptive mood so the major would be more likely to receive a positive answer regarding my possible employment.

I told him I would return to Egeln the following weekend and that I would like to know the outcome of his conversation with the kommandant at that time. I thanked the major for his efforts. At noon, I was ready to return to Magdeburg, and I expressed my appreciation to Abe and his family for their generous hospitality. Before I drove away, Abe told me something that had been bothering him for a long time. He said, "I have yearned for many years to see and speak to another Jew; I am very glad you came." I replied, "I enjoyed being with you; thank you for inviting me to your house. I will see you next week, my friend. Dosvedanje [Good-bye]."

I drove home feeling very satisfied. The Glanz family had been very hospitable. With my busy days in the office, the daily visits with Max and Bella, and my on-and-off relationship with Lizel and her Italian husband, the week passed quickly. When Saturday arrived, I was more than ready to go to Egeln. I went directly to Abe's house, and he told me the Soviet kommandant was willing to hire me as a full-time translator. This unexpected news pleased me greatly. I felt as though I had reached heaven; it was a joyful occasion. Finally, I would have peace of mind with regard to my relationship with the NKVD. I went to see the Jewish major, who confirmed what Glanz had told me. He was kind enough to introduce me to the kommandant in his living quarters, where I was politely received by a Russian colonel who missed no opportunity to drink vodka and offered me a toast to *nazdarovje,* or good health.

We discussed my duties, compensation, and the availability of daily meals in the officers' mess. Everything seemed fine, and I was to begin work within a week. Abe was pleased that I had been offered the job and would be living in his town. He said, "We will have a yiddishe mishpoche [family] here. Now I will be able to relearn my Yiddish, as I have not spoken it for so many years." It was evident that he longed for a Jewish soulmate in this gentile community. I had to secure living quarters with a local German family, since it would be impossible to commute daily from Magdeburg. The Pfestafings, a mother and daughter, were willing to take me into their home in Westeregeln. After making the necessary arrangements, I returned home.

I was a very happy man again, not so much because of the new job as for the opportunity to honorably and safely distance myself from the eventual struggle for reorganization in the Magdeburg Police Department. My friends, the kacetniks, heard about my new job in Egeln and were pleased for me but did not know the real reason I was giving up my prestigious police job. Lizel was upset that I was leaving her; she told me my presence made her feel at ease. At the time, she was still engaged in the legal battle for possession of her house, and she still wanted to have me around. I needed to leave Lizel's house on good terms so that if things did not work out in Egeln, I would still have a home in Magdeburg to which I could return.

The next day, I went to see my department chief to tell him I was resigning from my job. His kind face registered amazement; because of our good relationship, he had never imagined I would consider leaving the department. I felt very bad about not being more truthful with him, but under no circumstances could I reveal my reason for leaving the police force. I thought, If only I could tell you, my dear friend, that it is time for you to leave your position as well. The NKVD is after you, and you will eventually be removed forcibly. You do not deserve such disgraceful treatment. The chief accepted my resignation, and I left his office wishing him the very best; he, too, wished me good luck in my new endeavor. On my last day in the office, I cleaned out my desk and looked around the large room where I had spent several happy months trying to erase the mountain of crimes committed by the Nazis during the reign of Adolf Hitler. I would miss my extraordinary German co-workers, who were always willing to help me in any way they could. Before saying good-bye, I thanked them all for their friendship and camaraderie. This was the first paid job I had ever held, and working in this environment had taught me a lot, but I was forced to leave all of that behind and start a new chapter in my life.

By the middle of that week, I was ready to move. Lizel and her mother helped me pack, assuring me that their house would always be available for me. I packed my belongings in two large suitcases, which I said I would pick up over the weekend. My essential clothes and personal belongings were packed into my rucksack and a box that could be secured to the rear seat of my motorcycle. I left Lizel's house with the understanding that I would be back within a few days.

In under two hours I was at the Pfestafing's house in Westeregeln. The mother and daughter were happy to see me and showed me around their home, guiding me to my room. It was a comfortable, one-story house on an unpaved street, and the small grocery store they owned was attached to the front of the house. In the rear of the house was a large garden where they grew a variety of vegetables. The Pfestafings also had a cage that contained several domestic rabbits, which they raised for their own consumption. Mrs. Pfestafing was a slim, soft-spoken, very likable woman. The daughter, Fridel, looked a few years younger than I and was very welcoming, so the environment was extremely hospitable.

That evening I discovered that Mr. Pfestafing was an active member of the National Socialist German Worker's Party—the Nazis, for short—and had been a minor official in Westeregeln. When the U.S. occupational forces evacuated the region and the Soviets took over, he had been arrested and sent away; his wife and daughter did not know his whereabouts. This was the third time I had become the security shield for an unhappy German family. I had lived among German people for over a year, and my dislike for them had diminished somewhat, but I was shocked to discover I had taken up residence in a Nazi household. In days past, the smiles and kind words of my hostess could have brought bitter tears.

The following day I got up early so I would be on time for breakfast in the officers' mess, located in the Soviet kommandanture building in Egeln. When I arrived, every officer was seated at the table. Before anyone had his first bite of food, it was customary to have a drink of vodka, and the men were gulping it like water. I was hesitant to drink alcohol on an empty stomach, since I had never done such an unconventional thing. The officers sitting nearby convinced me, so I partook of some of their favorite alcoholic beverage; within a week, I had learned to gulp a good portion of a glass at once. The food was simple but well prepared. After the morning meal, I joined the kommandant in his office, where he gave me several assignments to translate various documents.

A few days later, the kommandant had to attend a morning meeting with the burghermeisters of the surrounding towns, and I went along in case a translator was needed. When we arrived the colonel went into the building, and I remained outdoors, waiting for him to call me. As I stood there a Jewish girl about my age came out of the building; she was the translator for the local kommandant. She approached me and said, "You are Jewish"; I affirmed that I was. She continued, "I have not seen a Jewish face for a long time. Are there any Jews in this part of the country?" I replied, "I know many Jews in Magdeburg." She revealed that her name was Minna and that she used to live in Vilna; she was a survivor of several work and concentration camps in Poland and Germany. Her last labor camp, not far from Berlin, had been liberated by the Soviet Army, and she went to work as a translator for the men who had liberated her. When the Americans evacuated the area, her unit was assigned to take over the military administration of this small town, which was how she came to be here.

Minna was so busy that she had no time to visit the surrounding towns. The Soviet officers treated her well and with great respect, and she felt comfortable among them, but she still yearned to see another Jewish person. She invited me to visit her over the weekend. I explained that it would be impossible, since I spent my weekends in Magdeburg with my old friends. We had to end our conversation, as the officers were leaving their meeting. Before I left, I promised Minna that I would visit her for a short time on my way to Magdeburg.

The next weekend it was time to see my friends and pick up my suitcases at Lizel's house. When I got to Lizel's, the entire family was already up. After friendly greetings, I was told the most bizarre story I had ever heard. In sad, hysterical voices, Lizel and her mother said, "We were robbed! We were robbed by Russian soldiers! They stole your two suitcases!" Everyone became very excited, as though the robbery had just taken place. When they had calmed down, I asked when it had happened, what their personal loss had been, and how the Russian soldiers had gotten in.

The unpleasant story then unraveled. The day I left, two armed soldiers had forced their way into the house. Everyone was very scared and did not know what to do, but Lizel, who was pregnant, was brave enough to beg the soldiers to leave their home and not harm them. She told them there was nothing valuable in the house, but the soldiers ignored her. After searching the main floor, they went upstairs, where the bedrooms were located. They checked out the other rooms and did not take a thing; when they entered my room and saw the two suitcases, they grabbed them and left the premises without saying a word.

I listened quietly to the story and did not know what to make of it. I could not believe this was how the "robbery" had taken place. "From all of the closets filled with clothes, the robbers took only my suitcases, without knowing what was in them? Is that not a little bit odd?" I asked. Lizel replied that it was very strange but insisted it had happened exactly as she told me. "Did you tell the robbers there was nothing valuable in the suitcases?" I pressed. "No, I did not, because I was very frightened. I was glad to see them leaving the house," she answered. The greatest irony was that nobody had bothered to call me in Egeln when this alleged incident had occurred. "Why did you not call me right away? Why did you wait for me to come to you?" I asked. Several mumbled replies followed, all lame excuses that were not worth pursuing. I was very angry and abruptly ended the conversation. I could not accuse them of lying, since I did not have the facts as to what, if anything, had happened.

There were two plausible explanations for the disappearance of my suitcases. One possibility was that Lizel and her unemployed husband had taken them and later convinced her elderly mother that a robbery had taken place. I knew they were having financial difficulties and were the only ones who knew about the valuable contents of the suitcases, which could bring a decent price on the black market. The second possibility was more serious—that there really had been two armed soldiers and that they had been sent by the Soviet secret police. Was it possible that the NKVD was looking for me? I thought fearfully. Knowing the character of those people, it was possible that when they discovered the contents of my suitcases, they had kept the valuable loot for themselves and dropped the case against me, lacking enough evidence to accuse me of anything. Either way, I never learned the exact circumstances that surrounded the disappearance of my suitcases.

It was heartbreaking to lose so many of my personal belongings. I had worked diligently to afford such a select wardrobe and had also saved some choice textiles for my father. By far the most damaging loss, however, was that of the concentration camp outfit. All the clothes were replaceable except for those. The gray-and-blue-striped gown I had found on the first day of my liberation marked the end of my Nazi slavery. It symbolized the loss of many of my basic human rights and my loved ones; it also represented thousands of Jewish camp inmates who had died and were buried wearing similar clothes. I had not lost an old, worn-out concentration camp outfit—I had lost the token of the darkest days of my life. The picture I had taken of myself in the Berlin train station was insignificant at the time, but it became a treasure I have kept to this very day.

The baffling loss of my possessions subsequently left me with unpleasant thoughts about the family who had been so close to me and considered me one of their own. It was sad and discouraging to see such a negative aspect of our relationship; still, I left Lizel's family in a friendly manner, despite the tense atmosphere. I followed my plan to see Max so I could hear about the latest happenings in town. At this time a massive number of refugees were passing through the city, and the Germans were being forcibly expelled from the Balkan countries as disloyal citizens. From Eastern Europe, the Jews were fleeing the Soviet sphere of influence that had been agreed upon at the Potsdam Conference. The Jews were disappointed with the Soviet system and the renewal of anti-Semitic activities in Poland.

The Jewish and German refugees arrived penniless, with only the belongings they could carry. Some of the gentiles tried to settle down in Magdeburg; others proceeded to the next towns. The Jewish people, however, had set their final destination as Palestine; to them, Magdeburg was only a stopover and a gathering place. Their journey was guided and organized by the Bricha, a Zionist organization that had developed an underground route that ran from Vilna to various seaports in Italy. From there, the refugees secretly boarded boats and hoped to reach the shores of Palestine by circumventing the stringent British coastal blockade. A large majority of the illegal immigration boats were intercepted; the people were transferred to the island of Cyprus, and the boats were confiscated by the British forces.

When I arrived at Max's, I asked whether any of the Jewish refugees—participants in what was known as the aliya—were from Latvia. He replied, "To my sorrow, none of them was from our homeland, but I will keep asking about my brother and your father." I spent the rest of the day at his house, since I wanted to tell him and my other friends about my new job and the people in the small town of Egeln. When I told of the misfortune of losing all of my clothes, everyone was amazed that such a thing had taken place; robberies had become very rare in Magdeburg. In the evening, I returned to Lizel's house for my overnight stay. The next morning, her mother again expressed sorrow over my loss, but I had little to say to her. I said good-bye and left for the Pfestafing's, where I spent the rest of the day building a new friendship in Westeregeln.

I did not return to Magdeburg for several weekends for fear of the NKVD agents who might be after me, as well as to allow things to cool off at Lizel's house. This gave me an opportunity to become better acquainted with the officers of the kommandanture on their days off; I was particularly interested in developing a closer friendship with the Jewish army major. Not a day went by that I did not see Glanz or some of his family. The majority of my time, though, was spent with the major and his close Russian friend, a lieutenant who was a co-worker. Both men were chemical engineers who had been sent to Germany on assignment. A third chemist, a female lieutenant, was also part of their work unit. They had little to do with her socially, for she was very bitter. The major and lieutenant told me they thought she was vicious and had strong anti-Semitic feelings.

Working in Egeln, I felt a deep sense of contentment and satisfaction. I enjoyed my tasks in the kommandanture, but after I had worked for the kommandant for a week or more, the Jewish major requested that I be temporarily transferred to his small engineering unit, which consisted of the three chemical research engineers. Their workplace was located in an old chemical manufacturing plant in Westeregeln. The main products they manufactured were a variety of fertilizers. The unit was known to all as a chemists' research unit, but that was just a cover-up; the team was actually copying the production manuals and patented chemical formulas of the products that were manufactured in the plant, and the female engineer was making scale drawings of the machines. This proved to me that Soviet technology and the manufacture of chemical fertilizer products and other items were underdeveloped. During the war, Nazi Germany had dismantled the Soviet industrial plants; now, as the victorious nation, the Soviet government was gaining knowledge without destroying the plant.

My work consisted of translating the plant's secret, patented formulas and manuals into Russian so they could be applied to and used in chemical factories in the Soviet Union. The plan was supposed to be kept secret. When I began, some translations had already been done by the three Soviet chemists. Since they knew no German, they had used a commonsensical method of translating the materials. From me, however, they expected much more; I was handed a stack of technical papers to translate. I worked on them for several days but was not pleased with my accomplishment; I had to ask for a technical dictionary. My request was ignored, the engineers told me, because Moscow would not be able to reply in time, but the truth was that the chemical "experts" were afraid to request a dictionary because doing so would have caused their superiors to suspect that they were not competent enough to complete their assignments.

The officers and I concluded that better results could be obtained if we all participated in the project together. To everyone's surprise, this plan worked well. The three chemists and I met in an empty room in the plant's office building and analyzed the complicated chemical procedures and manuals one by one. When they explained the different technical expressions and their functions, which I did not understand at first, we were finally able to determine the proper translation into Russian. In time, the difficult puzzles became an enjoyable game of words for us all. After several weeks we had progressed so far with our translations that the officers decided to relax a little and skip the afternoon work, so I found myself with a good deal of free time.

I began to visit the plant and office facilities more frequently and became acquainted with one of the office workers named Trudel. She had a small apartment on the factory premises where I often saw her after working hours. At first, these visits had to be kept secret; I sneaked in so nobody could see me. She wanted to avoid vengeance from the local villagers because she was receiving a non-German visitor. I respected Trudel's wishes, since I understood how clannish the people of this small village could be. When we saw each other during the day, she would guide me through empty fields to avoid meeting the locals. Holding hands and laughing, we would stroll down a path, admiring the beauty of the nature around us. We truly enjoyed each other's company, for there was always something to discuss.

Our closely guarded secret could not be kept for long in this village, and everybody eventually knew we were dating regularly. The name Trudel sounded too harsh to me, so I called her Trudchen. She had lost her parents when she was a small girl and barely recalled them; she had been raised by an aunt who lived in Westeregeln. Trudchen was left alone after high school when her aunt died, so she got a job at the chemical plant. Since she had no family, the managers felt sorry for her and offered her an apartment on the premises. Her living quarters were some distance from the manufacturing buildings, which enabled us to enjoy our privacy. I felt very comfortable with her; I often shared my most intimate, deep-rooted feelings and always received the gentle reply I sought. Perhaps, because Trudchen had experienced a lonesome childhood and had grown up without parents, she could understand my feelings better than anyone. I always took her advice seriously, since I knew she was sincere and logical in her thinking. Our relationship became so intimate that I often wondered what could come of it if Trudchen had been Jewish.

A few weeks had passed, and I decided it would be safe for me to renew my regular visits to Magdeburg. My first stop, as always, was Lizel's house; when I walked in, I did not like what I saw. Lizel had given birth to a little girl; her nanny, a young female German refugee, now occupied my room. She told me she had been there only a few days to take care of the newborn. I asked Lizel and her mother whether anyone had asked for me. "No, nobody has been looking for you," they replied, which pleased me very much. I was disappointed and hurt that I had not been informed about all that had happened during my absence; I felt like an unwelcome guest. We had little to say to each other, and I thought it was time to end my relationship with this family. I left Lizel's house, never to return; the long-lasting tie between us had finally ended.

Upon my return, I spent the evening with the Pfestafings. Fridel asked about my friendship with Trudchen, and I admitted that I saw her frequently, because she was a fine and respected lady in the village. I sensed a certain jealousy in Fridel's eyes, and she finally said what she really had on her mind: "I would like it if you spent some evenings with me, too." I did not want to hurt her feelings, so I promised to spend more time with her. In this small, sleepy village, there were few social activities for the locals; the Pfestafings spent most of their evenings listening to the radio or reading the newspaper. Fridel had some close girlfriends, but there were no men her age for her to date. When she sought my company in the evenings, I knew it was because she was bored and lonely. I felt I had to do my part to maintain good relations in this house, so I did my best to be a good companion whenever time permitted.

Mrs. Pfestafing spoke at great length about her husband and defended his membership in the Nazi Party. She hoped he would soon be released by the Soviet authorities. She and her daughter told me about their frequent visits to a fortune teller who lived in the next village. I asked them to let me know when they planned to go again; Mrs. Pfestafing promised she would do so.

Slowly, I got to know the Westeregeln villagers; they were mostly elderly people and young women, some single and some married with children, whose husbands had not returned from the war. There were no men in the area, and the women were very sad. The married women were frustrated because a long time had passed since the end of the war, but their loved ones had not yet returned. The Americans had released all of their German war prisoners, but for some reason the Soviet Union had not done the same. Out of desperation, a few women sought the friendship of the Soviet officers, but most kept to themselves. I was initially considered a stranger by the villagers, but in time I gained their trust. At many private or public gatherings, they talked to me freely; the women sometimes spoke frankly about their boring lives and how lonesome it was not to have a man around the house.

My stay with the Pfestafing family was very pleasant. Mrs. Pfestafing tried hard to please me and often prepared German dishes for my sake. The most memorable meal we had was a roasted rabbit with all of the trimmings, just like an American Thanksgiving feast. Fridel took care of the house and helped in the grocery store. She, too, was always kind to me and would do anything I asked. I appreciated the generosity of these women.

They soon planned another visit to the fortune teller, so I joined them. The fortune teller was well-known in the area and had many clients. When we arrived, I was soon called into a dimly lit room. An old lady with a severely curved back occupied a seat at a small, square table; opposite her was a chair, where I sat. This was the first time I had seen a psychic. She looked at my palms, then took out a deck of playing cards and placed them on the table with their faces up. After a few minutes of thought, she began to tell me what she saw as she looked intently at the lines on my palms and compared them to the cards. She predicted so many positive events for me that I have forgotten most of them, but even now, half a century later, I still remember the old lady's basic predictions, which were later fulfilled. She told me, "You will hear extraordinarily happy news; you will travel through deep water on a long voyage, and you will become a wealthy man." She did not tell me of the high mental price I would have to pay to reach these goals, nor did she say what she meant by "a wealthy man."

I continued my visits to Magdeburg. On my way, I would visit Minna for an hour or two. She always planned something special that would not take too much of my time, such as a well-prepared breakfast, a nature walk, or a simple conversation. In Magdeburg, I was always welcomed at Max and Bella's house, but because my time was limited, I could only see those friends who came to see me there. I always made sure I met up with my buddy Frieda. During my visits, I always asked about my father and encouraged others to do the same among the transient Jewish refugees.

After one of my trips to Magdeburg, I was returning home on my motorcycle when I saw a bicyclist approach from the opposite direction. When he came closer, I recognized his face—it was the evil supervisor I had pursued from the very first day of my liberation, the one who had vanished. By the time I could turn my motorcycle around in the heavy highway traffic, he was far ahead of me. When he saw me coming, he abandoned his bicycle and fled into the high cornfield. I waited for him to come out. After a while, I finally gave up and continued on to Westeregeln. I received great satisfaction from the fact that I had scared him so much. Now I knew his hiding place was in one of the villages in the area.

My undiminished perseverance in finding my father soon paid off, and the psychic's prediction came to fruition. On one of my visits to Magdeburg, Max surprised me by informing me that his cousin Ezka was among the Jewish refugees; he had managed to escape from Soviet Latvia and had stopped in Magdeburg on his way to Palestine. I was speechless at such unexpected news. I thought, He is my moshiach, my messiah, who has fulfilled my lifelong dream. I called out excitedly, "Where is he? Where is he? I have to talk to him." "He should be back soon," replied Max. I did not leave the house; I could not afford to miss Ezka. I sat tight, waiting to hear what he had to say about my father.

After a short time this brave young man appeared, and I immediately pressed him for information. I found out that Ezka had also been a concentration camp survivor and had been liberated by the Soviet Army, at which point he had returned to Riga. He told me he knew my father and had seen him frequently at the Peter synagogue, the only prayer house that remained in Vecpilseta, the old section of town. This place of worship had become the only legal gathering place for the Riga kacetniks.

On Saturdays, our people came for the Sabbath services, but most of them stayed in the courtyard, where they could see and greet each other and converse with old comrades of misfortune.

Ezka had seen my father only a month before, and he said he had looked well and seemed to be in good health. Unfortunately, he did not know where Father resided. He did, however, have the address of his cousin Adolf, Max's brother who had disappeared; he also lived in Riga. I knew Adolf, since we had been in the same barrack at Polta. As I had suspected, he and Father had been stranded in Magdeburg, but they were on the other side of the Elbe River. After the liberation, they, along with many other inmates, were so terribly homesick that they decided to return to Riga. This delightful news brought me tremendous mental relief; after so many hardships, I would finally be able to locate my father. My solemn vow was now fulfilled, and all that remained was to find a way to get in touch with him. This posed a difficult challenge, since regular postal service to the Soviet Union was not yet functioning. I busied myself with finding ways to write to Adolf first.

Ezka left Magdeburg before I could thank him for his message. I was told he successfully reached the shores of Palestine and fought in the war for Israel's liberation. He remained in the Israeli Defense Forces and participated in the other Arab-Israeli wars. This Jewish patriot, hero, and warrior retired as Colonel Itzhak Leshem and devoted his free time to his family.

On the next workday, I told my Jewish major what had happened over the weekend, and he was pleased to hear that my search had finally come to an end. I asked whether he would send a short letter to Riga by way of his military postal service. I explained that it would be addressed to a friend of mine, since I still did not know my father's address. The major was willing to do so as long as he could read the letter first; he wanted to make sure its contents met with his approval, as all military mail was closely censored. I agreed, and that same day I prepared a letter a few sentences long, telling Father I was alive and that a detailed letter would follow after his reply.

After two weeks I received a short but very moving letter from my father, the words of which are deeply embedded in my mind: "I read your letter, and tears are dripping down my cheeks. I do not believe what I am reading. Did I really find my son? I thought he perished a long time ago. Now I am not alone anymore. Write to me." I read this letter over and over and began to cry as I did so. I turned to the major and the lieutenant and burst out jubilantly, "I found my father! I found my father!" The officers were emotional as well; they understood how I felt at this moment. They encouraged me to continue writing to my father, for which I was grateful. From then on, I received mail from my hometown every two weeks.

In my letters, I could not express my thoughts as freely and thoroughly as I wished, since everything went through the military and ended up in a totalitarian state. Consequently, I had to be concise and find indirect ways to relay information. To notify Father that I would not return to Riga, I wrote, "I plan to visit my Aunt Betty." He understood what I meant, since she lived in the United States. I expressed a great desire for him to come to me so we could renew our life together: "It will be very good for you to see Ezka; you will be very well received by him." Father understood me and replied in his next letter: "My health does not permit me to leave Riga, since I would not survive another Polta." He meant that it was dangerous to escape; if caught, he would not survive the Soviet gulag. With the stroke of a pen, all of my hopes and dreams of being reunited with him were shattered. For almost two years, I had made many sacrifices to find my father and be with him again, and now I found it was not to be. This disturbed me deeply, but I finally found contentment within; I realized I would have to live alone without his kindness, devotion, and guidance as part of my life. My father's letters gave me the mental strength I needed to overcome the difficulties of living in a foreign country.

I was now faced with new challenges and the painful process of recuperation. Once again I had to rely on the instincts that had served me so well during the darkest days of my life. I felt as though I was floating without purpose or aim and did not know what to do. Two forces kept me going: the presence of my dear friends in Magdeburg, whom I considered my mishpoche, and my love for Trudchen, who had become my confidante. I often wondered whether I was following in Abe's footsteps. After World War I, he could not return to his hometown because it was occupied by Lenin's Bolshevik forces; I now chose not to return to my home because Stalin's Soviet regime was in place there. Abe had remained in Germany, fallen in love, married, and settled down in a gentile world.

I had been too victimized by his countrymen; if I followed his example, my guilty conscience would haunt me forever. I could never forsake my heritage and turn my back on family traditions. My life would be meaningful only if it were spent in a thriving Jewish community; I had to find a way to free myself.

My translating work with the Russian chemists was slowly coming to an end; I was now working only a few hours a day. The woman on our team was eager to return to her family in Moscow, whereas the two men enjoyed their leisurely life in Westeregeln and were not in the mood to leave. They stretched out the assignment as long as possible, spending more time socializing than working on the project. Eventually, they released me from my duties and sent me back to the kommandant in Egeln.

In the kommandanture, I was surrounded by Soviet officers; there was no fooling around here. Even if there was nothing to do, I had to create work or pretend I was busy. I resumed my meals at the officers' mess. My father's letters came regularly, for which I was very glad. I tried to put my life into perspective, but I lacked a strong enough will to change its course. My reliable intuition, or some mysterious superpower in heaven, was telling me the time was near to abandon my leisurely life in Egeln. I had to move on to the permanent country of my choice—the United States of America, if at all possible. Without warning, I was soon forced to choose my road in life. There were tragic repercussions at first, but my decision had a very happy ending.

16

My Escape From the Soviets and Life in Weilheim

By fall of 1946 I had definitely determined that I would not return to Riga, for it seemed an evil city to me. I could not see myself living under the Soviet system or in the midst of Latvians who had directly or indirectly collaborated in the destruction of the Jewish community. Indeed, they had helped to make Adolf Hitler's "final solution" a great success in Latvia. Meanwhile, the psychic's second prediction, "You will travel through deep water on a long voyage," lingered in my mind. I could not imagine how or when such a journey would take place. Despite these thoughts, my intuition mysteriously guided me in that direction.

I had not seen my friends in Magdeburg for a few weeks, so I decided I would visit them the following Sunday. Before the weekend arrived, though, I received a call from Minna, who told me that a well-known Moscow entertainment ensemble was coming to her village on Saturday to entertain the Soviet troops stationed in the area. The entertainers were popular Russian singers and dancers, and she advised me not to miss this unique performance. She was willing to make arrangements with her landlady for me to stay overnight. I had no urgent reason to go to Magdeburg, so I decided to accept Minna's invitation and spend the weekend with her.

I arrived at her house late Saturday afternoon; in the evening we attended the performance, which we greatly enjoyed. When the time came to sleep, Minna led me to my bedroom, which was next to hers. Before we parted I jokingly remarked, "I will not disturb your sleep during the night." The next morning she said, "You sure kept your word about not disturbing me." I wondered whether she had expected something more from me. I spent the rest of Sunday in the small village, admiring the serene country atmosphere and the beautiful landscape. Before I left, I kissed Minna for the first time and thanked her for her hospitality and the good time she had shown me. My visit with Minna had been enjoyable and memorable, and I left with every intention of seeing her again, but it was not to be.

I returned to Westeregeln, but my day was far from over. Before I left on Saturday, my dear friend Trudchen had been stricken with stomach pains. The doctor had advised her to stay in bed and take some medication. Although I was very tired from my weekend activities, I wanted to see her that evening. After comforting her for a while, I left for home. The Pfestafings had waited up for me; they wanted to hear about my visit with Minna. I told them briefly how much I had enjoyed the Russian entertainers, then went to sleep.

On Monday morning I geared myself for another routine day. I joined the other officers in the mess hall, where everyone was talking about his weekend. I told how I had attended a wonderful performance of the Moscow entertainment ensemble in a nearby village. As I was about to leave the table, one of the lieutenants whispered, "I received an order to put you under my supervision." "Is this a joke?" I asked, to which he replied, "No it is not. You will be repatriated immediately to your native home, the Soviet Union." "What is the urgency? I am working for the Soviet government," I responded. "The order came from Moscow. All Soviet citizens have to be sent back to their hometowns," the lieutenant answered, and he ordered me to follow him. I felt betrayed, since we had amused each other at the breakfast table just a few minutes earlier, but an order was an order, and he had no choice but to carry it out.

I was so shocked that all of my senses went numb; I knew what awaited me in my native land. I quickly composed myself and asked the young lieutenant to give me some time to pack my belongings. He would not let me leave the kommandanture alone, since the order called for him to stay with me at all times, but he was willing to accompany me to my house and help me pack. That plan did not suit me, as my goal was to escape repatriation. I was persistent in my efforts to convince him that I was happy to be sent back home: I was grateful to the Soviet government. . . I had been waiting for this moment to arrive . . . I was a diligent worker in the kommandanture . . . I worked here only because I wanted to help the Soviet military authorities in Germany. The ploy was futile; the lieutenant would not let me go. I became desperate and pleaded with him to change his mind. "We just had breakfast together as friends; we toasted our camaraderie, and look what you are doing to me now. I am only asking for two hours to pack my belongings and say good-bye to my Soviet friends here." My persuasive words finally worked, and he was willing to let me go. Before I left he reminded me, "I am responsible for you—be back in two hours without delay."

I was relieved beyond words. I ran home immediately and told the Pfestafings that I was in a hurry to leave Westeregeln. I packed essentials into my lucky rucksack; the rest of my belongings I packed into two pillowcases, which I took to my dear friend Abe's tailor shop for safekeeping. I told him what had happened and that I was escaping to the West; I would send someone later to pick up my things. He assured me he would keep them in a safe place and told me not to worry. He wished me good luck, and I departed with a hearty handshake. Then I went to say good-bye to Trudchen and told her I was forced to flee immediately to the western part of Germany. We expressed our mutual sorrow that we were being separated. I expressed concern about her health and wished her a speedy recovery. After a hug and a kiss, I hurriedly left her apartment; I had to return to the Pfestafing's to get my rucksack and leave Egeln. To disguise myself, I put on an old German-style jacket, and Mrs. Pfestafing gave me her husband's Tyrolean-style hat. I said a heartfelt good-bye and thanked Fridel and her mother for all they had done to make my stay in their home a pleasant one.

To avoid detection by townspeople, I rode my motorcycle through muddy side roads and open fields to get to the highway. When I reached it unnoticed, I was going faster than I ever had before. I periodically checked my wristwatch to see whether I was still within the two-hour limitation. I knew I was racing against time; the farther I got from Egeln, the better my chance for escape. I passed the gravel road that led to Minna's village, where only yesterday I had enjoyed myself so much. Today, however, I was running for my life. I wondered whether she had awakened that morning to face the same nightmare. The traffic on the highway was very light, and I made good time in my race to reach Magdeburg. My destination was Max's house, where I would decide my next move. I had to know whether he, too, had received notice of a mandatory repatriation. My frightened mind could not function; my hands were glued tightly to the handlebars of my motorcycle, and my eyes were staring into the distance, far ahead of the speeding bike.

Finally, I arrived at Max's and knocked at the front door, but nobody answered. This seemed strange, for Bella was always home at this hour. I called on the landlady to see whether she knew when they were expected home. To my surprise, she replied, "Oh, they left Friday morning. They were in such a hurry that they did not tell me when they would return." I knew right away that Max, Bella, and, most likely, the rest of my friends had left the city in a hurry, just as I was doing now; they had probably been warned about the repatriation. So as not to arouse suspicion, I told the landlady I would be back the next day. I found myself standing on the sidewalk with no idea of what to do or where to go. Although I could not have known what repercussions my actions would have, I angrily thought about how dumb it had been for me to spend the weekend with Minna; my trip to see a show might have cost me my precious freedom. I had always visited Max on Sundays, but this one—the most important—I had missed. If I had learned the fate of my friends on Sunday, I would have had more time to plan my escape and would not be in such a predicament.

I knew the Soviet authorities in Egeln would begin looking for me very soon; I was now a fugitive. I could not stay in Magdeburg much longer, since my face was familiar there. Calmly, I analyzed my options. The safest place to be was the American zone in Berlin, but I would never make it by motorcycle, since the Soviet military police patrolled the Autobahn that led there. Thus, I would have to take the train, which posed the problem of how to get a ticket, as train rides were restricted for official business use. My situation looked bleak until I decided to seek the help of the president of the Jewish Gemeinde in Magdeburg, who I knew very well. I took him by surprise, since I had not spoken to him for some time. I explained my problem and told him I needed his help to get to Berlin. Realizing the seriousness of my life-threatening situation, he agreed to do what he could. He quickly filled out a Gemeinde travel assignment to Berlin in my name, affixed the official seal, and signed it. I left my motorcycle in his backyard, and he drove me to the train station. We parted, expressing best wishes for each other.

With my official document, I was able to get a ticket and soon boarded the train for Berlin. I looked at my wristwatch; I was thirty minutes over my allotted two hours. I realized the Soviet lieutenant, whose trust I had betrayed, would be searching for me. I took a corner seat, pulled my Tyrolean hat over my forehead, and picked up the newspaper I had purchased at the station. I was not as interested in its contents as I was in covering my face to prevent anyone from recognizing me. When the train finally pulled out of the station, I relaxed somewhat; my first hurdle was behind me. Halfway to Berlin, we made a sudden, unscheduled stop. A dozen Soviet soldiers mounted the train and began to check every passenger's official travel documents. I was very nervous, as I was convinced the military police were after me. My heart was pounding so hard I thought it would tear my chest apart. I prayed, as I had so often in the camps when danger was upon me: "O God, O God Almighty, O my mother in heaven, please save my life."

When the soldiers neared me, I pulled the Tyrolean hat lower on my forehead and wrapped the green jacket I had taken from the Pfestafings around me. When they asked to see my papers, I looked straight at them with a seemingly calm face. They checked the document issued by the Magdeburger Jewish Gemeinde and then returned it to me. Without saying a word, they moved on to the next passenger. I kept pretending I was busy reading the newspaper, but I peeked out at intervals to see how far the Soviet soldiers were from me. I was relieved when they left and the train was on its way again. This frightening confrontation with the enemy lingered in my mind for a very long time.

A short while later, the train stopped at the Berlin station I had visited several months ago for another purpose. Inside, I met two Jewish men I recognized as being from Riga. We realized we were Jews with a common purpose. We struck up a conversation, during which I learned that one of them, Shelkan, was a well-known singer, and the other was a cellist named Arnov. It was obvious that they had undergone the same experience I had, for they, too, were on their way to the Berlin refugee shelter in Schlachtensee to seek asylum. We eventually reached the camp, which was managed by UNRRA. After we registered, we were fed and assigned to a room. The officials told us the camp was overcrowded; the Soviets were blocking the traffic on the Autobahn, causing a delay in the transport of refugees to Allied-occupied Germany. This was the begin-

ning of the Cold War between the Soviet Union and the United States. I
did not mind the delay, for I felt safe in the shelter of the camp and could
recuperate from my journey from Egeln. I was happy that my daring
escape from the Soviet authorities had been successful; my life had changed
beyond recognition.

When the formalities ended, I went to find the room assigned to me.
I met people of many nationalities, although most were Jews. They all
had one thing in common: They were seeking asylum from Communist
countries. Some were on their way to the West: others sought to reach
the shores of Palestine. This UNRRA camp in the American zone of
Berlin was like a small island in a Communist sea, serving as a protector
of human rights for all who sought help. The standing policy of the
camp administration was that refugees fleeing the Soviet-occupied zone
received utmost priority for transport to one of the Allied-occupied parts
of Germany.

As I made my way through the masses of people, I found myself
face-to-face with my dear friend Frieda; we were surprised and delighted
to have met here. We embraced each other and were speechless for a
moment; we looked at each other as though we had been liberated from
the Nazi camps all over again. None of my friends from Magdeburg had
dreamed we would ever meet again in a Berlin refugee camp, of all places.
We had many things to discuss, such as what had happened to our friends
and how each of us had reached this haven. At last, I found my room,
then Frieda and I found a spot where we could talk. She revealed that she
had arrived at the camp on Saturday after discovering that everyone had
left Magdeburg in a hurry the previous day; they had come here and been
immediately transported to the West. A day later, when she arrived, the
Soviet military authorities began the blockade of the Autobahn, and she
was trapped.

We decided to stick together and help each other in our unfamiliar
surroundings. We were sure that within the next few days we would be
able to join our mishpoche (family) in the West. The few days we had
anticipated, however, became several weeks; new refugees sought asylum
every day, but none could be sent to safer areas. The living quarters became more crowded every day, and the beds were so close together that it
was difficult for anyone to reach his or hers. In some cases, men and
women slept in the same room, yet as uncomfortable and completely

lacking in privacy as the situation was, nobody complained. Everybody tried to be helpful and accommodating. Because of the increase in the camp population, our food was rationed, and the buildings soon became so crowded that I could go nowhere without finding myself in the midst of people.

Some of the refugees quickly became entrepreneurs, peddling edibles to supplement the tasteless food we received. I went to the city to find something I could sell in the camp and was able to get a bag of onions without a ration card. When I returned to the camp and showed Frieda what I had bought, she laughed at me, but she accompanied me to help me sell my onions. I sold them by the piece, according to size; they were soon gone, and I had made a nice profit. Frieda thought I had become a smart businessman, but my second attempt did not work out as well. I bought a bucket of herring, many of which sold quickly; I decided to wait until the next day to sell the rest. Unfortunately, our supper that evening consisted of herring and boiled potatoes, so nobody would buy any more fish from me. I stored the herring under my bed, but the odor was so strong I was forced to either sell them below cost or give them away. All of my efforts had been for nothing, for this undertaking left me with no profit. From this experience I learned the truth of the saying "Never put off until tomorrow what you can do today."

As the days and weeks passed, the sleeping arrangements became so bad that those refugees who had the financial means rented furnished rooms in the city to get a comfortable night's rest. Frieda and I checked our finances; together, we had enough money to rent a small, unfurnished room. The only furniture we needed was a large bed to accommodate us both; we could buy a used one very reasonably. It took a few days, but we found an apartment on a small street named after the well-known German writer Goethe. We introduced ourselves to the landlady as husband and wife and gave her a small deposit with the understanding that the balance would be paid on the day we moved in. Frieda and I were pleased with our new home and went back to the camp to make plans to purchase an old bed.

The next morning, a bulletin was posted at every building in the camp: The Soviets had partially lifted the blockade of the Autobahn, and the first ten priority displaced persons were to be shipped out at night to Munich with a U.S. military convoy. Frieda, my friends Arnov and

Shelkan, and I were on the list. Our plan to sleep away from the camp as husband and wife was abandoned; after many weeks of living in congested quarters, we were happy to leave this UNRRA camp in Schlachtensee. At the appointed time, a tarpaulin-covered truck that contained U.S. soldiers pulled up to the camp's gate. The ten evacuees climbed in and were guided to seats near the cab of the truck; the soldiers sat in the rear to camouflage us. The truck pulled away and later joined a convoy of other army trucks. The Soviet military police stopped the vehicles a few times to check the contents; during these stops, we were told to keep very quiet. It was scary to sit in the darkness, knowing we were considered illegal cargo by the Soviet authorities.

Our first rest stop was in the city of Hannover. I still remember vividly the sight of the city on that clear night. A full moon backlit the skeletons of collapsed buildings with protruding smokestacks, visible only in the distance. The landscape looked like a volcanic surface, and no signs of life or sparks of light were evident. It was strange to see the extent to which the war had turned Hannover to rubble. We were soon on our way again, speeding down the highway. There were signs of destruction whenever we passed through a village or town, and scars of war could be seen for many miles. At daybreak, the convoy arrived in Munich. I was tired from the long, sleepless night; still, it had been a relatively pleasant trip, and I was glad to reach our destination without incident. The ten of us were let out, and the truck continued on.

We dispersed to search for a brighter future in the free world. Arnov and Shelkan had an address at which they knew they could find shelter in Munich. They wished us luck in our endeavors, then Frieda and I were left alone. We found out where our friends might have gone, so we boarded a train that took us to a large UNRRA camp in Feldafing. There were many barracks-type buildings, which reminded me of the Nazi concentration camps. I did not like this place, although only Jews lived there; it served as their temporary home until they could be resettled in the country of their choice. I was glad when we learned that our friends had not come here. We were advised to check at the next UNRRA site, less than ten miles away. Frieda and I boarded the next train and got off in a small town, Weilheim, where the camp was located. We were told by some Germans that we would find Jewish people in the Bierstube (tavern) Brauwachsel, which was considered the Jewish Community Center where people met and spent their free time. When we reached the tavern nobody was there, but our friends soon appeared, and Frieda and I were surrounded by the old group from Magdeburg. Everyone was happy to see us, and our mishpoche was reunited again. We told stories of our escape from the Soviet authorities and the unpleasant experiences along the way.

After greeting and conversing with our friends, we were ready to report to the camp authorities. Next to the Brauwachsel was the city hall, which was shared with the UNRRA camp officials. Frieda and I were received politely; in fact, from the first moment, I felt I was among friends and could talk to them as though I had known them forever. The Jewish Committee, which was under UNRRA auspices, resembled a miniature United Nations: The president was from Salonica, Greece; the police chief was from Kaunas, Lithuania; and the secretary was from Vilna, Poland. There were office workers from Latvia, Hungary, and Romania. Everyone was ready to help Frieda and me obtain food and lodging.

We soon received identification documents and were considered full-fledged members of the community. We were no longer referred to as refugees; according to the official documents, we were now called displaced persons. Although these people were supported by UNRRA, they did not live in a camp setting. Weilheim was unique in that DPs there were placed in individual homes among the farmers and townspeople, despite the objections of the former. In this part of Germany, called Oberbayern, the farmers' houses were not on their farmland; they lived instead on the outskirts of town, where they had animals and small vegetable gardens. The land they cultivated was a few miles away, and the farmers left their houses early in the morning to tend to their crops, then returned in the evening.

The UNRRA committee could not find lodging for me that first day, as the town could absorb no more people. I would have had to sleep on a wooden bench had it not been for the kindness of my good friends Zamka and Basja Esaksohn. They took me in and generously shared with me the little food they had for themselves. I spent a few nights with them, then a room was found for me on the outskirts of town in the farmhouse of an elderly couple with a married son and his ten-year-old child. I was told they had been forced against their will to give one room to a DP. When I arrived at their home, I was very coolly received, and my conversation with them was limited.

The next morning, the wife told me they had just enough food for their own family and would not be able to feed me. I politely explained that I would manage on my own and would not need their help. I understood how unhappy they were to have me there, but as time passed and they got to know me better, they became used to my presence. Slowly, they became convinced that the vicious anti-Semitic propaganda they had heard for many years was not accurate. Early each morning, everyone in the family left to work in the field except for the ten-year-old and the elderly woman, who remained in the house and did the cleaning and cooking. Once in a while, she would offer me food or some fresh vegetables from the garden. I was not home most of the day, since I spent my time outdoors or at the Brauwachsel with my friends.

Our Magdeburg mishpoche (family)—Max, Bella, and the others— had developed a daily routine. After having breakfast at home, we met at the Brauwachsel, where everyone occupied a regular booth; there we discussed current world events. We quickly became thirsty from the gusty debate, so everyone ordered beer, which was served in tall Bavarian steins. When we felt we had "solved" all of the world's and Jews' problems of the day, suggestions were made regarding what we should do for the rest of the day. Some people often had to take care of personal chores, others planned to participate in sports events in or out of town. If no general consensus was reached on how we would spend the day, each person went his or her own way. In the evening, our family of friends attended social events or played cards in someone's home.

To others, we must have seemed like lazy loafers until we had an opportunity to further ourselves. In reality, everyone was making plans for the future, as we considered our stay in Weilheim to be temporary. Letters were sent and received by DPs to and from all parts of the world in attempts to find relatives far away, and official approval and denial documents came from various embassies regarding final settlement in their countries. I heard encouraging news and happy letters from France, South Africa, Argentina, the United States, Canada, Palestine, and other lesser-known countries. We rejoiced when people received emigration papers and commiserated when a relative could not be located or a visa was denied. Everyone in our mishpoche was concerned for each other, and good news received by one pleased us all.

I wasted no time finding my relatives in the United States. I sent a request to the American Red Cross to find my aunt, Betty Delson, in Chicago; within a week I received a reply from her. I asked her directly whether she would be willing to send me an affidavit to admit me to the United States. I did not know how she would respond, since she knew little about me. The last time we had seen each other was many years before, when she had visited Riga, and we had spent only a few minutes together.

Days later, I received an affirmative reply—my mother's sister, Betty (once known as Rebecca) and her husband, Herman, were more than happy to help me get to the United States. She had received notification from the Red Cross some time ago that I was the only survivor from our family. She had tried to learn my whereabouts but without success, so she was very happy to hear from me directly. It was thus that I discovered that my friend Sam, the U.S. soldier from Brooklyn, had fulfilled his promise; he had found Aunt Betty in Chicago, but his sudden evacuation from Magdeburg had prevented him from telling me the good news. I considered Sam a soldier of honor and wished I had his full name and address so I could express my overwhelming gratitude to him.

I was sorry the correspondence with my father had been interrupted, but I no longer felt lonesome for relatives, since Betty and Herman wrote and sent me packages regularly. Somehow, she always knew what I needed, just as a mother would feel for her needy child; I received underwear, socks, and cigarettes—a particularly vital commodity. Of the five cartons I received in every package, I kept only one for myself; the rest were sold for spending money. The local street price for cigarettes was low, so I traveled to Frankfurt am Main to a DP camp called Zahlsheim, where the price for cigarettes was considerably higher. The several trips I took to Zahlsheim were for both business and pleasure, as I often spent the day meeting old friends from various Nazi camps.

I became very good friends with Fedka, the barber from Kaiserwald and Buchenwald. In the evenings I was his "guide dog," as he had night blindness. He and I both faced the problem of how to retrieve the clothes we had left behind, his in Magdeburg and mine in Egeln. We found a German woman who occasionally visited her sick parents in the Soviet-occupied zone; for a generous reward, she was willing to go to

Magdeburg and Egeln to pick up our belongings. She had no problem obtaining Fedka's possessions, but I was not as lucky. When she introduced herself to Abe as the person who was supposed to pick up Boris's clothes, he said there was nothing to give her. To erase any evidence that I had visited him before my escape, he had been forced to get rid of my clothing as soon as I left Egeln. He tried to justify his actions by telling the woman that Soviet officers from the kommandanture were searching for me all over town.

These men had stopped in Abe's tailor shop to find out whether he knew where I could be found, but he had told them he had not seen me for several days. The kommandant had been extremely upset and angry about my disappearance, and Abe became very frightened. After the officers had left, he decided to dispose of the clothes. Once again, I had lost my only possessions. Had he truly considered himself my devoted friend, as he had stated on so many occasions, Abe would have found a way to hide the few, unmarked items. As Lizel had done before, Abe had broken a promise to keep safe the belongings of a friend. I felt betrayed, but I realized Abe was probably sorry he had taken my clothes, since he could have been accused as an accomplice in my escape.

One day, I decided to break up the monotony of my days by undertaking an adventurous hike through the countryside. I left home early in the morning, telling the farmer's wife I would be gone for a few days. I packed a small satchel with essentials for the road and enough food for one meal. I took the scenic route—an unpaved country road—and walked for miles, admiring nature and the neatly cultivated fields in the distance. The air was pure and clean, and the fresh aroma of wildflowers gave me an extra lift as I continued on. At times, I stopped to admire the twisted trunk of an old tree or to watch the colorful butterflies zigzagging in the green pasture. The beautiful scenery in this part of Bavaria in no way resembled the structural and human destruction in and around Magdeburg, for nowhere was there a trace of the devastating war. The day passed so pleasantly that I felt no exhaustion or hunger.

The sun was slowly lowering on the horizon, so I began to look for lodging. As I walked, I noticed two brick posts beneath an old, ornamental iron gate, where high-grown bushes substituted for a fence. On one of the posts was a sign, upon which was inscribed the name of a convent and the Catholic order to which it belonged. I decided to stop here, so I entered the gate and followed a long, narrow road that led to a red-brick building. As I neared it, a nun stepped out of the open door and told me that dinner was over; she had assumed I was a beggar seeking a meal. They did distribute free meals to needy Germans, but only at certain hours of the day. I told her I had come not for food but to see what a convent looked like, since I was Jewish and had never visited such a place. I also said I had been recently liberated from a concentration camp, where I had been incarcerated for over three years, and that I was presently living as a DP in Weilheim.

She asked whether I lived with my parents, and I replied that I was in search of my father and that my mother and siblings had been killed by the SS. I could see that my words touched her deeply; she seemed unaware that the Nazis had inflicted any atrocities on the Jewish people. She expressed her sorrow and said, "Of course, I would be very happy to show you around our convent." She asked me to follow her into the building, and I found myself in a visitors' waiting room with benches along the walls. We then entered a large dining hall with several long tables set up for the poor to receive their free meals. My stomach was growling with hunger, and I wished I could indulge in such charity myself.

The soft-spoken nun guided me through the small chapel and then out to a beautiful flower garden. A short distance away was a farmhouse where the convent raised a variety of domestic animals for their own consumption. Among them was a sow feeding her newborn offspring. I was fascinated, for this was new to me; I had never been on a farm, much less seen an animal feed its young. I asked several questions about raising and feeding pigs, and the nun noticed my curiosity and interest. She asked, "Would you like to have one of the baby pigs?" "I would be glad to," I replied, with no thought as to where I would house the little animal or how I would be able to continue my hike with it in my possession. "You can have one if you promise to raise her to full size," the nun said; I assured her that I would fulfill her wish. When I had been shown around the rest of the grounds, we returned to the dining hall, where we engaged in a lengthy conversation; she was interested to know about every member of my family. Finally, she suggested that I have supper and stay overnight. I accepted her gracious offer and was served a bowl of meat and vegetable soup with fresh bread.

After the meal, I was led to one of the rooms that contained a few beds with crucifixes over each one. They were reserved for travelers who needed shelter for the night. I was the only person in the room that evening and was happy to finally get a good night's rest. It felt strange to have these religious symbols displayed over my bed, although I had nothing but warm feelings for my Christian host.

The following morning, I had to rise early to make sure I was on time for breakfast; when I reached the dining hall, the poor were already there, waiting to be served. Most were ethnic German refugees who had been expelled from their native countries. I had breakfast and was preparing to leave the convent when the nun who had been so kind to me appeared with a burlap sack over her shoulder. "Here, take your baby pig," she reminded me. I took the sack and thanked her for the generous hospitality that had been extended to me and especially for the piglet. As I departed, I told her, "Your convent is doing marvelous charitable work for the needy and hungry people. God bless you." She replied, "God bless you, too—go with God's blessing." We respected one another's religious beliefs. I never forgot the extraordinary hospitality and care the nuns had rendered to a young Jewish man.

I knew I could not proceed with my adventurous hiking trip with a pig over my shoulder, so I decided to return home. It was still early morning, and everything around me was quiet and serene; only an occasional squeak from the pig was heard. As I walked, I thought about my once-in-a-lifetime experience in the convent; I had witnessed good deeds performed for unfortunate, helpless people. I was probably the only Jew to have ever set foot on this property; on top of it all, I had been rewarded with a baby pig. I suppose life had a different purpose and meaning to the people of this secluded institution. The nun who had guided me had shown an unusually deep and sincere concern for me; I was perhaps the only Jew to whom she had ever spoken. Her passionate words about me and my vanished family, as well as her kind expression, left me feeling very humble. I wondered, Did she do all of this to seek repentance for her German brothers who had bestowed so much pain and suffering on the Jewish people? I felt mentally and spiritually uplifted; I had a new, inexplicably satisfying feeling. I tried to imagine why I had been treated with so much kindness; after all, I was just one of many daily visitors. Was I something unique in the eyes of the Catholic nuns?

By the end of the day, I had returned to the farmer's house. I told the wife I had a baby pig and asked whether I could let her loose in the backyard; I was granted permission and let her go free. When the farmer returned from work in the fields and saw the piglet, he was so angry he was ready to slaughter her. I told him that despite his rage he could not harm her, for my sake. I explained how I had obtained the pig and that I had promised the nuns that she would not be slaughtered until she was fully grown. The farmer took my words seriously, and we struck a deal: He would keep the pig, and in return I would receive a portion of bacon on a regular basis. We were both satisfied, but I hoped to be in the United States by the time the pig was ready to be slaughtered.

This agreement changed the attitude of the farmer's family toward me. Suddenly, products that had been denied me appeared on the kitchen table and were offered to me. I received bacon, beef, and cheeses daily and was no longer told there was a shortage of food. Our relationship improved greatly; in fact, to please them I bought some coffee beans on the black market, knowing they were great coffee lovers. From then on, I was no longer considered an unwanted Jewish intruder but was a welcome guest in their home. I was invited to join the family at their meals and often accepted the offers. My short, stimulating adventure had changed my way of life at the farmer's house.

The World Zionist movement—which consisted of individual progressive, liberal, and conservative organizations—was extremely active throughout Europe, and its activities were very prominent in Weilheim. A few miles from town, an agricultural school had been established, with practical fieldwork for the benefit of the future settlers of Palestine; the volunteer students lived and learned there until they were ready to leave for the new land. They were primarily taught farming, how to handle domestic animals, and the community lifestyle of a kibbutz; with these tools, they would have an easier adjustment in their new homeland. One day, I noticed several unfamiliar men and women in the Bierstube Brauwachsel. I learned they were Revisionists, members of the conservative Zionist movement, whose founder and late leader was Zeev Zabotinsky.

Most had come from Munich for a special gathering. They held their meetings late into the evening and had no means of transportation to return to their home base. No arrangements had been made for them to stay overnight, so they had to sleep on the benches of the bierstube. Among the group was a good-looking young woman named Tamara who lived in Munich. I struck up a conversation with her and found that she worked as a secretary for the Revisionist organization, which was headquartered in Munich. She was part of the aliya staff in charge of sending settlers to Palestine to break the stringent British blockade. Since Tamara had no place to spend the night in town, I naively offered her my room, where she could have a comfortable bed after a hectic and tiresome day. She did not know me well enough and refused my offer, but we departed in a friendly manner, hoping to meet again someday.

After several weeks, the joyful day finally arrived when I was notified by the U.S. consulate in Munich that my immigration affidavit had arrived to be processed. I was to supply them with a passport-sized photo; without delay, I had my picture taken and delivered it in person to the consulate office. As I made my way to the train station, I stopped for a light at a busy intersection several feet from a commuter bus stop. Among those waiting for the bus was a short, dark-haired woman with two small children, a boy and a girl, at her side. I could not see her face, but I could see those of the children. I admired them; they looked Jewish, and at the time it was rare to meet small Jewish children in Germany. As I smiled at them, the mother turned in my direction; she now looked very familiar. I thought, This woman looks like my Aunt Minna from Riga. I looked at her again and became convinced that it was my aunt, so I came closer to her and asked, with a trembling voice, "Is your name Minna? Are you from Riga?" She replied, "Yes, but who are you?" "Look at me once more; maybe you will recognize me," I said to her. She gazed at me intently but still did not know who I was.

At this point my excitement overwhelmed me, and I could no longer withhold my identity. "I am Boris! I am Fanja's son!" Minna's face instantly lit up happily as she recognized me, and we embraced on the busy sidewalk. The two children were my cousins, Bella and Leiba, who I barely knew. My aunt told me what I already knew: that her entire family had escaped from Riga before the Germans entered the city. During the war years, they had been in the Soviet Union, and she had been able to return to Poland after the war, since it was her birthplace. She had come to Germany intending to immigrate to Argentina, where her brother resided, and she presently lived in an UNRRA camp a distance from

Weilheim. We had many things to discuss, but a street corner was not the proper place for such a conversation. She gave me her address, and I promised that I would visit as soon as possible. I would never have dreamed I would meet relatives at a crowded bus stop in the city of Munich.

After a week, I was ready to visit Minna and her children; it took a few hours to reach her UNRRA camp in Airing-Frailassing by train. My aunt received me graciously and tried to make my stay as comfortable as possible. We exchanged information about ourselves and our perished family, and we reminisced about sad and happy times in Riga. Minna told me that her husband, Wulf, had died of natural causes in the Soviet Union. My cousin Chaim, her eldest son, had been killed fighting the Germans, and her older daughter, Tanja, had been married and settled down in Riga and then moved to Israel. After a short stay in Poland, Aunt Minna had smuggled herself and her youngest two children out, and they went to Germany. The journey was very strenuous and dangerous, and most movement was done on foot at night, with little nourishment, and they had to climb mountains and walk on muddy country roads. Ultimately, she and the children reached their destination; with the help of the Red Cross, she got in touch with her brother, Max Perlman, a well-known Yiddish singer and actor who lived in Argentina.

I had time to walk around my aunt's UNRRA camp, which was located in beautiful natural surroundings. I spent quite a while taking in the skyline of the glorious Austrian Alps, with their snow-covered peaks and green valleys; it was the most gorgeous sight I had ever seen. I returned home, glad to have been in the company of my relatives and to have had the opportunity to see the outdoors at its finest.

During my short absence, news had arrived that transports of DPs from various parts of Germany were on their way to the United States. I was very happy; within a few days, I was called to appear at the consulate in Munich for the second time. When I got there, I was informed that I was required to have a character witness testify for me; without the appearance of such a person, they could not proceed with my immigration papers. I needed to find someone in Munich who could testify for me, and I tried to think whether I had an old friend there upon whom I could call. The only name that came to mind was that of Tamara, the woman who had refused my offer of lodging in Weilheim.

I went to her workplace, the headquarters of the Revisionist organization. She was typing some documents, so I approached and asked whether she could do a favor for me and testify as a character witness for me at the U.S. consulate nearby. Tamara replied, "You seem to be a fine fellow. When I was in need, you offered me lodging in your house without even knowing me. Although I am very busy, I will go and help you." I was delighted with her decision. Her testimony satisfied the interrogator, and my immigration papers were sent on for processing.

On the way back to her office, I asked Tamara where she planned to settle. She replied, "I am obliged to go to Palestine, but my uncle in America wants me to come to him, since I am the only survivor of our entire family. He would have to do a great deal of convincing to persuade me to come to America, though." She gave me her uncle's name and address in Gary, Indiana. When I arrived in the United States, I was to convey Tamara's regards to her uncle, Jake Dalkoff. I thanked her for coming to my rescue; we said good-bye and wished each other good luck. Neither of us would have guessed that she had just served as a character witness for the man she would marry a year later in his new homeland.

17

America, My New Home

February 1947 was coming to an end, and the U.S. immigration authorities began to enforce the Displaced Person Immigration Act. The first Liberty-class boats, used to transport troops during the war, were arriving at Bremenhafen to take the DPs to the United States. As I waited for my legal documents to come through so I could join them, I improved my English with the help of a retired English teacher in Weilheim.

Although a great deal of time had passed, my love for Trudchen had not diminished. I wrote her a farewell letter, in which I told her I now felt safe enough to reveal my whereabouts, as I was preparing to leave for the United States. I expressed concern about her health and asked how she was spending her time. Within days, I received an answer: "Dear Boris, I am glad you are about to embark for America, for I know that is what you desire. I have completely recovered from my illness and have returned to my job. Not long ago I met a young man, a native Westeregelner, who was released from the Soviet war prisoner camp. We are very much in love, but the vicious rumors about my relationship with you stand in the way of our marriage. It would make me very happy if you would please describe our friendship in writing to stop the gossip." I addressed her concerns as well as I could, since I wanted what was best for her. My letter was intended more for the young man than for Trudchen; in it, I praised her character and her ladylike behavior during our friendship in Westeregeln. He should consider himself a very lucky man, I wrote, to have a woman such as her by his side. I told him I did not doubt he had made the perfect decision to choose Trudchen as his lifelong mate. I closed by wishing them both much luck and happiness.

The day finally arrived when I had my immigration papers and a ticket for the steamship that would take me to the other side of the Atlantic Ocean. I was delighted; at last, I would be able to grow to adulthood in "the land of the free and the home of the brave." The news of my departure spread rapidly through the town, as I was the first person to leave UNRRA team 194 from Weilheim, Oberbayern, U.S. Zone, Germany. Everyone was happy that my stalled emigration was finally taking place, and friends came by, offering good wishes. I was given the names, addresses, and telephone numbers of family members residing all over the United States, to whom I was to relate greetings from various friends.

I needed little time to prepare for my voyage. Someone gave me an old, large suitcase, into which I packed my belongings, including the lucky rucksack. My old friends from Magdeburg—Max and Bella, Zamka and Basja, Fedka, and Frieda—and my new acquaintances, Grunja and her girlfriend Mirjam, got together to celebrate my departure. Each friend gave me a picture with a kind inscription; I still cherish these photos of my devoted, unforgettable friends. Before I could leave, I had another celebration to attend; Frieda had received the papers authorizing her immigration to Paris, France, where her elderly cousin had lived for many years. The day of my departure, everyone gathered at the Weilheim train station to say a last farewell. After hearty embraces and kisses from each of them, I boarded the train that would take me to Bremenhafen. Some of my friends had tears of happiness in their eyes. Our Magdeburg mishpoche was slowly dissolving.

It was March 20, 1947, when I arrived at the steamboat dock, carrying my battered suitcase. Some passengers were already at the boarding ramp, although we had been notified that we would not be allowed on the boat for a few hours. I decided to do some window shopping and stopped at a store where a man was making all kinds of leather goods. I went in to see whether there was anything I could purchase with the several German marks I still carried in my pocket. I noticed a leather wallet, and the face of the old fortune teller appeared to me. I could hear her third prediction: "You will become a wealthy man." Her first two predictions—those regarding the discovery of my father and the long voyage over water—had come true. I figured that if she was right again and I became a wealthy man, I would need a wallet. I had just enough money to buy it. I still have the wallet, and it is as new as the day I bought it, as I found only opportunity, not wealth, in America.

I returned to the dock as people were boarding the boat. My documents were inspected; my name was on the boarding list, so an agent put a blue badge on my lapel. It had the letters "HIAS" (Hebrew Immigration Aid Society) in English and Yiddish, as well as the inscription "Bremen 1947." As I was about to board the boat, I saw another agent giving a ten dollar bill to anyone with a blue HIAS badge such as mine. I discovered that this was spending money for the boat, and I was humbled to receive something without having earned it. It was a noble gesture for the HIAS to think so much of us, the penniless survivors of the Holocaust.

I boarded the boat with uncertainty and was slightly confused, as I did not know what to expect in a strange new country. My first task was to find a place to sleep. I reached a large sleeping hall with little privacy. I found the bed to which I had been assigned and put some of my clothes there; I was making sure nobody took my place, as though I were still in the barracks of a concentration camp. This room was strictly for sleeping. It was windowless and dimly lit, and a common washroom was located to one side. I sat on my bed and waited for others to occupy theirs so I could see who my neighbors were. After a while, I went up on the main deck to find out more about the boat, the SS *Ernie Pyle.* Everybody was soon on board, and the ship began to move; it was not long before only the endless waters of the Atlantic Ocean could be seen.

The boat was not a luxury liner, but none of the passengers complained; we did not care by what means of transport we reached the "Golden Land" as long as we got there. The sleeping quarters were comfortable enough to allow a good night's rest. During the day, most of my time was spent on the main deck, where I watched the boat stream through the Atlantic. A recreation room was available where I actively participated in various games or watched movies. I met a few people I knew from Riga but had not seen after the liberation, and our common past kept us together. Dinner was served cafeteria-style in the dining room, and a large selection of tasteful food was available at every meal. On the main deck was a canteen in which a variety of tropical fruits, chocolates, and cigarettes could be purchased at minimal cost. I was one of many steady customers. I yearned for bananas, grapes, and chocolate, as well as my favorite cigarettes, Pall Mall. Of the ten dollars I had been given, I kept three in case I needed streetcar fare in New York.

On the third day of the voyage, I reached the limit of my endurance. Walking through the cafeteria I suddenly lost the strength in my feet, and my full tray dropped to the floor. Everything began to spin, which was one of the symptoms of seasickness. I could not eat or even look at food. I ate no more meals in the cafeteria, and my movement on deck became very limited.

The next day, I noticed that we were not moving, for our boat had broken down the night before. We floated in the calm waters of the Atlantic until a tugboat arrived to tow us to Plymouth, England. An excerpt from a local newspaper was handed to every passenger; it read: "Some 800 displaced persons on board the crippled 12,000-ton U.S. steamer *Ernie Pyle* anchored in Plymouth. They played cards, sang, and took lessons in the jitterbug from the crew yesterday. This ship, on its way from Bremen to New York, put in with engine trouble. A cable was sent to New York yesterday, asking for a turbine part to be flown to the ship. Meanwhile, officials are trying to arrange for another ship to take the displaced persons across the Atlantic." Within a day, the new ship arrived—the SS *Marine Marlin.* The passengers were transferred, and we were back on our way to the United States, but we were disappointed about the many extra days we had spent at sea.

We reached New York harbor on the morning of April Fool's Day; our long trip across the Atlantic Ocean had finally come to an end. At times, I wondered how the old German fortune teller could have predicted my extended voyage over a large body of water, for she was very precise. When I came up to the top deck, I was disappointed to find that I had missed the Statue of Liberty, which I had been so eager to see. When I disembarked, I recognized my distant cousins Ester and Harry Schneider waiting at the dock. As a small boy, I had attended their wedding in Riga just before they left for the United States. We embraced, and they told me Betty and Herman were vacationing in Florida and had asked them to pick me up, which they said they were happy to do. After claiming my suitcase, we left for their apartment in Brooklyn, where I spent two splendid, unforgettable weeks. Their daughter, Sylvia, who was in high school at the time, showed me the splendors of New York and all the tourist attractions. We went to Broadway and Jewish Theater productions, Rockefeller Center, Radio City Music Hall, and many other places that seemed fantastic to me. Their son, Sammy, was a small boy; I kept him with me, like a little brother, whenever possible.

I loved to help Ester with her daily shopping, when I was introduced to the Jewish butcher, baker, and grocer. No English was spoken—all transactions were conducted in Yiddish—and I saw few signs in English over the business establishments. One could apparently live in this neighborhood for a lifetime without needing to know the U.S. national language. At Ester's house I met my first cousin, Frieda; she was the daughter of my favorite uncle, Aron, and had come to the United States in the 1930s. I later met her husband, David, and their son, Bert. My Aunt Hanna's youngest daughter, Lisa, also came to see me; she and her husband lived in Holland but had come to the United States for a short visit with his relatives, as well as for the birth of her first child, a boy named Jerry. When I had visited with both cousins, they could rest their thoughts about the fate of their relatives; from the sole survivor, they heard the sad facts about our family being trapped in Riga under the Nazi occupation. It was painful for me to disclose to Frieda that her brother Boris's tragic decision to separate from Father and me had cost him his life. It was also difficult to tell Lisa that her oldest brother, Moisey, with whom I had worked, had perished in the Stutzpunkt.

After two weeks in Brooklyn, I boarded an overnight train to Chicago. I was looking forward to meeting my American relatives who had been so concerned about my well-being when I was in Germany. When the train arrived at the station, I grabbed my suitcase and looked eagerly through the windows of the car to see whether I could find my family. Betty, Herman, and my Aunt Debora's son, Ralph (who used to be called Rafa), were waiting; this was the most joyous greeting I had ever experienced. Ralph took my suitcase, and we walked to their Buick Roadmaster. I enjoyed the comfortable ride on the streets of Chicago, as well as our conversation.

I expected to be led to a luxurious apartment, since I perceived that I had come to stay with rich American relatives. Betty was considered the wealthy, devoted daughter who sent money to her parents each month in their retirement years and, at times, also sent five dollar bills to her youngest sister, my mother. Instead, Herman stopped at the entrance of the Guyen Hotel at the corner of Washington and Pulaski. We entered the lobby and an elevator brought us to the second floor, where I received my first disappointment. I walked into a small, furnished hotel apartment that had one bedroom, a living room, and a kitchen big enough to seat only three people at a small table. I was granted the Murphy bed hidden in the wall; to use it, I had to open two doors on the side and pull it down. This was to be my new home for the next several weeks.

Betty was very excited to see me; when she left Riga, I was only two years old, and she remembered teaching her sister Fanja how to bathe me. The last time I had seen Ralph was in 1939 in Riga on the eve of his departure to the United States. Most of our conversations were about our perished relatives; the usual questions were raised about the Nazi atrocities toward the Jews and toward our family in particular. This was a lengthy subject, but after a few days we put the cruel past to rest. Ralph told about his experiences as a soldier in the U.S. Army fighting in Africa and Italy, and I was told how lucky I was to have survived the Holocaust and come to the United States.

I thanked Betty and Herman for their generosity several times, but before I went to bed on my first night I experienced another disappointment. Betty handed me a new wristwatch as a gift and asked whether I would consider giving mine to Herman as a token of appreciation for what he had done for me. I liked my old watch much better than the new one, and it served as a memento from the old country, but I did as my aunt requested. I would not have minded the exchange if Herman had worn my watch occasionally; instead, he put it in a drawer for safekeeping.

These few disappointments were followed by many more pleasant surprises. On my first Sunday in Chicago, Betty and Herman drove me to a man's haberdashery to buy me a new wardrobe. They watched with great interest and devotion as the salesman fitted me with my first American-made suit. I was grateful that they wanted to help me become acclimated to the society. From that moment I felt an extraordinary closeness to my aunt and uncle and held them in high regard, second only to my parents. They had grown fond of me as well, since they had no children, and introduced me to their friends as "their boy." That same weekend I met Herman's relatives, who had moved to Chicago some years earlier from Libau, Latvia; it was a large family that consisted of his parents, three brothers, and two sisters. I became well acquainted with them and visited them often. Although I had some sad memories, I was generally very happy; I had realized I could not bring back my old home, but I could bring a "home" back into my life. My longtime friends were gone, but I was surrounded by people who cared for me.

In the mornings, Herman would leave for his law office downtown, but Betty was a physician, and she began her rounds of house calls to see her sick patients. I became her companion; riding with Betty, I received my first advanced English lessons. She made me read every sign and billboard we passed, which was a practical teaching method that helped me to absorb the language; I also became more familiar with the American way of life. One day, we drove by the Western Electric plant, and Betty decided to ask whether any openings were available for an electrician. I filled out an application, took an aptitude test, and was hired immediately.

I started my first job in the United States at a salary of thirty-seven cents an hour. There was another Holocaust survivor in my maintenance department; he did mechanical work, whereas I was employed as an electrician and was sent all over the plant to do repair work. I soon discovered that we were the only Jewish workers there. I tried hard to fit in with the rest of my co-workers; as poor as my English was, they understood me, and over time we built a friendly relationship. I was pleased with my new job and received a raise of five cents an hour every few weeks. When I got my first paycheck, Betty rendered financial planning advice "the American way." She said the first week's paycheck each month should be used for rent, the second for food, and the third for miscellaneous expenses and clothing; the fourth should either be deposited in the bank in a savings account or used to purchase a U.S. savings bond.

I quickly relieved my aunt and uncle of their obligation to support me. Since no apartments were available to rent because of the housing shortage, I lived in various furnished rooms with Jewish families. At times, I shared an apartment with Ralph and his friend. I moved from one place to another on the west side of Chicago; I liked the neighborhood and was proud to become a "west-sider."

Several thousand people were employed at Western Electric. Working for such a large company, where workers came from a variety of ethnic backgrounds, made it easier for me to understand my new homeland. My immediate supervisor, a Swedish man named Peterson, took a liking to me and often asked how I was getting along. I usually replied that things were fine; after a while, though, I decided to tell him what I really thought. The next time he asked, I answered, "I am fine, but I would be even better if I could earn more money; I am sure I would be much happier." He asked, "Do you want to work on Saturdays?" I said, "Yes, of course." "I will see what I can do for you," Peterson told me. The kindly supervisor soon created work for me on Saturdays so I could earn more money.

Working among people with different cultural upbringings, I was occasionally confronted with unpleasant feelings of racism and prejudice. As a newcomer to the country, this surprised me to the point that I became outraged. I would like to share a few of those instances.

In the course of my daily work, I passed through several offices many times a day and became well acquainted with most of the secretaries. At first, I simply said a friendly hello; this was followed by complimentary remarks, and I eventually chatted regularly with some of the women during breaks. I asked one girl for a date, but she refused; every time I asked, she found an excuse not to go out with me. When I eventually asked her the reason, she hesitated, then said, "You are a likable fellow, and I would not mind going out with you, but my parents would throw me out of the house if they found out I was dating a Jewish boy." I understood and stopped asking her for dates but continued my complimentary remarks.

One day, I received a work order to do some electrical repairs in the Cable Department, which was a separate building some distance away from the main plant. I had started my work when a middle-aged man came up and watched what I was doing. After a while he asked, "Are you Jewish?" I answered yes, and he whispered, "I am Jewish, too, but nobody here knows that." I asked him the reason, and he replied, "They would not have hired me. During the Depression, I needed a job very badly to support my family, so I marked 'Christian' on my employment application." He came and went constantly as I was busy with my repair work. I soon realized he was not interested in what I was doing as much as he enjoyed being in the presence of a Jewish co-worker, something he had never seen here. Just as Glanz had yearned to see a Jewish face in Egeln, this devoted company worker yearned for a Jewish face at the plant.

My department chief asked whether I would be the company's representative at the funeral of a senior worker. I was flattered to have been chosen, so I agreed and was told a limousine would pick me up the next day. When the car pulled up to my house, I noticed that the Jewish mechanic from my department was in the limousine as well; we were the sole representatives of the plant, but neither of us knew the worker whose funeral we were attending. At the funeral home we saw that we were the only white men present; all of the other mourners were black. We expressed our condolences to the widow as Western Electric Company representatives. My friend and I were bewildered, and we wondered, This man who was laid to rest worked for the company for many years. Where are all of his "devoted" white co-workers? We were shocked that management had seen fit to send two Jewish, newly employed workers as the company's representatives to the funeral of a black man they had never known.

On the Fourth of July, Betty and Herman took me with them on their long weekend vacation to Elkhart Lake, a resort in Wisconsin. The trip was worthwhile because, for the first time, I was exposed to the landscape of two states and the Main Streets of several American towns. The most fun I had was at the small, private beach; without difficulty, I was accepted by the young Americans and had a good time in their company. A young man approached me. "I overheard your conversation; you speak with a heavy accent. Where are you from?" I replied, "I came from Germany." He told me, "My cousin, who is staying with us, recently arrived from Germany, too." I asked the young man, "What is your cousin's name? I might know her."

When he said her name was Tamara, I thought of the girl who had been my character witness not long ago. "Is she from Munich?" I wondered aloud. I got the answer I wanted: "Yes, she came from Munich over a month ago." I told him I knew her very well and would like to talk to her. He said his name was Irving Dalkoff, and he lived in Gary, Indiana; he gave me his telephone number before he left. When I returned to Chicago after the holiday, I called Tamara, who already knew I had met her cousin. Her uncle Jake picked up the receiver as I was about to hang up and invited me to come to Gary for the weekend. I did so, and his wife, Ethel, prepared a special Sabbath dinner so I could meet the rest of the family. This memorable weekend was the beginning of a courtship between Tamara and me, and our engagement was soon announced; the wedding date was set for December 19, 1948.

From the first day I arrived in the United States, I was filled with new hopes and dreams about life in my new homeland. Betty and Herman received me with open arms and warm feelings, showing me the love and compassion I had craved for so long. As much as they tried, though, my dear aunt and uncle were unable to satisfy my urgent desire to achieve my goals quickly and in my own way. They could not give me the necessary guidance and advice to prepare me for my future, and I soon realized that my "good job" at Western Electric, as they assured me it was, would not lead to the realization of my lifelong dreams. To fulfill my ambitions, I had to use every avenue of opportunity in this new, free country. I had been denied the educational tools I needed to cope with the diverse society in which I would live the rest of my life; therefore, I began attending two schools in the evening while working full-time during the day.

Herman's youngest brother, Norman, who everyone knew as Nick, made an extra effort to show me a good time in Chicago. He and his buddy Max often invited me to join them and go dancing. We three bachelors would go to the Aragon Ballroom, which was popular for young people's entertainment. The ladies there were happy to be invited onto the floor to dance to a large orchestra. Nick became a devoted friend; after his death, Max and I remained close, and we reminisce about the times we used to have every time we see each other.

I wanted to go into the shoe business, as my father had. I visited several shoe wholesalers, and they all had equally distressing advice for a newcomer to this type of undertaking. They said they were willing to give me all the merchandise I needed on consignment but warned me that I should have enough resources to withstand a loss the first year, an even break the second year, and a limited profit the third year. Since I had no investment capital, I was forced to give up my dreams of following in my father's footsteps.

My wedding day was slowly approaching, and Tamara and I did not have a place of our own. With Betty's resourcefulness and a hefty payoff to the landlord, we were finally able to secure a small apartment. The previous tenant had neglected the place to such a degree that it took Nick—who was a professional painter—three coats of paint, as well as my scrubbing and varnishing the hardwood floors, to make the apartment an enjoyable place to live.

On the day of our wedding, the banquet hall on Roosevelt Road was beautifully decorated. Almost all of our relatives and friends responded to our invitation to marry off the *greene kuzines,* or newcomers. I was guided to the chuppa (wedding canopy) on a white "magic" runner by Betty and Herman, and Tamara was given away by her aunt and uncle, Ethel and Jake. Our marriage vows were officiated by a rabbi and concluded with the traditional breaking of the ceremonial wine glass, to remind us of past sorrows. Kosher food and drinks were then enjoyed by the guests. Popular Jewish and American melodies made the wedding more festive; the floor creaked loudly under the weight of the joyous dancers. Our traditional Jewish wedding was followed by a week-long honeymoon at the Excelsior Springs in Missouri.

Now we were both residents of the west side, which was unique; the Italians, Irish, and Jews made the neighborhood very pleasant. The beautiful Douglas and Garfield Parks were replete with greeneries, ponds, and places for children to play. On hot, muggy summer nights, people could spend time outside without being molested or disturbed by anyone. The churches and synagogues carried the names of every major country in Europe, and the Catholic and Hebrew parochial schools taught children tolerance for and understanding of their neighbors. The Jewish People's Institute served as a gathering place and cultural center, and the Judea Temple was popular with the young people.

I often walked down Roosevelt Road, passing Silverstein's Deli and Royal Cafe, Jewish bakeries, fish stores, and Lazar's kosher sausage factory, where delicious pastrami, corned beef, hot dogs, and a variety of sausages were available. There were landmarks like Weinstein Chapel and the Yiddish daily newspaper, *Forwards.* I cannot forget the Sears and Roebuck store. It was a neighborhood in which baby buggies in parks and on the sidewalks were the main attraction.

Slowly, I became acquainted with the entire city. I was intrigued by the beauty of Chicago's skyline, its beaches, old State Street, the financial district on LaSalle Street, the various museums, and the observatory and conservatories, which I visited often. The resourceful Mayor Richard J. Daley made the city prosper. Chicago became known as the "city that works." Whenever I was in the vicinity of the mayor's Bridgeport neighborhood, I would try to drive by his modest home.

With time and much work, I finally graduated from electrical school, received my license from the city of Chicago, and finished my high school studies. I now wanted to leave my job at Western Electric and start my own contracting business. I allowed myself to be laid off from my first American job to take advantage of the generous company severance benefits. I never regretted it, as it helped me to overcome the financial difficulties that followed.

I had a rough and difficult road ahead. I opened my business with no knowledge of how to run it, no car, and very little money. I still remember that to get to my first job, I had to use public transportation, carrying my tools and materials in a large briefcase. As I got more work, I needed a car, but I did not know how to drive, so Tamara's cousin Irving took it upon himself to teach me; I mastered the necessary skills and soon had my driver's license. I was still faced with the problem of getting a car, since I did not have enough money to buy a used one, but Uncle Jake, who was in the car business, came to my rescue. He had an old Packard trade-in that was supposed to be in good running condition; I bought the car with the understanding that I would make monthly payments. The first few weeks it performed beautifully, but then every few days minor problems kept it from running. I returned the Packard and got another car free of charge as compensation for the difficulties I had endured.

I now had a means of transportation, but no work was available; my only income was a check from the unemployment office. I called on Jewish and gentile contractors for work but received only unfulfilled promises, so I decided to visit the Electrical Union Hall on Ogden Avenue. When I came to register for work, there were already four long sheets with the names of unemployed electricians; nonetheless, I put down my name, knowing I would never be called. I was given the telephone number of a prominent union business agent named Murray; I called him the next day and explained my financial problems. He was willing to help me and told me confidentially that the Pullman Railcar Manufacturing Company had received a large order from the Canadian government to build passenger cars and would need electricians. Early the next day, I left for the Pullman plant, which was on the south side of the city. It took two hours to get there, but the effort was worth it: I was hired and automatically became a union electrician with a high hourly rate. While I was employed there, I began building up my own business.

At this stage in my entrepreneurship, I sought every opportunity for help and advice. I knew the job at Pullman would last only until the Canadian order had been filled; luckily, I was able to find a variety of freelance jobs. Many men hired me and helped move my career along. An electrical contractor named Demsetz understood my needs as a newcomer to this country; he gave me fatherly advice on how to increase my business in a competitive market. Essarov, the wholesale electrical supplier, was kind enough to extend unlimited credit and give me some recommendations. Luigi, the Italian contractor, loaned me tools and ladders until I was able to purchase my own and find a place to store them. Last but by no means least, my good friend Nick, a paint contractor, introduced me to some people in real estate who became steady customers. I was faced with challenges but undertook them with all the passion a man could muster. I printed specially designed business cards; mailed postcards to businesses in the neighborhood, offering my services; and advertised in *Forwards*.

I received favorable responses from all these methods; when I left my job at Pullman, my business was on the right track. My one-man business developed to the point that I was doing electrical contracting work throughout Chicago and its suburbs. My ambition forced me to work long, hard hours. Tamara woke me early in the morning; I left the house without a wristwatch, for I worked by my own schedule. After sunset, I knew it was time to go home.

In 1951, we decided to raise a family, and Tamara soon gave birth to a girl; she was named Sharon Faith, in memory of both our mothers. Tamara did not have to return to her office job and could now join other mothers with their baby strollers. My perseverance and skillful and efficient work in my craft eventually paid off, and I had the financial freedom to move to the northernmost outskirts of Chicago. Tamara and I enjoyed our improved lives; we no longer had to walk three flights of stairs to reach our apartment or spend our leisure time on the sidewalk, for we now had a lush backyard with a child's swing and sandbox. We were surrounded by homeowners who were willing to help at any time. In 1955, we had an addition to our family—a baby boy. He was named in memory of Tamara's father, Nathan, and my beloved grandfather, Schleime, the patriarch of the Lidowsky family; in English, he was called Steven Neal.

After a few years, we were ready for the second wave of the exodus from the city; this time, the builders utilized farmland for their home development, and I became a suburbanite. I went to the bank to apply for a mortgage loan, and the vice president said, "I have watched your banking habits from the first day you opened your account with us, and I like what I have seen. Your credit is good without documentation." I was very flattered by what he said, for it meant the fortune teller's final prediction had been fulfilled; I had become a "wealthy man" in the eyes of others. My financial credibility was so well established that it has endured to this day.

My only cousin in Chicago, Ralph, graduated from dental school, set up an office in the city, and married a beautiful young woman named Shirley. They, too, became a family of four with the additions of a girl, Debbie, and a boy, Cary. Our family in Chicago expanded and grew closer. Aunt Betty served as the matriarch, making sure there were festive celebrations for birthdays, anniversaries, and Jewish holidays. She often invited me to her professional gatherings, and I was flattered when she continued to introduce me as "her boy." I was glad my aunt and uncle felt close enough to present me as such to those who did not know me.

My happiness extended further when I was able to reestablish contact with my father in Riga and send him suits of clothing. I lived a normal and comfortable life but still missed the gentle touch of my mother, whose memory lingered with me. I often dreamed about her and my siblings; some nights I woke up and allowed the tears to run down my cheeks into the pillow—quietly, so as not to be noticed by Tamara. Some days I could not get my mother's distant image out of mind. I yearned for her to such an extent that I finally decided to visit Riga and see the place where the massacre had occurred and where she rests in peace.

It was 1963 when I left for my old hometown alone; at the time, very few people traveled to the Soviet Union, especially alone. I arrived in Moscow and had the pleasure of seeing my Uncle Alexander, known to the family as Sascha, for the first time. His son, Jefim, was not present, but I met his wife, Helena, and daughter, Frieda, during my short visit to his home in Nekolskaja, a town outside Moscow. After visiting all of the tourist attractions, such as Lenin's Tomb, the marble interiors of the subway stations, the walled-in buildings of the Kremlin and its museum, and the Bolshoi Theater, I was on my way to Riga. I was greeted with flowers by my father and his new wife, Lea; we were extremely happy to see each other again, having been separated for so long.

After registering me at the hotel, we boarded the familiar Brivibas Street trolley to get to my father's apartment. I could only stay in town for one week, and we had a lot to catch up on, with the many lost years behind us; we had many unanswered questions that could not be addressed in regular correspondence. I was soon walking the cobblestone streets of the medieval city that I had once called home. I remember that nothing looked the same. The warped walls of the old buildings portrayed unspoken images of the way in which I was put into the shackles of slavery, first by the Latvians and then by the Germans. When I visited the building where my family had lived, a frightening feeling came over me, for I saw no one who was near and dear to me. A cold sweat started to develop on my forehead, and my cheeks were covered with tears as I walked into the courtyard where I once had played with my siblings and friends. This spacious yard, once filled with laughter, smiles, and happy faces, now stood empty. No playing children, no crying infants in their buggies, no human beings could be seen. Two benches that had once stood there were gone. Now the yard was only an access route to the rear of the building.

I would not have been fully satisfied if I had not gone to see my father's business establishment around the corner on Terbatas Street. The store had a large window and a glass door protected by shutters. Everything stood as it had when I last saw it, around twenty years ago. Time stood still here. There was no one in the store. The shutter door was still secured by the familiar lock on the latch. Although it had become a little rusty, to me it was an old friend. As a small boy, I held it each day with gentle fingers. I would open and close it and make sure to keep it in a safe place for Dad and Mom to find.

Father always came to my hotel early in the morning and waited for me in the lobby. One day I asked him, "Why do you come so early? You know I will still be sleeping." Looking straight at me, he replied, "I come here because I know you sleep upstairs. I want to be as near to you as possible while you are still in this hotel; after all, you are my son." He caught his breath and continued, "I missed you very much during all of these years—I love you." After this emotional explanation, tears came to our eyes. I embraced him, and we walked to the coffee shop for breakfast.

I told my father I had come to Riga not just to visit him but also to see the Rumbuli forest, where Mother and the children had been murdered by the Nazis. He looked skeptical; he suggested that it might be impossible to go there, as it was off-limits, but I was obsessed with the idea and said, "I have to see the forest at any cost." I contacted two of my childhood friends, Zama and Sascha, and asked them to help guide me to this scary, forbidden place I felt compelled to visit. They refused but were willing to describe how to get there; I accepted this compromise and was daring enough to go by myself, despite all warnings. They told me to take the Maskavas Street bus and to get off at the end of the line; across the road, I would see the Rumbuli forest. I was to go into the forest and walk until I reached a stream. On the other side of the stream, I would have to walk a few hundred feet to reach a flat, open pasture—the spot for which I was searching.

I had decided to fulfill my lifelong dream by myself the following morning, but my father called before I went to bed. He told me, "I cannot let you go alone to this restricted area in the forest—I will accompany you." I did not want to accept his offer, since it seemed to be something I alone needed to do; I also had to make sure he would not be hurt in any way. My father was very insistent about accompanying me, because he had not visited the site either, so I finally gave in.

The next morning we were ready to begin our dangerous journey. I hid a camera in my raincoat and followed in detail the instructions my friends had given me. I took the bus, went into the forest, and found the stream. We reached an open field that was lower than the ground around it; the entire area was covered with young, small trees and wild bushes with tall weeds and grass, all of which were surrounded by a variety of much older trees. Some of the trees had markings on them, which told us that automatic machine guns had been mounted on them. On one side of this plateau was a tall, black board with a small framed picture of colorful flowers attached to it; there was no inscription. It had been erected by anonymous men as a commemorative plaque to the perished Jewish community of Riga. Everything was solemn and quiet. There were no sounds, not even birds; it was the most lonesome, isolated place anyone could imagine.

Father and I stood motionless, looking at every tree, every branch, and everything that covered and surrounded this land soaked with Jewish blood. Tears began to gush down my cheeks. I thought, So this is the place where thirty thousand innocent Jewish people were gunned down in cold blood by the German SS units with the participation of the Latvians. This is where Kaiserwald's Stutzpunkt work units were sent to exhume the bodies and burn them to ashes so no trace was left of the Nazi atrocities. With my camera, I took pictures of every spot in the area, thinking each might have been the place at which my mother and the children had stood. I was so fearful of being seen by someone entering the forest that I did not notice that my film was not winding; only much later did I learn I had developed unused film. I needed no pictures for myself, only for others; the images of this tragic place and the massacre of my family had been permanently imprinted on my mind and soul. Father soon became very nervous and constantly reminded me, "Let's go, let's go; we have seen everything." Ordinarily, I would have said Kaddish, the traditional mourner's prayer for the dead, but we had to rush to escape the secluded forest before a Soviet agent caught us. I left this horrible place with the satisfaction of having accomplished my mission.

On the way home, Father and I stopped in the area where the ghetto had been. The small house where our family had lived was gone; the street was extended over the garden where our valuables had been buried. To make our visit complete, Father guided me to the tiny house in the Little Ghetto where we had shared our room with my cousin Boris. Russian people now occupied the house, but they allowed us to come in, as they knew who we were. I was flooded with sad memories of the past. When Father and I went to the backyard, the Russian man handed me a shovel and said, "Go ahead; I don't mind. You can dig out everything you left here." I quickly replied, "You can have your shovel. Nothing was buried in this yard." With that, we left the premises and boarded the bus to return to Father's apartment. Now that I had seen everything my mind was at ease, and I hoped my loved ones had not died in vain. Their deaths had exposed to the world the terrible truth: They were annihilated simply because they were born Jewish.

Lea was preparing an elaborate dinner in honor of my departure, since I would be returning to the United States the next day. Many relatives and friends were at the dinner table, and I enjoyed their company. I thanked Lea and her family for their hospitality and embraced Father, expressing the hope that he would soon come to visit me in Chicago. When I reached my hotel room, I went straight to bed and fell asleep immediately from exhaustion.

In the middle of the night, I woke up and could not continue the rest I so desperately needed; the mental tension of the day had finally caught up with me. I began to cry hysterically and could not control myself; a few years ago, I thought my eyes had run out of tears, but I knew now that they had simply been held back. I was in complete disarray; the peaceful night's rest I needed had been interrupted, just as my young life had been shattered unexpectedly back in 1941. All night long, I tossed and turned and was finally able to fall asleep.

When I awoke, I had no time to think about the turbulent night. My transportation to the airport was waiting, and I was quickly on my way. The drive took me down Maskavas Street, where two decades before the Riga Jews had marched to their annihilation. We made a right turn, and I had a chilling feeling, for this was the intersection where I had gotten off the bus the previous day to reach the Rumbuli woods. The car continued to the airport, but I was looking back at the fast-fading sight of the forest. I was glad I had kept my promise to myself and made this trip, despite the powerful emotions it had aroused.

I flew back to Chicago, where my family waited eagerly for my arrival. I had been gone only a short time, but we had missed each other very much. At home, Sharon and Steven were happy to receive a variety of Russian dolls, and Tamara was given amber jewelry. I had small souvenirs and, most important, the unforgettable memories. Our family life soon returned to normal; I had seen the distant, secluded place where my loved ones had gone to heaven, and it was enough. With the passing years, the image of my mother in my dreams has slowly diminished, but the invisible bonds of love have not. The pictures of her and my father stood, unchanged, for many years on my nightstand. Every morning I gave them a wink and thought of them; these photos gave me a daily dose of inspiration to make my life more fulfilling.

My life changed in other ways as well. As busy as I was, I still managed to become involved in volunteer work for the sake of my fellow humans. The certificates and plaques on my office wall testify that I, in my own small way, have helped the sick, needy, and less fortunate. I supported the fight against anti-Semitism wherever it occurred and contributed to the welfare of the state of Israel. It was there that every visiting Jew could find a mishpoche and every persecuted Jew a home; the rebirth of Israel meant the best future for the Jewish people.

In summer 1980, my wife and I visited Israel for the second time. We traveled the width and length of that beautiful historical country. We traveled as far as we could to the north until we reached a sign that said "Danger; land mines; do not trespass." We were at the Golan Heights. The UN observers were stationed at the demarcation line between Israel and Syria. From a distance we could clearly see the devastated Syrian city of Qunetra. After the armistice agreement between Israel and Syria had been signed, the understanding was that President Assad would rebuild the city and let the refugees return to their homes, but the rebuilding never took place. What a beautiful gesture it would have been if he had honored his commitment of harmony and peace for the people of Syria and Israel. The concrete bunkers on the high ridge of the Golan Heights had served the Syrian military forces well, but now they were a tourist sight from which one could observe the beauty of the valley as the farmers worked their fields and fruit orchards.

From here we traveled south through the rugged Negev and Sinai Deserts until we reached artillery guns that faced the Red Sea's Strait of Tehran. This place was Sharm-El-Sheikh. The guns, which had once threatened Israel's shipping line into the southern port of Eilat, had led to one of the causes of the Six Day War with Egypt in 1967. I looked over every gun and even took a picture of Tamara sitting on one. The hot desert was all around us. Our small group was greeted by local Bedouin Arabs. Some were barefoot; others wore sandals, rode camels, or drove Mercedes-Benz automobiles. We left Sharm-El-Sheikh with the hope that the heavy guns would never provoke another war but would stand as a tragic reminder of the fallen warriors.

With great excitement we entered the city of Jerusalem, the ancient Israelite city that King David had made the capital of his kingdom of Judah in 1004 B.C.E. and in which his son Solomon built the First Holy Temple in 960 B.C.E. Although various conquerors passed through Jerusalem's gates and destroyed the First Holy Temple, it was rebuilt as the Second Holy Temple by King Herod in 69 B.C.E. In 20/19 C.E., warriors of the Roman Empire conquered Judea, destroyed the Second Temple, and changed the name of the land from Judea to Palestine

(Geoffrey Wigoder, *The Encyclopedia of Judaism*). The Jews were forced to flee their native country and were dispersed to every corner of the earth. Only the retaining wall of the ancient Second Holy Temple remains today; it is known as the Wailing or Western Wall. Annually, on the day called Tisha B'Av, Jews pray to commemorate the destruction of the Second Holy Temple.

By the time of our visit, Jerusalem was already united and had become the eternal capital of Israel. On a previous trip to Israel in 1964, when the ancient part of Jerusalem was occupied by Jordanian forces, we could only stand at the barbed-wire fence and ask others where the various holy places were located. We received answers such as "there on the right" or "there on the left" or "there in the rear of the Golden Dome." Only the top of the Dome of the Rock was visible from a distance. I was glad we could now enter the ancient part of Jerusalem, the home of three faiths—Judaism, Christianity, and Islam. With great enthusiasm I looked over every holy place. I saw Jerusalem past and present. Tamara and I did not forget to fulfill an old Jewish tradition—to leave a small wishful note between the old stone joints of the Western Wall.

One day, we met a dear friend from Chicago, whom we had known for many years and who now resided in Jerusalem. Our friend's name was Dr. Moshe Lev, and he was accompanied by his lovely wife, Lisa. As we discussed the latest events in the United States, Dr. Lev said, "I have a special invitation for you and Tamara. Prime Minister Menachem Begin has invited you to be his guests at a tea party next Saturday evening." We were flabbergasted at the opportunity to meet such a prominent freedom fighter and statesman. Begin had been the leader of the Irgun Zvar Leumi, the organization that fought to oust British rule in Palestine. He also served in the Knesset (Parliament) for many years. In 1977, he won the confidence of the Israeli people and became prime minister. He signed a peace treaty with Egyptian President Anwar Sadat, for which he received a Nobel Peace Prize. I thought, Such an opportunity only comes once in a lifetime. Without delay, we accepted the invitation.

Before we entered the prime minister's official residence, the guards politely looked us over and asked for proper identification. We were on the guest list. Dr. Lev introduced Tamara and me to the prime minister and his wife, Aliza. Mrs. Begin asked us to make ourselves comfortable in their home. I had the remarkable opportunity to chat with Mr. Begin and other dignitaries. My camera came in handy, as the prime minister posed with Tamara and me. To this day an enlarged picture of us with Mr. Begin hangs on my office wall. I thanked Moshe and Lisa for this memorable evening with Israel's prime minister.

This experience prompted me to become more involved in the Zionist movement, particularly in the fundraising campaign for the National Sick Fund of Israel. My second journey to Israel gave me the motivation and impetus to plan future visits.

As a survivor, I became a charter member and helped to lay the foundation for the U.S. Holocaust Memorial Museum in Washington, D.C., built so those who perished in the Holocaust would not be forgotten. The institution had many important objectives to fulfill to ensure that prejudice, bigotry, and hatred are erased in a pluralistic society. The eyewitness stories of survivors serve as documentation against the claim by anti-Semites that the Holocaust was nothing but a hoax. The museum, built in our capital city, will remain a constant watchdog and reminder to the world—long after books and human memories have faded—that a state-sponsored extermination must never again take place. Future generations will be able to see the inhuman evils perpetrated against innocent people in Europe during Adolf Hitler's Nazi era. Tribute should also be paid to the brave Allied soldiers who fought to liberate the surviving Jews. Respect and admiration should be given to the thirty-five Latvian Righteous Gentiles who risked their own lives to save Jewish people. Among them was Janis Lipke, considered to be Raoul Wallenberg of Latvia (*Latvian Jewish Courier,* March 1995, vol. 12, no. 1).

The time I spent in humanitarian activities did not prevent me from honoring my family obligations; in fact, it encouraged me to become closer to my family members. My son, Steven, was a soccer player in high school, and I was there to encourage him at every game. He also belonged to the school's Aeronautical Club; when they had a miniature rocket contest, I was with him. I attended Sharon's piano recitals and rarely missed a meeting with her teachers. I was devoted to my children; when they needed me, I never told them I did not have time.

On our first trip to Los Angeles, we met family members about whom we knew very little. We saw my Uncle Leon, known to me as Chone Lidow (shortened from Lidowsky), and his wife, Rachel, who had been saved from the Nazi hordes by a Polish couple in Vilna. Just before my arrival in the United States, they had immigrated to California to be with their son, known to me as Archik but now called Eric, and his wife, Lisa. I recall the happy faces of my children when they met my cousin's two boys, Derek and Alexander. The Lidowsky family tree began in the small town of Vilna and had grown to its fullest in Riga. After the Holocaust, the tree, now named Lidow and considerably leaner, had extended to the United States in the cities of Chicago and Los Angeles.

After the passing of my Aunt Helena, her family had joined Operation Exodus of the Soviet Jewry. Uncle Sascha, my cousin Jefim and his wife, Natasha, and Frieda and her son, Misha, came to Chicago. With their arrival in the United States, my family roots of centuries past were significantly diminished on the European continent. I visited Sascha frequently, and we grew very fond of each other. I had a great time engaging in lengthy conversations with my elderly uncle; he enjoyed telling, and I enjoyed listening to, his countless nostalgic stories of the Lidowsky family's life in Vilna the previous century. He died at age ninety-six, and I truly miss him and his enlightening tales of generations of our relatives. I also miss another patriarch of the Lidow family, someone I could not see as often as I wished: my late Uncle Leon, with whom I occasionally spoke on the telephone. It was a tradition for me to wish him a healthy and happy New Year on the eve of Yom Kippur after I had returned home from Kol Nidre services. Leon would say to me, "You do not have to say who this is. I have been waiting for your call all evening."

The kind and flattering words "our boy" that had been spoken so many times by my aunt and uncle still sounded loudly in my ears, even after many years had passed. To my disappointment, it took me a long time to comprehend that the words were shallow and had little sincere meaning; they were just the empty expression of a childless couple. When they died, neither left a little love note for "their boy." I regularly visited their simple, grass-covered grave but never noticed any other visitors or flowers there. They may have been forgotten by the greedy people who had undeservedly gained their love, but I continued to care for them in death as I had in life; I bore no grudge against them. Looking down at the beautifully engraved marble headstones, I could only tell them, "Betty and Herman, rest in peace. Thank you for bringing me to America." I then thought to leave one more message in this peaceful surrounding. "When the time comes that I am laid to rest, I will not be far from you—just up the hill. Our souls will meet, and they will discuss the state of our past affairs."

My eager wish and my father's greatest desire were fulfilled when he arrived in the United States for an extended visit. I was delighted to have him in my home; we were united again under one roof, even if it was temporary. Sharon and Steven got to know their grandfather for the first time, and although there was a communication gap, my father found a way to play with his newly discovered grandchildren; By the end of his visit, he had even learned a few words of English from them. He went back to the Soviet Union, but after the principles of glasnost and perestroika were adopted, he returned to the United States to live in the land with which he had fallen in love. Eventually, Father, his wife, Lea, and her family settled down in a southern state; we were in close touch, and I visited regularly. He had the good fortune to attend the weddings of both of his grandchildren and became acquainted with their respective spouses, Robert and Robin; a few years later, he was able to play with his great-grandchild, Benjamin. For many years, he enjoyed a happy life in his adopted country; I lost my father, Abram, when he was ninety-three.

I reached my senior years, and the darkest days of human history were behind me. I was able to recover from the terrible experiences of my youth and to shape a new life according to my own desires. After the disaster of World War II, the countries of the civilized world became so saturated with their own problems that they had no time to dwell on the past; nor did they make a great effort to create a more humane new world order. Armed conflicts still rage in every corner of our globe, and anti-Semitism and sympathy for the Nazi ideals have begun to rise again. I do not know whether I will live to see a world free of hate and filled with harmony and mutual understanding; perhaps that is just another of my many wishful thoughts—only time will tell.

My lifestyle has changed somewhat to allow me to enjoy the fruits of my years of diligent work. I am no longer in a hurry to get on with my day, although time has become an important and precious commodity in my life that cannot be wasted. I still live on a schedule: I have to determine when to do the little work of love, when to participate in sports activities, when to see my grandchildren, when to help somebody in need, and when to see the doctor to maintain my health. I am still very busy, but I am as happy as I can be, for the greatest challenge in my life was fulfilled, and I have Tamara, my children, and my grandchildren—Benjamin, Elizabeth, and Aaron. The efforts Tamara and I made concerning our children's education and Judean teachings have borne great fruits: the relentless ambition Sharon and Steven both possess has granted them the highest degrees that can be obtained in schools of higher learning, and they are both productive in the medical profession.

The love I have for my adopted homeland will never diminish; I will be laid to rest here. On every legal holiday, to express my supreme gratitude for what this country has done for me, I display my American flag—for what it stood for in time of war, as well as for what it represents in time of peace. I dearly hope the family roots I planted half a century ago will continue to grow and will become a mighty tree with lengthy branches for many generations to come. As a Holocaust survivor, I hope I serve as a lasting reminder to my family and others to see to it that such gruesome atrocities are never committed again against the Jewish people or anyone else. This should remain their solemn obligation so that those who sacrificed their lives, Al Kiddush Hashem, did not die in vain. Let my struggle for survival in war and peace serve as an example to my present and future relatives.

While I was blessed with life, I witnessed the realization of a two-thousand-year dream of the Jewish people: The state of Israel was established from the ashes of the Holocaust. The concentration camp intuition I gained, upon which my life so often depended, has remained with me. I envision that the decades of fighting to save and protect the Jewish state from evil forces will eventually end and that the peaceful understanding that has been initiated with the neighboring Arab states will continue. In Jerusalem stands the dignified Yad Vashem, the tribute to the Jewish people victimized by Hitler's Germany; it also passionately recognizes the courage of the Righteous Gentiles, who defied the Nazis and risked their own lives to rescue Jews. This solemn memorial represents one of the greatest landmarks of morality in the world. From the same holy city, a stream of knowledge, tolerance, and justice will reach the people of the world—the Jewish communities in particular. Every human being will be the beneficiary of this holy call, not for preservation but for the prolongation of a fulfilling, healthy life.

With unfavorable odds of survival and the terror of suddenly being free with nowhere to go, a young man found something of value—himself. The legacy of my life was discovered through a generation of unthinkable tragedy. The memories and life experiences found in this book can contribute to a new vision of life and make a better world for the old, the young, and the yet to be born. The text of this book took several years to compose; I hope it will be preserved as documentation from a survivor. In this way, it can serve as one of many educational remedies to fight off and immunize against that dreadful, widespread disease of the mind—anti-Semitism. This must be done in the spirit of brotherhood, love, and understanding, not only for some individuals but for society as a whole.

Painful to Remember . . .
Impossible to Forget . . .

Index